The Relentless Business of Treaties

THE
RELENTLESS
BUSINESS
OF
TREATIES

×××××××××× ◆ ××××××××××

How Indigenous Land
Became US Property

Martin Case

MINNESOTA
HISTORICAL
SOCIETY PRESS

www.mnhspress.org

The Minnesota Historical Society Press is a member of the Association of University Presses.

Manufactured in the United States of America

10 9 8 7 6 5 4 3 2 1

∞ The paper used in this publication meets the minimum requirements of the American National Standard for Information Sciences—Permanence for Printed Library Materials, ANSI Z39.48-1984.

International Standard Book Number
ISBN: 978-1-68134-090-6 (paper)
ISBN: 978-1-68134-091-3 (e-book)

Library of Congress Cataloging-in-Publication Data available upon request.

This and other Minnesota Historical Society Press books are available from popular e-book vendors.

You think nothing of the land, because the Great Spirit made you with paper in one hand and pen in the other, and altho' he made us at the same time, he did not make us like you.

Little Priest, Ho Chunk, 1828

Contents

The Relentless Business of Treaties

INTRODUCTION
The Lay of the Land

T he American myth, like the book of Genesis, includes not one but two creation stories. One American origin story celebrates the foundational documents that enshrine the country's ideals. The Declaration of Independence, though it was written by slaveholders and refers to indigenous people as "savages," expresses the ideal of equality among all people. The Constitution with its Bill of Rights, though it originally institutionalized chattel slavery, set the rule of law that would in theory guarantee the ideal of individual liberty. Through the words in these documents, the United States was created *in principle*.

The American myth also provides a story in which six days stand out as milestones in the United States' march of progress. On Day One, a treaty with Great Britain ended the Revolution and the United States was born. Subsequent days saw the Louisiana Purchase from France, the acquisition of Florida from Spain, the annexation of the Republic of Texas, the Oregon Treaty that settled the US title to the Pacific Northwest, and the Treaty of Guadalupe Hidalgo, ending a war between the United States and Mexico. Six days, six changes in colonialist regime, six giant strides across the continent; Americans saw that it was good and rested until Hawaii and Alaska made their later appearances.

When indigenous nations appear in this mythical version of the past, they are presented as a temporary impediment to US expansion. The American myth conveys a carefully constructed image of indigenous identity, meant to contrast a primitive social order with a superior civilization that supplanted it and relegated it to the past. Though the myth is essentially racist and demonstrably untrue, it still shapes public discourse in the United States, not least through the legacy of significant Supreme Court decisions.

But beneath the American myth, the history of North America has featured a long history of diplomacy among sovereign nations. Treaties are an important part of that history. One result of those agreements was the transfer of millions of acres from the control of indigenous people to that of the United States. The impact of that transfer on indigenous nations is widely known today but less widely understood. The treaties also played an essential role in creating and expanding the US property system. Like the Declaration and the Constitution, they are foundational documents of the United States. As living documents, they continue to operate on the political, legal, and social systems of North America today.

The US–Indian Treaties

As nation-to-nation agreements, the US–Indian treaties cover a full range of diplomatic relationships, including peace accords, military alliances, trade compacts, and—generating the most public discussion today—land cessions. Indigenous people brought their own traditions in international diplomacy to their negotiations with the United States, including protocols and ceremonies that solemnized their agreements. Their collective experience with diplomacy preceded the birth of the United States. Today the most famous treaty among indigenous nations is perhaps that of the Iroquois Confederacy, which united neighboring nations in an enduring compact long before the United States was created, possibly before Columbus set sail from Europe; negotiations over trade and territory were common. Indigenous people made treaties with European countries 150 years before the American Revolution. A Cherokee delegation, for instance, traveled to London to negotiate a treaty in 1730.[1]

These treaties, even from a colonialist perspective, have carried the weight of international law. From time to time—usually on those Six Days of the creation myth—the United States in effect *inherited* treaty obligations from other colonialist powers: Spain, France, Great Britain, the short-lived Republic of Texas. The Louisiana Purchase, for instance, bound the United States to abide by Spanish treaties with indigenous nations.

Early on, the federal government reserved for itself the exclusive power to make treaties on behalf of the American people. To be an official, legally binding treaty from a US perspective, the agreement had to be signed by multiple parties, ratified by the US Senate, and proclaimed (formally announced) by the president. Between 1778 and 1871, the United States signed about 375 official treaties with indigenous nations. Although states, corporations, and individuals occasionally tried to reach agreements on their own with indigenous nations, usually in order to acquire land, as a general rule only federally negotiated treaties carry the weight of law.

The accurate recognition of US–Indian treaties as agreements among sovereign nations carries profound consequences. Along with the Constitution, international treaties—including those with indigenous nations—are the foundation of the US legal system. As Article 6 of the Constitution itself says, "This Constitution, and the Laws of the United States which shall be made in Pursuance thereof; and all Treaties made, or which shall be made, under the Authority of the United States, shall be the supreme Law of the Land."

American public discourse about the treaties is often hampered by a persistent misperception that the United States granted rights to indigenous people through treaty making, with the implication that those rights can be unilaterally taken away by the federal government. But indigenous "treaty rights" are not a product of the US political and legal system. They spring from widely diverse traditional social structures, national histories, and relationships to land that evolved long before the creation of the United States. When negotiating land cession treaties, indigenous people often successfully retained certain rights that they had always enjoyed as sovereign nations: the right to hunt and fish even on the land they ceded, for instance. Indigenous nations have skillfully maintained these rights ever since, by engaging in the legal and political systems of the nation that acquired much of their land. In contemporary American society, the assertion of treaty rights is an expression of enduring national sovereignty that was never given up by indigenous people.

The idea that rights might originate outside the Constitution has proven to be a difficult one for many Americans to grasp, and indigenous sovereignty has been dismissed in public discourse on many levels. Politicians and some scholars have asked long after the fact whether the treaties were actually valid, legal documents. The treaties have been described, for instance, as "political anomalies." The American myth has made from the US–Indian treaties an example of political inequality, famous for removing the Indian from the United States. As the story goes, this removal was justified because Americans could use natural resources more effectively than indigenous societies did. So the American system unleashed a great tide of material progress that continues to wash over the world to this day. The United States distributed to settlers the cheap land that indigenous people had never fully exploited through, for example, the Homestead Act and the Oklahoma

Land Rush—important images from the myth. Hardy pioneers subsequently created the American ideal of hardworking individualists, kicked off an era of American triumphalism, and, in American public perception, relegated indigenous people (and their sovereignty) to the past tense. The treaties, when mentioned at all, are remembered as transactions that, while unfortunate for indigenous nations, belong in a bigger, more benign, more inspiring narrative of the good things that spread across the continent: democracy, liberty, Christianity, and (in the words of the man who coined the phrase "Manifest Destiny") "the irresistible army of Anglo Saxon emigration."[2]

Tellings of this story often refer to a history of broken treaties, the readily lamented but easily ignored failure of the United States to live up to its legally binding, treaty-generated trust obligations. If treaties are "broken," they can presumably be consigned comfortably to the past. Despite failures of the federal government, however, the treaties are still in effect, used in court cases to assert indigenous rights.

A Clash of Organizing Principles

The US–Indian treaties were the meeting grounds for nations with widely diverse social structures. The stakes were often high in these events: indigenous people retained certain rights and—closer to the subject of this book—the United States secured its title to millions of acres of property. But the fundamental transformation that treaties wrought was something even more profound, nothing less than a restructuring of the way that human beings relate to the natural world.

Individuals have a great capacity for complex relationships with the natural world. The landscape is our home, and home life is always complicated. It provides sustenance, inspiration, and entertainment; it shapes our transportation and commerce. But from these many possibilities, *societies* are structured on *specific* relationships with the natural world, and those selected relationships make a society distinctive. If, for example, societies are organized on the principle of *kinship* with elements of the natural world (as are traditional Dakota and Ojibwe societies), that organizing principle will be reflected in a family structure where rivers are relatives and shape the traditional political structures, cultural infrastructure, commerce, and international diplomacy of those societies. The organizing principle—in this case, kinship—defines moral behavior and determines which communally made decisions are politically acceptable.

The United States, too, is based on a relationship between people and the natural world: a property relationship. The westward growth of the United States—the business of territory making—was essentially the expansion of a system of property. In fact, the United States was the first nation to be founded on the idea (only recently developed at the time) that private property could be equated with personal liberty. The stories of Genesis echo in the background of this enterprise. On the sixth day, mankind was instructed to "fill the earth and subdue it." The US system—based on property rights and informed by that biblical directive—proved incompatible with the traditional political, economic, and social systems of indigenous nations. The treaties would determine which relationship with the natural world would serve as an organizing principle in a specific location on the continent.

In the rhetoric of the American myth, land cession treaties are often presented as real estate transactions, exchanges between landowners. The idea of land ownership is so deeply seated in American society that at times it can be difficult to imagine land as anything other than real estate. But rather than being property sales, the treaties were in effect moments when the natural world *became* private property in the United States.

Treaties in a Property System: The Doctrine of Discovery

In 1823, John Marshall explained this transformational process in a Supreme Court case called *Johnson v. M'Intosh*. His majority opinion for that case, a pillar of property law in the United States, assigned to the US–Indian treaties a critical role in creating the titles—public, corporate, and individual—by which land is owned.

Marshall was trying to explain why one person's claim to property ownership was more valid than another's. Backing far away from the facts of the case, he placed land titles in the context of what is now called the Doctrine of Discovery. He desperately wanted to claim that land titles are comprised of two rights: dominion (the right to rule a territory) and occupancy (the right to live there). He also wanted to claim that the right of dominion was created when a territory was "discovered" by a colonialist power.

To justify this dogmatically Eurocentric claim, Marshall might have pointed to a series of proclamations by various popes, beginning before Columbus went to sea, in which Catholic countries were awarded spheres of influence, first in Asia and then in the western hemisphere.

These proclamations at least offered a precedent for discovery resulting in a claim of dominion. But Marshall could not rest a US legal decision on papal proclamations: he was an advocate of the separation of
church and state; the Enlightenment, of which he was an intellectual
product, was in part a rebellion against the authority of the Catholic
church, and many of his contemporaries hated Catholics. So he felt
compelled to fabricate nothing less than "the history of America from
its discovery to the present day." And what Marshall found in that history was a remarkable (in fact, fictional) degree of consensus among
European governments on the importance of "discovery": "As they
were all in pursuit of nearly the same object, it was necessary, in order
to avoid conflicting settlements and consequent war with each other,
to establish a principle which all should acknowledge as the law. . . .
This principle was that discovery gave title to the government by whose
subjects or by whose authority it was made. . . . It was a right with
which no Europeans could interfere. It was a right which all asserted
for themselves, and to the assertion of which by others all assented."[3]

Of course, in the real world there was no "doctrine" that kept Europeans from "conflicting settlement" or "consequent war"; they inter-
fered with each other constantly. But the right of dominion became,
in Marshall's formulation, one of two components for a valid property
title.

The other component was the right of occupancy, or "right to the
soil." Easy claims of dominion are, in the words of economist and phi-
losopher Adam Smith, "fictitious possession" if they are not accompanied by the right to live on the land. Marshall acknowledged that,
originally, indigenous nations had the right to occupy the entire continent. He went so far as to say that "their right of possession has never
been questioned." This right was later called aboriginal title. But in the
bizarre world of the Doctrine of Discovery, indigenous nations could
never hold the right of dominion over the land where they lived, precisely because they were already there when Europeans arrived.[4]

The point of Marshall's Doctrine of Discovery lay in the relationship between right of dominion and right of occupancy. Discovery,
as the shaky foundation of dominion, "gave to the nation making the
discovery the sole right of acquiring the soil from the natives." So the
United States acquired dominion—and only dominion, not necessarily
the right to occupancy—over a huge territory from the British in the
Revolutionary War, and over an even larger area from the French in the
Louisiana Purchase. And to Marshall, this arrangement among colonial-

ist powers trumped any relationship to the land among indigenous nations: "Indian inhabitants are to be considered merely as occupants, . . .
incapable of transferring the absolute title. . . . [T]heir power to dispose
of the soil at their own will to whomsoever they pleased was denied by
the original fundamental principle that discovery gave exclusive title
to those who made it. . . . Absolute ultimate title has been considered
as acquired by discovery, subject only to the Indian title of occupancy."
    The practical, real-world point of *Johnson v. M'Intosh* was that
the United States needed to extinguish aboriginal title—primarily
through treaties—in order to make any practical claim to control land.
And indigenous nations could "dispose of the soil" only by ceding it
to the federal government—not to individuals, to corporations, or
even to states. Once the government held a "perfected" title (combin-
ing the right of dominion with the right of occupancy), it could sell or
grant property to anyone. And the government did this so effectively
that land titles are usually taken for granted today. Americans argue
about who owns what, but the more fundamental aspect of a property
system is that *everything* is owned by *someone*.

The US Treaty Signers

For each official US–Indian treaty, the federal government authorized a
commissioner or team of commissioners to conduct negotiations with
indigenous nations. These commissioners generally had the discretion
to involve whomever they wanted, or needed, in the treaty-making
process. Between 1778 and 1871, approximately 2,300 men represented
the United States at these events.
    Over the last ten years, as time has permitted, I have pursued what
became the Treaty Signers Project, an attempt to research the identities of the men who signed treaties on behalf of the United States. This
research project has collected biographical information that identifies
about 1,600 of the US signers. In this book, I use information from
the lives of the US treaty signers as a lens through which to view the
American process of treaty making.[5]
    Some of these men are famous around the world. Others played
prominent roles in their local communities. The identities of some are
lost to history. Taken individually, the lives of these men can be interesting in their own right. The signers include Founding Fathers; the
founders of towns, newspapers, historical societies, and Arbor Day;
the man who found Livingston in the Congo; the "Father of Copper

Mining" and the "Father of the US Cavalry"; Jedidiah Morse, the "Father of American Geography" (and father of Samuel, who invented Morse code); Dr. William Beaumont, who in his gruesome medical experiments on a human subject became known as the "Father of Gastric Physiology." Treaty signers ordered Marines both into the Halls of Montezuma and onto the shores of Tripoli. Their family members include Whistler's mother and the originators of the Girl Scouts of the United States of America, the Kentucky Derby, the "hollow earth" theory, and Texas. They are commemorated in the names of scores of counties and thousands of streets across the country. And many of their names are readily recognizable to tribal members across the continent who are aware of the specific treaties by which their traditional homelands were ceded to the United States.[6]

At first glance, the signatures of these men might serve to reinforce a received story about the treaties. The American myth presents these events as bureaucratic functions, the paperwork that validated unstoppable historical forces; the men who signed the treaties, then, are merely filling interchangeable roles. Taken one by one, the signatures—French names that might belong to fur traders, names attached to military ranks and political offices, famous "Indian fighters"—are seldom unexpected. The signers might have been chosen at random: men who happened to be on the spot at the time, soldiers assigned to a military unit in the West or paper pushers from a government office in the East or voyageurs who happened to paddle past the treaty site in their canoes, dragooned into temporary service at the very moments when a major colonialist power acquired a continent's natural resources.

The briefest reflection on this story would indicate its improbability, and from the first day of the Treaty Signers Project, a different story emerged. The men who appeared for the United States at the treaty signings represented as a group all of the interests that drove the country's westward expansion, from settlers who wanted land for themselves to land speculators who wanted millions of acres for resale, owners of trading and mining and timber companies and their employees, and political and military glory hounds. Upon examination, these were not distinct subsets: military officers were land speculators, bureaucrats were business owners, settlers were militia officers. And often enough to defy any expectations, these men were related to one another through family ties.

In fact, the extent to which US treaty signers were related to one another by marriage bears noting. Treaties often took place at the geographic limit of US expansion, in places where there were few settlers. So one might not be surprised to find that the signers of a treaty in Detroit, or in Vincennes or in St. Louis or in Prairie du Chien, were related by marriage. But family ties connected signers from *all* of these places, and those ties extended over generations.

Representatives from indigenous nations also signed treaties, of course, and one might ask why the US signers in particular form the focus of this book. Treaties were agreements among multiple parties, and certainly the treaties cannot be fully understood without examining each party's point of view. In fact, the Supreme Court developed canons for treaty construction that required ambiguities in the treaties to be construed in favor of indigenous interpretations of what the treaties said.[7]

The indigenous representatives—who account for more than 8,300 treaty signatures, nearly double the number of signatures for the United States—acted on behalf of scores of distinct nations. Each of those nations had its own social and political structures, and each signer had a (sometimes controversial) role in those structures, a role that might change over time and from treaty to treaty. The treaty signers are not from only two groups, indigenous on one side and the United States on the other, but instead are from many widely diverse nations. Telling their stories would require many voices.

So I want to be clear about the subject of this book. It is not the treaties themselves, the hundreds of convergence points where many cultures met. Instead, it is the US property system in particular, which spread through treaties across the continent. I am particularly interested in how the actions of these men, taken as a group rather than as individuals, challenge the assumptions of the American myth. Because so many settlers and pioneers benefited from the US acquisition of indigenous resources, the myth can present a simple proposition that the entire enterprise was undertaken primarily on their behalf. The lives of the US treaty signers tell a different story. In their networks of business, social, political, and family ties, we find a more reliable picture of the motivations and mechanisms that drove US expansion.

Treaties and Territory

Most Americans become aware of treaties when indigenous groups assert their retained treaty rights. The treaties themselves are considered less often. They are usually discussed as part of a tribal or state history, or studied as individual events, or tracked through a single era of US history (e.g., the Indian Removal Act). Behind these important but local or narrow concerns, however, US–Indian relations run like a spine through all of US history.

In this book I have tried to connect the treaties—and the property system that grew through them—to a broader narrative of US history. In six sections, I trace the evolution of the Northwest and Louisiana Territories, two vast areas that together span the Mississippi and cover more than a third of the United States. Details from several territorial and state seals are used at each section's start; the irony in this iconography is discussed in the Mythmakers section. In each of the sections, a "Territory" chapter demonstrates how a particular business interest or social force—land speculation, for instance, or the formation of race—shaped the history of those territories during a specific period; another chapter, "Signers," provides a broader treatment of the section's theme. By focusing on the evolution of the story as it affected the center of the continent, the area the colonialists knew as the Northwest and Louisiana Territories, I am able to address nearly the entire treaty-making period and to demonstrate how the waves of treaty-making interests affected one specific part of what is now the United States, the area that became Minnesota.

Using the lives of the signers as the connective tissue, I present in this book a suggestion of how treaty making intimately shaped the broader history of the United States—not only in its territorial expansion, but also its trade networks, its industrial development, its bureaucracies, and the very stories that Americans tell about themselves. The actions of treaty signers demonstrate with unnerving clarity the operations of an expanding property system and the mechanics of the relentless business of treaties.

1 Speculators

Though the pioneer—the rugged individualist—is a central character in the American myth, corporate land speculators were the initial drivers of westward expansion of the United States. From Day One, prominent Americans were eager to make fortunes by acquiring indigenous land and selling it to pioneers. Even before the American Revolution ended, speculators held political and military positions from which they could take charge of land policies, territorial governments, and US governmental relationships with indigenous nations.

Private land speculation changed in scope over the course of the treaty-making era. Initially, speculators accumulated millions of acres at a time. Later, townsites and transportation routes became the more narrowly targeted objects of speculation. But land speculation of varying scope remained a primary motivation for US treaty making with indigenous nations. Consequently, land speculators attended treaties to shepherd the transfer of natural resources from indigenous control to the United States.

More than eighty years after the Revolution began, the governor of Minnesota stated the continued importance of turning the natural world into property:

> Give us the capital of more men and we will vivify [and] infuse the breath of life into the dead capital of millions of acres now growing only prairie flowers.
>
> *Alexander Ramsey, signer of treaties with Dakota and Ojibwe*
> *Inaugural Address as Minnesota Governor, 1860*

TERRITORY: 1783–1800

At the 1783 Treaty of Paris with Great Britain, the United States claimed a territory that stretched from the Atlantic Ocean all the way to the Mississippi River. How often has it been stated that this treaty

---

Top right: Great Seal of the State of Ohio (1803), detail.

"doubled the size of the United States," and what little sense does this statement make? There *was* no independent United States until the treaty, when the area of US dominion grew from zero to nine hundred thousand square miles. Both before and after the treaty, European colonialists occupied half of this area where aboriginal title had been extinguished; indigenous nations occupied the rest. What doubled was the size of US colonialist ambitions.

The leaders of the new federal government were well aware that claiming dominion over a territory is very different from actually living there. The Treaty of Paris ended a revolution, but a war continued north of the Ohio River. The Miami Confederacy of indigenous nations was defending its homeland in present-day Indiana and Ohio, and it was joined in this defense by a multinational alliance: the Shawnee, the Lenape Delaware, the Wyandot, and the powerful Council of Three Fires—the Ojibwe, Ottawa, and Potawatomi.

This conflict not only put a brake on colonialist settlement; it also threatened the financial survival of the United States. The federal government was broke, and it had no authority to raise money. Pleading with the individual states for the power to levy taxes was not a strong option, given the rhetoric of the recent war against Great Britain. Tariffs on imported goods generated revenue, but that revenue went to the individual states. The bankrupt federal government did have one avenue to income: its exclusive power to make treaties. If indigenous nations could be induced to cede their land, the United States would hold both the right of dominion and the right of occupancy there and could then sell that land to the private sector.

And the private sector—in particular its wealthier members—were ready to buy. In fact, many of the Founding Fathers and their families had been frustrated for a generation in their desire to acquire land. Beginning in the 1740s, the Virginia government had granted hundreds of thousands of acres west of the Appalachians to Washingtons, Jeffersons, Lees, and other prominent families. These new private owners were expected to encourage colonialists on the Atlantic seaboard to move west. Until this point, colonialists had made their money by owning land; now they would make their money by selling it.

Their dream of enormous wealth was soon crushed. Great Britain found in the "French and Indian" War (1754–63) that antagonizing indigenous nations was expensive. In the Proclamation of 1763, Great Britain changed its Indian policy, cancelled the grants, and forbade any settlement west of the Appalachians. The colonialists in North America were simply incapable of taking the Proclamation seriously. George

Washington hired a boyhood friend, William Crawford, as his western land agent, and instructed him to carry on as usual:

> I can never look upon the Proclamation in any other light . . . than as a temporary expedient to quiet the Minds of the Indians. . . . Any person therefore who neglects the present opportunity of hunting out good Lands and in some measure marking and distinguishing them for their own . . . will never regain it. If therefore you will be at the trouble of seeking out the Lands I will take upon me the part of securing them. . . . By this time it may be easy for you to discover, that my Plan is to secure a good deal of Land.[1]

The American Revolution eliminated the detested British ban on acquiring indigenous land. The need of the Founding Fathers to finance a federal government converged with their desire to make money from land speculation. Their first target was land north of the Ohio River.

In creating the Northwest Territory, Americans added a new definition to the word *territory*. For centuries a territory had been a particular place associated with a particular people. The boundaries of the place might be vague and changeable and contentious, but within those boundaries, the landscape over time shaped the people who occupied or controlled it—and vice versa—until people and place developed a common identity.

It can take a long while to create such an intimate relationship between people and place. The word *territory*—until the United States was born—evoked a sense of history, of the evolution of relationships over time. But when the United States formally incorporated its territories, it dismissed local history. US territories were transitional spaces, a kind of political limbo where the important thing about land was not what it had meant to people, but what it would become. Within the temporary boundaries of these new territories, land would be incorporated into the US property system and then carved into states.

Exactly two weeks after Great Britain finally ratified the Treaty of Paris, Congress passed the Land Ordinance of 1784. Written by geometrically minded Thomas Jefferson, the ordinance divided the vast territory north of the Ohio River—170 million acres—into squares marked "by parallels of latitude . . . and by meridians of longitude." The legislation confidently asserted "that so much of the territory . . . as is already purchased or shall be purchased of the Indian inhabitants, and offered for sale by Congress, shall be divided into distinct states."[2]

The confidence was premature. Distrustful of centralized authority, the states had disbanded the Continental Army, and the United States was losing the Northwest Indian War. Nonetheless, in preparation for selling the land it did not control, Congress passed a second land ordinance in 1785. This was a plan to survey, acre by acre, the entire Northwest Territory—all 250,000 hotly contested square miles occupied by other nations—and then encourage citizens to buy the land (to which there was still no clear title) in lots of one square mile each. The plan was a disaster. Two years later, fewer than two hundred square miles had been sold, at a dollar per acre. The government was still broke.

The United States tried desperately to engineer a land cession from any indigenous nation in what is now Ohio. The Miami Confederacy, led by Little Turtle, was absolutely committed to resisting US expansion; no olive branch or financial inducement was adequate to secure a land cession from them. So the United States brokered two treaties with allies of the Miami. A US negotiator at one treaty, Samuel Holden Parsons, succinctly expressed what was at stake: "Here Congress places its expectations for paying the National debt." Though the treaties were signed, they were not effective. As recorded in the federal government's official Schedule of Indian Land Cessions, the first, negotiated in 1785, "was never carried into effect, owing to the hostile attitude assumed by a large proportion of the Ohio tribes." The second, in 1786, "was never carried into effect, owing to the continued acts of hostility on the part of the Shawnee toward citizens of the U.S." The United States would not even attempt another treaty in the Northwest Territory for three years.[3]

Thus by 1786, in spite of its inability to gain a clear title to land north of the Ohio River, the United States had created a dream of dividing that land into states and had devised a scheme, inadequate as it was, for selling the land. Congress next grappled with the question of how to govern an area from Pennsylvania to present-day Minnesota, 99 percent of which was controlled by other nations. It was at this point that impatient land speculators seized control of the territory-making process.

In March 1786, a group of ex-officers from the Continental Army met in a bar in Boston to form the Ohio Company of Associates. The leaders of the company included General Samuel Holden Parsons, negotiator of the abortive treaty with the Shawnee in that same year. General James Mitchell Varnum and Major Winthrop Sargent would soon join the company. These men had been promised land in payment for their military service, and they intended to claim it in the rich northwestern region they had seen during the Revolutionary War.[4]

Samuel Parsons soon proposed to Congress that the syndicate purchase 1.5 million acres north of the Ohio River and orchestrate a land cession treaty at their own expense. Cash-strapped though the federal government was, Parsons made no headway. But in June 1787, key members of the government—including General Arthur St. Clair, who was president of Congress—were given shares in the Ohio Company. The clock was ticking for the Ohio Company. A new constitution was being written, and it would go into effect when ratified by the states. The company needed to exploit its political connections quickly.

A director of the company was soon helping to draft the 1787 Northwest Ordinance, which incorporated the first official territory of the United States. When Congress passed the ordinance in July, the influence of the Ohio Company was apparent. The legislation invested all political power over the territory in the hands of a governor, who would serve as superintendent of Indian Affairs; a secretary; and three judges. These positions would be appointed by Congress, rather than elected by residents of the territory—much to the dismay of Thomas Jefferson.

By September, the Ohio Company had signed not one but two contracts to purchase land in the Northwest Territory. A 1.5-million-acre tract was acquired for fifty cents per acre—half the amount set in the Land Ordinance of 1785. An additional 3.5 million acres was also sold to the Ohio Company through the machinations of a consortium that included company member Winthrop Sargent; its members would pay for that land in a secret side deal. The company had purchased nearly 20 percent of the current state of Ohio. The capital of the entire territory—all the way to the Mississippi—would be located on Ohio Company land.

But the great triumph of the Ohio Company lay in the selection of government officials for the Northwest Territory: governor Arthur St. Clair, secretary Winthrop Sargent, judges Samuel Holden Parsons and James Mitchell Varnum. The third judge, Congressman John Cleves Symmes, fronted another consortium that was negotiating with Congress for hundreds of thousands of acres on the Miami River.

As government officials, these men were granted the exclusive authority to extinguish aboriginal title to land in the Northwest Territory and to decide how it would be distributed. As speculators, they would be the purchasers of the land, and they would resell it for a profit: among their fellow officers and other avid land speculators, they had a pool of ready customers. This was an event that the Founding Fathers had not planned and that John Marshall forgot in his "history of America": a corporate takeover of 170 million acres and of the government that would control it.

In 1787, the Northwest Territory was *incorporated* by Congress: it would be a formal part of the United States, where the federal government would guarantee rights such as trial by jury, habeas corpus, and compensation for any personal property that the government might seize. The territory would also be *organized*; that is, it would have a government, with territorial officers and a process for electing a territorial legislature and a non-voting representative to Congress. (*Incorporated* territories of the United States have not always been *organized* into governmental units.) One fundamentally important job of the governor and other officials would be extinguishing aboriginal title to land and, as the ordinance put it, to "lay out the parts of the district in which the Indian titles shall have been extinguished, into counties and townships."

As the land opened for settlement, the population would grow and the territory would be divided into "not less than three nor more than five States." And as states were admitted to the union, the territory would diminish in size. Sixty years after its incorporation, nothing was left of the Northwest Territory. But one clause of the ordinance continues to resonate in the political life of the United States even today: "The utmost good faith shall always be observed towards the Indians; their lands and property shall never be taken from them without their consent; and, in their property, rights, and liberty, they shall never be invaded or disturbed, unless in just and lawful wars authorized by Congress; but laws founded in justice and humanity, shall from time to time be made for preventing wrongs being done to them, and for preserving peace and friendship with them." In the ninety years after the Northwest Ordinance was enacted, scores of indigenous nations would cede their homelands and transform their ways of life, depending on the "utmost good faith" of the United States.[5]

In April 1788, forty-eight settlers arrived in a boat at the confluence of the Ohio and Muskingum Rivers to push the limits of that good faith. A small fort had been built there to keep American squatters from antagonizing indigenous nations; now Fort Harmar would protect the interests of the Ohio Company. The new settlers erected walls of their own around an area they called the Campus Martius (Marching Ground). The typical images of pioneer life—a farm family huddled in a sod house on the prairie, or a bonneted woman riding in a Conestoga wagon while her husband walks alongside, whipping the ox—did not apply to these first settlers. These were heavily armed corporate foot soldiers with combat experience who conducted military drills every day in Campus Martius. Within those walls, they would start a city and call it Marietta.

Prominent among the initial settlers in Marietta was a man named Ebenezer Sproat. He had attained the rank of colonel in the army and helped conduct the government survey in Ohio. Sproat became the leader of the Marietta militia and a cofounder of the first Masonic lodge in Ohio. Months after his arrival, he was joined by his father-in-law, Commodore Abraham Whipple; his wife, Catherine; and his daughter, Sarah. A legend has developed that the local indigenous people called him "Buckeye," a possible source of the Ohio state nickname. Sproat and all of the settlers in Marietta were shareholders in the Ohio Company.[6]

They wanted to make money by acquiring indigenous territory and selling it. But their presence in the new territorial capital was in itself a speculative venture, in that it required an act of the imagination. Situated fifty miles from Pennsylvania but looking west for a thousand miles into the continent's interior, standing in territory occupied by indigenous people for millennia, these speculators envisioned the absence of "Indians." Removal of indigenous people from their homelands was a necessary condition for expanding the US property system and the fortunes that grew with it, and their removal was imagined before it was accomplished.

Governor Arthur St. Clair joined the settlers in July, to live in Marietta and conduct business at the tiny Fort Harmar. Within six months, he organized another treaty intended to finally extinguish aboriginal title to the land on which he now lived. His hopes for success were bolstered by greater military support: to strengthen its position in the Northwest Territory, the United States had expanded its standing army from eighty to seven hundred soldiers.

St. Clair's treaty in 1789 was in many ways a reiteration of the abortive 1785 treaty. Many of the same indigenous nations attended, and like the first treaty, this one was a failure, "never carried into effect, owing to the uninterrupted hostilities on the part of the Indians."

As desperation mounted on the part of government officials and land speculators, the United States abandoned treaty making. General

Josiah Harmar was ordered to attack the heart of the Miami Confederacy, in present-day Indiana, with half of the total manpower of the US Army—320 men. To supplement this force, St. Clair organized 1,100 hapless militia members from Pennsylvania and Kentucky. An investor in the Ohio Company, Lieutenant Ebenezer Denny of the Kentucky militia, observed, "Many are without guns."[7]

In the ensuing two-month campaign, which came to be known as Harmar's Defeat, 225 regular army combatants were killed or wounded. Undeterred, Congress fired Harmar and replaced him with Arthur St. Clair. The United States quickly raised more troops at reduced pay, and St. Clair assembled another thousand raw, untrained militia members. In October 1791, St. Clair set off with two thousand soldiers; half of his men deserted before reaching Little Turtle's village. Meanwhile,

1780s: Failed Treaties of the Northwest Territory

The Miami, Wea, Kickapoo, Piankeshaw, and Eel River peoples—members of the Miami Confederacy—were the most adamant opponents of early US expansion along the southern shores of the Great Lakes. Their homeland at that time was centered in present-day Indiana and extended into western Ohio and Michigan, an area that was not adjacent to the settled areas of the United States. Desperate to extinguish aboriginal title to land that might be sold to speculators, the United States focused on treaty making with the allies of the Miami: the Wyandot, Delaware, Ojibwe, and Ottawa in 1785, joined by the Potawatomi in 1789, and with the Shawnee in 1786. With the Wyandot and their allies, the United States proposed a border beyond which it would not expand, where the right of indigenous nations to "live and to hunt" would be secured, and where

> If any citizen of the United States, or other person not being an Indian shall attempt to settle on any of the lands allotted to the Wiandot and Delaware nations . . . such person shall forfeit the protection of the United States, and the Indians may punish him as they please.
>
> *Article 5, Treaty with the Wyandot, Etc., 1785*

With the Shawnee in 1786, the United States invited prominent leaders of the Wyandot and Delaware, who had signed the 1785 treaty, to apply diplomatic pressure.

The determination of the federal government to extinguish indigenous title to land north of the Ohio River was symbolized in the presence of General Richard Butler, the only American to attend all three treaties. He was one of the five Fighting Butler Brothers, the fiercest champions of centralized federal power. Butlers appeared like knights errant wherever the early federal government asserted its will against

Chief Buckongahelas of the Lenape, Little Turtle of the Miami, and Blue Jacket of the Shawnee assembled a thousand seasoned fighters. The result—St. Clair's Defeat—was the worst casualty rate ever suffered by the United States in battle. Eighty-eight percent of the officers were killed. The United States now had no army, and its claim to dominion over the Northwest Territory was empty.

✕✕✕✕✕ ◆ ✕✕✕✕✕

The Legion of the United States—America's permanent army—was formed to defeat the Miami Confederacy. Arthur St. Clair was retained as governor of the Northwest Territory after his military fiasco but was replaced by Anthony Wayne as commander of the legion. While 3,300 soldiers trained for two years in western Pennsylvania, St. Clair

indigenous people, the British, state governments, or private citizens. The five brothers fought in the Revolution. When Georgian settlers encroached on Cherokee territory, Thomas and Edward Butler negotiated a treaty that thwarted their expansionist ambitions. When insurrectionist citizens roamed the Pennsylvania countryside during the Whiskey Rebellion in 1794, they threatened Fort Fayette. Thomas Butler "prevented the deluded insurgents from taking it more by his name than by his forces, for he had few troops."[1]

At the 1786 treaty, George Rogers Clark gave his own demonstration of US determination. A Shawnee leader, refusing to make a land concession, placed on the negotiating table a string of white wampum, indicating a desire for peace, and a string of black wampum, indicating a desire for continued warfare, and left it to the Americans to make a choice. George Rogers Clark knocked both strings off the table and stomped on them.[2]

The financial aspirations of the government, and of the land speculators who drove its policies, were not served well by these treaties. Claims of dominion meant nothing without the right of occupancy, and the heavy-handed, paper-only extinguishment of aboriginal rights merely provoked a deeper commitment to resisting American expansion.

Eventually, the United States abandoned treaty making, and four of the five Butler brothers fought in St. Clair's defeat. Richard Butler's Shawnee son fought on the opposing side. At the end of the battle, brother Edward removed the wounded Thomas from the field, and Richard was buried on the site. Through ten years of treaties and military action, the United States proved willing to undertake any cost—financial or human—in its aggressive pursuit of indigenous land.[3]

huddled within the confines of Campus Martius, "a poor Devil banished to another planet."[8]

In 1794, Wayne assembled the largest military flotilla ever to travel the Ohio River. The legion fought its way toward the present-day site of Toledo, where the Miami had allowed the British to build an illicit fort. The indigenous combatants retreated after a major battle that was fought in a stand of fallen trees, only to find the doors to Fort Miami barred by the British. They were forced to surrender to Wayne.[9]

The Battle of Fallen Timbers was a decisive victory for the United States, and the men who fought in it became famous. William Clark served with Meriwether Lewis there. Wayne's aide-de-camp, twenty-two-year-old William Henry Harrison, began his rise to national prominence in the battle. James Wilkinson, second-in-command at Fallen Timbers, immediately began a vicious smear campaign against Wayne while vaunting his own contribution to the battle.

The Treaty of Greenville in 1795—the last (and only lasting) treaty signed in the Northwest Territory—marked the end of the Northwest Indian War. In the aftermath of military defeat, indigenous nations accepted a boundary line that would separate them from US settlers and ceded much of present-day Ohio, plus land in Illinois and Indiana. The United States "perfected its title" to the Ohio Company Purchase, to John Cleves Symmes's Miami Purchase, and to a tract set aside for Virginia military veterans; the cession included the future sites of Cincinnati, Dayton, Columbus, and Cleveland.

By 1800, forty-five thousand Americans had arrived in the territory. In preparation for Ohio's admission to the Union, the Northwest Territory was reduced to the area of the state, plus western Michigan. (Eastern Michigan was still occupied by British forts, in violation of the Treaty of Paris and the principle of discovery.) Arthur St. Clair moved to a new capital in Chillicothe.[10]

The remainder of the territory—present-day Indiana, Illinois, Wisconsin, and eastern Minnesota—was organized as Indiana Territory. The territorial secretary, John Gibson, arrived in the new capital of Vincennes in the middle of July 1800. He had been a British soldier before the Revolution and a militia general during it; as an early trader near Fort Pitt, he had once been captured by the Lenape Delaware and was sentenced to be burned at the stake until he was rescued by an old woman (a surprisingly common story). While waiting for the new governor to arrive, Gibson arranged the affairs of the territory.

It was six months before William Henry Harrison appeared in Vincennes to assume control. His career thus far had been meteoric.

Orphaned in his teens, he had been taken into the home of Robert
Morris, the wealthiest man in the United States. In his early twen-
ties, he had been aide-de-camp to Wayne at Fallen Timbers. In 1795,
he signed the Treaty of Greenville and married the daughter of John
Cleves Symmes, owner of the Miami Purchase. In 1798, he had become
secretary of the Northwest Territory, and the next year, he became

1795: Treaty of Greenville

The most notable indigenous military leaders of the "Northwest Indian War" attended the Treaty of Greenville in 1785: Little Turtle of the Miami, Buckongahelas of
the Lenape Delaware, and Weyapiersenwah, or Blue Jacket, of the Shawnee. But
nearly half of the indigenous signers of the treaty (forty-two out of ninety) represented
the Council of Three Fires of the Ottawa, Ojibwe, and Potawatomi. The Ojibwe played
a large (and largely unstated) role in indigenous resistance to early US expansion.

The backgrounds of several US signers illustrate the complex relationships
among indigenous people and colonialists. Jacques LaSelle, an interpreter at the
treaty, was married to the daughter of Blue Jacket. And two other signers had
stepped out of a legend. As long as indigenous nations held a significant land base,
the colonialist imagination was engaged by "Indian captivity" stories. By the mid-
1800s, these stories were used to illustrate the depravity of indigenous people, but
earlier and more common captivity stories had a different tenor, and came in two
varieties. One was the tale of kidnapped white children who were adopted into tribal
societies with such care that they either refused to return to British or American
society as adults or retained after their return a nostalgic fondness for their "Indian
families." The other captivity story involved a trader or soldier, taken prisoner and
about to be burned at the stake, but saved at the last moment by an old Indian woman
who later adopted him.

Characters from these stories—a dozen different men—showed up to sign
twenty-one of the fifty-two official treaties that the United States signed with indigenous nations before the War of 1812. Two of these men were at the Treaty of
Greenville. Christopher Miller had been captured at age fifteen by the Shawnee, with
his brother Henry. Henry returned to his birth family, but Christopher continued to live
among the Shawnee. Just before the Battle of Fallen Timbers, he was recaptured
by a party of legion scouts led by Captain William Wells and, ironically, his brother.
Christopher Miller signed the Treaty of Greenville as an interpreter.

Captain William Wells had himself been kidnapped by the Miami at the age of
twelve and eventually married a daughter of Little Turtle. He led Miami sharpshooters
against US artillery at St. Clair's Defeat. In 1794, however (possibly with the "permission" of Little Turtle), Wells joined the legion while it was fighting its way through
Ohio and served it as a scout. At Greenville, he interpreted the exchange between
his commanding officer, Wayne, and his father-in-law, who was the most reluctant
of the indigenous leaders to sign the treaty.[1]

the territorial delegate to Congress. When he assumed the office of territorial governor, he was twenty-eight years old, harbored limitless political ambitions, and was committed to overturning the Northwest Ordinance's prohibition against slavery north of the Ohio River. He would negotiate millions of acres in land cessions from indigenous nations, and within four years he would become, briefly, the autocratic, unelected ruler of two-thirds of the area of the United States.[11]

Sixteen years after its incorporation, the Northwest Territory had been reconfigured into the state of Ohio and the Territory of Indiana. Land speculators had successfully shaped US territorial expansion in their own interests and aboriginal titles to millions of acres had been extinguished. But the end of the Northwest Territory was only the beginning of US expansion. The United States signaled its unwavering intent in the Treaty of Greenville. The boundary established there between indigenous nations and the United States was defined in detail, but it was temporary: "The Indian tribes who have a right to those lands, are quietly to enjoy them, hunting, planting, and dwelling thereon so long as they please, without any molestation from the United States; but when those tribes, or any of them, shall be disposed to sell their lands, or any part of them, they are to be sold only to the United States."

SIGNERS: A SPECULATIVE ENTERPRISE

Private land speculation grew out of public poverty.
◆——

Historian A. M. Sakolski, 1932

After the opening chapter of the American myth, in which the Declaration of Independence inspired yeoman farmers, led by philosophers, to throw off the shackles of tyranny, the second chapter of the American myth turns to "westward expansion." This is the story of hardy individuals spreading the blessings of liberty, first into Kentucky with their long rifles and axes, later picking rocks from Wisconsin fields to transform a wilderness into productive farmland, eventually arriving at the Pacific in Conestoga wagons, scared witless every step of the way by indigenous people who already lived where the hardy people were just arriving.[12]

This mythological version of US expansion has its contradictory aspects. On one hand, the myth celebrates individualism, the willingness of individual settlers to undertake sacrifice and hardship: the painful farewell, the arduous journey, the herculean task of breaking the land,

and most of all the danger posed by "merciless Indian Savages whose known rule of warfare, is an undistinguished destruction of all ages, sexes and conditions," as the Declaration of Independence so flatly puts it. On the other hand, one of the central images of westward expansion is the homesteader: somewhere along the way a benevolent, egalitarian government, according to the myth, gave away land— free!—to homesteaders and most evocatively to boomers in the Oklahoma Land Rush. These images—rugged individualists creating a new life through their own hard work and the government handout that made America great—coexist in their separate compartments of the American imagination, components of a system designed at all points for the benefit of mythological "ordinary citizens," men of northern European extraction and their nameless wives.

The giveaway, however, happened late in the game. The Homestead Act was passed during the Civil War; the Oklahoma Land Rush was held in 1889, the year before the University of Kansas started playing intercollegiate football and US census takers announced that the American frontier was a thing of the past. Earlier westward expansion was driven not by distributing land in small lots to individual farmers, but by land speculation. Private interests would acquire tens of thousands of square miles from the government for resale to pioneers at a profit. Westward expansion in its beginning was a corporate, not an individualist, enterprise.[13]

Just eighteen months after the Declaration of Independence was signed, the first heady rush of revolutionary fervor had cooled. Farmers and cobblers and shopkeepers needed an inducement to enter pitched battle with British soldiers. So throughout the Revolution, cash-poor states recruited soldiers with the promise of land. The federal government and nine state governments offered warrants that could be redeemed for acreage in the West if the war was won. The size of these bounties depended on the rank of the soldier: the federal scheme offered one hundred acres to each enlisted man, increasing to 1,100 acres for a major general. Virginia, with the largest territorial claim, offered the largest bounties, up to fifteen thousand acres for a major general.[14]

Most enlisted men needed ready money and sold their land warrants for pennies on the dollar, often to their trusted commanding officers. The 2,200 men who had been officers in the army, on the other hand, held warrants for millions of acres. So the original impulse to expand US settlement beyond the Alleghenies was spearheaded by officers of the Continental Army. They became a special interest group, pushing Congress to extinguish aboriginal title to land and distribute that land to soldiers, as promised.

As the Treaty of Paris was negotiated in March 1783, the army was gathered in Newburgh, New York. Congress was planning to disband the troops, because states did not trust the federal government to maintain a permanent army. The officers did not trust the government to deliver on its promise of land, so before they disbanded, they sent a message to Congress. General Henry Knox and more than two hundred other officers signed the Newburgh Petition, warning that "the uneasiness of the soldiers, for want of pay, is great and dangerous; any further experiments on their patience may have fatal effects."[15]

George Washington visited the camp to defuse the immediate situation, and the signatories denied that the petition's stern language was meant to threaten a coup d'etat.

The next month, General Henry Knox (owner of five hundred thousand acres in Maine) created the Society of the Cincinnati. This was ostensibly a social club with membership open only to Continental Army officers for "defense of liberty, the promotion of union, and the preservation of friendships forged in war." But the organization demonstrated an attitude of elitism, to say the least. Membership was hereditary, passed from each member to only one of his male heirs (down to the present day), and members wore a gold medal. If society members shared a political position, it was support for a strong federal government, capable of aggressively extinguishing aboriginal rights to the soil above all else. Society member Nathaniel Gorham, for instance, while president of Congress in 1786, reportedly wrote to inquire if Prince Henry of Prussia was interested in becoming the king of America if its democratic institutions failed. The very existence of the society alarmed some of the more democratically minded Founding Fathers, such as Jefferson and Franklin.[16]

Within a year, half of the officer corps had joined state chapters of the Society of the Cincinnati, and founding members were ready to cash in their land warrants. They included the shareholders of the Ohio Company: Arthur St. Clair, James Mitchell Varnum, Samuel Parsons, Winthrop Sargent, Ebenezer Sproat. When the Ohio Company met with difficulty in making a payment to the federal government on its land north of the Ohio River, shareholders redeemed warrants for 250,000 acres. John Cleves Symmes, another society member, paid the government for the Miami Purchase in part with military warrants—and named the major settlement within the boundaries of his purchase Cincinnati.[17]

Eventually, land warrants of the enlisted men were sold on the open market, where any speculator could buy them at a deep discount. It took years for the federal government and some state governments to set aside land where warrants could be claimed, and longer to extinguish aboriginal title to some of this land, so speculators were buying only the paper promise of real estate. But they could sell those promises for a profit if the market allowed or hoard them until the market did.

As the 1780s progressed, states faced the administrative challenge of distributing land, rather than land titles. They reserved "military districts" for the redemption of warrants. Pennsylvania set aside 500,000 acres, New York 2 million. Virginia reserved 4.2 million acres for bounties in Ohio, plus the southwestern third of Kentucky. (Unequalled in its territorial ambitions among the states, Virginia had once claimed all of the area of the Northwest Territory plus Kentucky for itself and ceded this land to the federal government only on the condition that some of it could be used to meet obligations for military bounties.) Some of this land was still controlled by indigenous nations when the districts were created, and warrant holders would have to wait for land cession treaties in order to claim their land.

In North Carolina, a military tract was already reserved by 1783. As part of a larger scheme that came to be known as the Land Grab Act, state legislator William Blount sponsored a bill creating the military district in an area that later became Tennessee. In addition to reserving land for military bounties, the bill opened four million acres to private purchase; though the law limited the amount of land that any individual could claim, Blount and his brother, along with other leading politicians, claimed hundreds of thousands of acres for themselves. "Enter as much land as you can," Blount advised his cronies. "Make use of any Names fictitious ones will do I suppose."[18]

The mantra of early land speculation was "cheap land." People today are still amazed at the opportunity that was presented to the early American land speculators: tens of thousands of square miles to be had for as low as pennies per acre, in a country where much of the population was a market for resale. "Cheap land," however, is a euphemism. The financial desperation of post-Revolutionary governments, federal and state, certainly deflated the price of land. But nothing brings down the price of real estate like tragedy does—the flood, the factory closing, the murder in the basement. Western land stayed "cheap" during America's expansionist period because the epic, continually unfolding tragedies inflicted on indigenous people—epidemics that were among the most devastating in the history of the world, intentional ethnocide, the displacement of nations—were never entered into the ledger books. At land cession treaties, the page on which those stories of hardship were written was turned to a new blank sheet, where small expense and massive profit might be entered.

Speculators made New York and Ohio the early targets of their attempted "killings." In June 1787, the state of New York auctioned 640,000 acres of land to the private sector. The state's intention was to set aside some of this land for sale to individuals, in small tracts of one square mile, but when the bids were in, the state had bowed to the interests of land speculators. A single syndicate of land speculators purchased the entire tract of land.[19]

A thousand square miles—640,000 acres—may sound like a large real estate transaction, but the leaders of this syndicate had large appetites for land. Alexander Macomb, the front man for the purchase, already owned 173,000 acres in the Adirondacks and 89,000 acres in Ohio. He made his money during the Revolution by selling supplies to the army, but because he sold to the *British* army, he needed patriotic partners. Fur trader and shipping magnate William Constable also engaged in trade with England at the beginning of the war but eventually became aide-de-camp to Lafayette, so his patriotic pedigree was good. A partner further in the background of the deal was Robert Morris, the richest man in America, who handled the finances of Congress during the Revolution. Morris and Constable had opened trade between the United States and China, and their pockets were even deeper than Macomb's.

Over the next ten years, these men were part of a revolving cast of characters—prominently featuring Robert Morris, William Blount, and a Massachusetts politician named Oliver Phelps—who organized syndicates that captured millions of acres.

Even while bidding on land in New York, Macomb and Constable were also minor shareholders in the Ohio Company, which would in a matter of weeks secure its purchase of five million acres in the new Northwest Territory. Near the Miami River, just west of the Ohio Company holdings, US Congressman John Cleves Symmes was selling land that he did not own to soldiers. His request to buy a million acres—the Miami Purchase—was not yet approved by Congress, but he trusted that the influence of one of his partners, ex-president of Congress Elias Boudinot, would secure his title. (He eventually acquired three hundred thousand acres.)

Later in 1778, the western third of New York went up for sale. Massachusetts and New York had settled competing claims to land south of Lake Ontario in a unique agreement: the land would be part of New York, but Massachusetts would sell it. In a single purchase, a syndicate led by Oliver Phelps and Nathaniel Gorham paid a million dollars for the entire six million acres. Phelps was part of the powerful Governor's Council in Massachusetts; as commissary in the Revolution, he had purchased goods for state troops. Gorham had just finished his term as president of Congress. Other players in the deal included Robert Morris and Jeremiah Wadsworth, director of the Bank of the United States and president of the Bank of New York, who met Phelps while serving as commissary general of the Continental Army.

The Phelps-Gorham purchase was a complicated deal involving exchange rates between US dollars and Massachusetts scrip, mergers with companies that claimed to have leases on land from the Iroquois, and a heavy debt load. For their million dollars, the syndicate acquired *preemptive* rights to the land: their title was dependent upon the extinguishment of aboriginal rights. A portion of the purchase—2.5 million acres—was covered in a 1788 treaty with the Iroquois at Buffalo Creek, New York, held not by the federal government but under the auspices of Massachusetts. (The boundaries were later confirmed in a federal treaty.) The financial burden of the project led Phelps and Gorham to sell the remaining 3.5 million acres directly to Robert Morris, who quickly resold all but five hundred thousand acres to front men for the Holland Company, a publicly traded corporation in the Netherlands.

By 1791, Alexander Macomb was a member of the New York legislature when a bill was passed to eliminate any restriction on the sale of land within the borders of the state: no need for an open bidding process, no consideration of the ordinary citizen who might want to buy a farm. In responding to this opportunity, Macomb and William Constable enlisted Daniel McCormick, cofounder of the Bank of New York, who had made his substantial fortune in the Revolution as the auctioneer of Loyalists' property. Over the next six months, the state sold 5.5 million acres of land, and Macomb's syndicate bought 3.7 million acres of it for about eight cents per acre.[20]

By 1795, Oliver Phelps and Nathaniel Gorham had unloaded 1.2 million acres of their land in New York (again to Robert Morris, unsurprisingly). Phelps was financially free to turn his attention to Ohio.

Three million acres lying just south of Lake Erie were claimed by Connecticut—the Connecticut Western Reserve. Phelps, with thirty-four minor associates, bought it all, for $1.2 million.

⋈⋈⋈ ◆ ⋈⋈⋈

Of course, these monumental land deals were not the only land speculation ventures in play in the early days of the republic, though most of the major land speculators before 1800 partnered at some point with Macomb, with Phelps, or especially with Robert Morris.

The most enthusiastic of all speculators, Morris purchased land throughout the United States, both on his own and as the founder of a dizzying array of land companies. He owned more than 7,000 building lots in Washington, DC. His American Land Company held 650,000 acres in Pennsylvania, 900,000 acres in Virginia, 700,000 acres in North Carolina, 950,000 acres in South Carolina, 2 million acres in Georgia, and 400,000 acres in Kentucky. And the biographer who painstakingly tallied this accumulation of capital noted, "When the tracts assigned to this company were disposed of, Mr. Morris was still so extensive a landholder that he owned real estate in Pennsylvania estimated to have a value of $1,000,000 with which in 1797 to organize the Pennsylvania Property Company."[21]

Below the level of "major land speculator," many individuals and family groups acquired land that measured in hundreds of thousands, rather than millions, of acres. John Smith, who added T (for Tennessee) to his name to make himself distinctive, owned a quarter million acres, mostly in Kentucky; his unorthodox land acquisition methods, which included creative use of weapons from his extensive personal armory, earned him a reputation as a "land thief." James Wilkinson was a partner in Symmes's Miami Purchase. He was an earlier speculator in Kentucky, acquiring at least thirty thousand acres there. (His biographer, Andro Linklater, noted that "by 1783, wealthy speculators in the east owned . . . up to one third of Kentucky.") Wilkinson was driven by land lust to extraordinary lengths. At various times he was the highest-ranking officer in the US Army, but he became a paid spy for Spain in the hopes of acquiring sixty thousand acres in what is now Mississippi.

⋈⋈⋈ ◆ ⋈⋈⋈

The promise of wealth, the desperation that arose in managing heavy debt, and the cupidity of treaty signers such as Phelps, Gorham, Blount, Constable, McCormick, and Wilkinson steered massive land speculation schemes toward massive fraud. Morris's Pennsylvania Population Company was one of the most intentional and organized of these frauds. Morris's partner in the scheme, John Nicholson, was Pennsylvania's comptroller general, in charge of the state's finances. Investors also included Aaron Burr, treaty signer Ebenezer Denny, and other members of the Society of the Cincinnati. For some investors, the Pennsylvania Population Company was the culmination of their shady careers. For Morris, it was merely a place to hold clouded land titles in a financial juggling act.

The fraud began in the 1790s, as soon as Pennsylvania opened the sale of public land to all citizens. Buyers could claim land at a central office in Philadelphia, supervised by Nicholson, and pay the state to conduct a survey of it. Nicholson eventually shepherded through his system 1,150 warrants for 440 acres each, using 1,150 false names, then transferred them to the company. This scheme netted the cabal a half million acres—still a fraction of the four million acres that Nicholson would at one point claim to own.[22]

Francis Johnston, who signed the Treaty of Greenville, became receiver general of the Pennsylvania Land Office. As the person who registered the land warrants and guaranteed their validity, he was in on the scheme; so were state surveyors who took bribes from speculators to identify choice land. The conspiracy was eventually investigated by the state legislature, but it was complicated and involved many prominent people. Nicholson resigned his office but was acquitted on charges of corruption.

Farther to the south, William Blount's early personal land fraud proved the precursor to a more organized and complicated conspiracy. In 1795, Blount's speculation partner, John Sevier, wrote to James Glasgow, the secretary of state in North Carolina, for help in fraudulently registering 128,000 acres in the Southwest Territory in his own name. That was not the conspiracy, but only an indication of how crooked the local land distribution system had become.

Land speculators controlled every aspect of that system, from setting public policy to surveying land west of the mountains to running the offices where land claims could be registered, right to the final certification of deeds by Secretary of State Glasgow. The conspirators included William Terrell, a clerk in Glasgow's office; surveyor William Polk, a speculator with partners in the federal Treasury Department; and surveyor Stockley Donelson—son-in-law of Glasgow and brother-in-law of Andrew Jackson.

Investigators later identified fourteen distinct methods of fraud that the conspirators used to accumulate as many as seven hundred thousand acres for themselves. As the scheme fell apart, several of the participants burglarized the state capitol in Raleigh to destroy records; Philemon, a slave of William Terrell, was captured and hung. At a subsequent meeting at William Blount's house, the conspirators considered burning down the capitol building to cover their tracks.

Before prosecution of the conspirators could begin, John Sevier was elected governor of the new state of Tennessee, and he claimed that North Carolina had no jurisdiction over the records of the land offices. Several of the conspirators became fugitives, and Glasgow was ruined politically, but none of the cabal went to jail.[23]

Before the American land bubble burst, speculators had the chance to participate in the grandest and most corrupt venture of all—the Yazoo Land Fraud. Four corporations purchased thirty-five million acres— more than half of the current states of Mississippi and Alabama— from the state of Georgia. Every member of the Georgia legislature but one accepted bribes, including shares in the land companies, and were in effect selling the land to themselves.

Public outrage was overwhelming. The next legislature rescinded the deal, and eventually Georgia was forced to cede its western land to the federal government. But in the weeks immediately following the sale, land speculators from throughout the United States converged on Georgia to get a piece of the action. In rapid-fire transactions that clouded land titles for generations, involvement in the scandal expanded to include treaty signers Robert Morris, Oliver Phelps, William Constable, John Smith T, William Blount, and William Hull; their cronies John Nicholson and John Sevier; and many others. Members of one of the Yazoo land companies built a boat, raised an army, and started down the Tennessee River to take their land by force, but they turned back when they encountered Thomas Butler of the Fighting Butler Brothers stationed with artillery on a bluff overlooking the river.[24]

The Yazoo Land Fraud coincided with the collapse of major land speculation ventures all over the country. The largest speculators, needing a quick turnaround to meet their heavy debt loads, put more than fifty million acres on the market in a country with a population of five million people. Land sales to Europeans were wiped out by an economic crisis in England, and economies on both sides of the Atlantic struggled for decades. Few people went to prison for the fraud committed in these enterprises, but John Nicholson of Pennsylvania and Alexander Macomb went to debtors' prison; Oliver Phelps died there. Even Robert Morris wound up in debtors' prison and would also have died there if his friends in Congress had not closed the debtors' prisons down.[25]

XXXXX ◆ XXXXX

The fortunes of all the major land speculators depended on land cession treaties. They might *buy* their land preemptively (assuming that aboriginal title would later be extinguished), but they could not *sell* it until indigenous groups had ceded their rights to the land. In fact, several of the syndicates—notably Phelps and Gorham, and the Ohio Company—were required as a condition of their purchase to cover the cost of the treaty negotiations and even of the payments to indigenous nations for their land.

This critical juncture in land speculation was too important to leave in the hands of bureaucrats. Consequently, major land speculators and/or their representatives attended the treaties that affected their fortunes. Some of them were actually mentioned in the treaty text, because their purchase was the whole point of the enterprise: Oliver Phelps in a treaty with the Seneca, 1802; his Connecticut Land Company in a treaty with the Wyandot and others, 1805. Most of the speculators mentioned previously—Phelps, Constable, Gorham, Wadsworth, Morris, McCormick, Wilkinson, Smith T, Polk—trekked to places like Buffalo Creek and the mouth of the Great Miami and Pushapukanuk in Mississippi, or met with indigenous delegations in New York, to witness the transformation of the natural world into their own private property.

After the Louisiana Purchase, large-scale land speculation became unfeasible. If unloading a million acres in New York on a short time line was difficult, it would have been impossible in early Montana. The epic early acquisitions east of the Mississippi would be rivaled west of the river only by infrequent, extraordinary phenomena such as railroads and Texas. The brake on massive land purchases also resulted from a new federal land policy that emphasized land sales in small lots at set prices of more than a dollar per acre. Land offices were established to conduct this business.[26]

Consequently, the objective of speculators changed from quantity to quality. A lot of money could still be made if the right land was selected for purchase. Augustus Porter, for instance, greatly increased his wealth in 1805 by buying only four hundred acres: it was a mile-long strip of land that controlled the US side of Niagara Falls, including a road along which all American fur trade traffic had to move. In general, the focus of land speculation became townsite development, where a few thousand acres could turn a profit with the sale of a few city lots. Of course, the early speculators had created hundreds of towns in New York, Ohio, and the South, and sixty years later, railroads would create hundreds more towns. In the intervening years, speculators with just as much ambition but working on a smaller scale would create cities and towns in the Midwest.[27]

Location and timing became the keys to successful townsite development. The first person to claim a thousand acres at the confluence of rivers, for instance, had a greater chance of making money than a person buying a few thousand out of millions of acres of farmland. Many of the most successful early opportunists in the Midwest were fur traders. Licensed to enter "Indian country" long before any settlers, they set up trade at locations where people had been gathering for centuries. Fort Wayne and Indianapolis, Pierre and Yankton in South Dakota, Prairie du Chien and Green Bay in Wisconsin, Chicago, Kansas City, and many other trading centers of white settlement were already established as trading centers among indigenous people.

Another early factor in the selection of townsites was the construction of military forts. These were situated at prime locations on rivers or along major roads used by indigenous people, and communities developed around them to serve the needs of soldiers, both legitimate and illicit. Examples include Fort Wayne, Indiana; Fort Dodge, Iowa; Chicago, which grew around Fort Dearborn; and St. Paul, Minnesota, which grew near Fort Snelling.

Traders and military personnel were familiar with local landscapes *before the land was ceded by indigenous nations.* This gave them a great advantage over other would-be founders of towns, and many Midwest speculators entered the game from those professions. Attendance at a treaty also created advantages for locating promising sites and securing them quickly. Joseph Barron, an interpreter for William Henry Harrison, finished his work at a treaty and, while the document was still being signed by the participants, rode out of the fort in a wagon to claim a salt mine.

Attached to the bottom of treaties, the names of the government witnesses might be easy to ignore today. The articles of a typical treaty are often so monumental—the transfer of vast territories—that the signatures at the bottom of the document can seem insignificant. The presence of a military officer at a treaty makes sense, but at first has no meaning. A French surname might indicate a fur trader, but so what? Treaties are often dismissed in the American popular imagination as the bureaucratic paperwork of an inevitable historical movement. But treaty sites and ceded territory were more than "hunting grounds" (important as those were). They included important traditional meeting places that fostered cohesion among indigenous communities. On the US side, men known as founders of towns signed virtually every treaty in the Midwest, though many of those townsites had been occupied for generations.

In the mid-1830s, as indigenous nations began their forced diaspora in the East and ceded extensive territory west of the Mississippi, the amount of land sold by the federal government skyrocketed: 4.5 million acres in 1834, 20 million acres in 1836. Though the demand for this newly available land was apparent, the government did not raise its prices. Anyone who purchased public land felt that profit was assured. Given the burgeoning demand for land, banks were willing to loan money for unsecured real estate purchases, even if the buyer was a second- or thirdhand purchaser getting into the market at an inflated price.[28]

At the same time, banking regulations changed. Until the 1830s, most banks were private enterprises chartered by state governments. Corruption was rampant, as politicians appointed themselves or their cronies to lucrative positions as trustees of the banks. And these banks limited the amount of money in circulation; speculators had difficulty securing cash even for down payments on land. Reform-minded "free banking" laws increased currency and started a speculation boom. Virtually anyone could open a bank and issue notes that could be traded like cash. According to banking historian Bray Hammond, "It might be found somewhat harder to become a banker than a brick-layer, but not much."[29]

John P. Arndt was a man of substantial means, a boat maker and tavern keeper who supplied beef for Fort Howard in Wisconsin. In 1835, he was starting a new career as a creator of towns. His first step was to incorporate, with influential friends, the Fox River Hydraulic Company, which was authorized by the Wisconsin legislature to build a dam. With state money secured, the company issued certificates that ostensibly were redeemable for cash, and began operating as the Bank of Fox River. Arndt also invested in the Fond du Lac Company with some of the same partners. These two companies started the towns of De Pere, Two Rivers, and Fond du Lac, Wisconsin. Arndt was a speculator who survived financially in the long run, in part because one of his partners in both the Fox River Hydraulic Company and the Fond du Lac Company was James Duane Doty—the largest speculator in the history of Wisconsin. When Wisconsin Territory was formed in 1836, Doty successfully lobbied the legislature to use one of his townsites, Madison, as the territorial capital.[30]

Millions of acres of land were purchased using notes like those issued by the Bank of Fox River. And as the land craze continued, the bureaucrats in land offices—receivers of public moneys, registers of deeds—were increasingly tempted to corruption. They might take ownership of choice land before it could be publicly sold or take bribes to withhold those titles until a particular customer made it to the front of the ever-growing line of aspiring purchasers.

Banking and treaty-making: some men left banking to take potentially more lucrative positions and signed treaties as Indian agents; others made enough money from US–Indian relations to open a bank later. Many were pillars of their communities, stoking the local financial engine and processing the paperwork for people's dreams; others were wildcat bankers and corrupt bureaucrats. They were on hand at treaties to witness the perfection of land titles on which they hoped to make their fortunes. This is another untold story written in the signatures at the end of treaties.

The infrastructure of land speculation depended upon land offices and banks, and the most successful speculators controlled these aspects of the enterprise. Another ancillary aspect of speculation was land surveying. Surveyors were often paid for their work *in land*. In 1784, for instance, James Wilkinson signed a contract to survey eleven thousand acres of land for a speculator and as compensation would receive half of that land. The financial risk was minimal, the return for labor was highly lucrative, and the resulting land claims of surveyors were more solid than those of the men who hired them. When claims were disputed, claimants who had made "improvements" to the land usually won the dispute, and conducting a survey was considered an improvement.[31]

Surveyors, bankers, and land office personnel were personally interested in the transfer of indigenous land to US control. At some point in their careers, nearly one out of every ten Americans who ever signed a treaty with indigenous nations worked in a land office, founded or directed a bank, or worked as a land surveyor. But in 1836, the entire mechanism of land speculation ground to a temporary halt. Andrew Jackson "ordered that the land offices should accept only gold or silver or 'land scrip' (i.e., soldiers' warrants) in payment for public lands." The land bubble of the 1830s had been built not with these resources, but with worthless notes from wildcat banks. Land sales stopped and land prices crashed. Exacerbated by financial decisions in England that year, the bursting of the land bubble generated the Panic of 1837. The American economy would not recover for seven years.[32]

XXXXX ◆ XXXXX

The same year—1837—Dakota and Ojibwe people made the first land cessions in what is now the state of Minnesota. These treaties were, from a colonialist perspective, less about land for speculation purposes and more about territorial boundaries and the extraction of natural resources. Speculators in what would become Minnesota would have to wait years for an opportune moment.

By 1851, settlers were moving to the new states of Wisconsin and Iowa, and speculators in Minnesota wanted a piece of the action. In reporting to Congress on the massive Dakota land cession of that year—nineteen million acres, virtually all of the Dakota homeland—treaty commissioners Luke Lea and Alexander Ramsey wrote, "It is needed as an additional outlet to the overwhelming tide of migration which is both increasing and irresistible in its westward progress."[33]

The Dakota were told that they would be isolated from white settlers on their small reservation in the western part of the state. But within two years, Henry Sibley was selling land on the very edge of that reservation, and townsite development had begun in Minnesota. Again, many of the leading speculators were also leading politicians; many had started in the fur trade. And not coincidentally, many were signers of treaties with the Dakota, Ojibwe, and other nations. The Minnesota townsite developers who signed treaties included Sibley (who also invested in the development of Mendota, Hastings, and St. Anthony Falls); George Fuller, who developed Chaska; Alexander Faribault, who started the town that bears his name; D. George Morrison, Reuben Carlton, and D. Cash, who incorporated Duluth; and Joseph Brown, who started Henderson and Stillwater.

On the eve of Minnesota statehood, land speculation had reached such a fever pitch that it was noted around the world. The *Boston Traveller* newspaper ran an article about Midwest land prices in July 1857:

"The land mania in the West is wholly irreconcileable with any reasonable view of industrial advancement and prosperity. . . . We have had many land speculating manias before, but none so very wild, absurd and extensive, as that which has prevailed for two or three years past. The fever has subsided somewhat in Michigan, Illinois, and Wisconsin, but in Iowa, Minnesota, and Kansas, there seems to be yet no abatement."[34]

And again demonstrating that that "cheap land" is produced by human misery, the article links the high prices of American farm products to the potato famine in Ireland. In October, the article was reprinted in the *Sydney* (Australia) *Morning Herald*. In the intervening months, however, land speculation had come to a halt, with the Panic of 1857.

As long as indigenous people held extensive homelands, speculators were on the lookout for ways to make money in the transition of that land into US property. Clark W. Thompson was a powerful Indian agent and railroad booster in 1863, when the Ho Chunk were removed from Minnesota; Clark Brothers real estate company was in charge of selling their land. Six years later he started the town of Wells, Minnesota, on part of the nine thousand acres he reportedly had acquired for $1.25 per acre, a site situated to take advantage of a new railroad. He held onto much of his land for twenty-five years, when he sold it for $80 per acre.[35]

Land speculation was a prime motivation for westward expansion. From soldiers to settlers, from townsite developers to land office agents, men involved in speculation dreamed of making fortunes by being the first buyer when indigenous land went on the American market. This fact runs counter to the American myth, which presents the idea that indigenous land was taken for the benefit of the "little guy," the sergeant or store owner in the East who wanted to start a new life by picking rocks from a field in the Midwest. Certainly the ultimate benefits were spread around, but settlers were often the secondary beneficiaries of treaty making, the customers of speculators who engineered the treaties.

Land speculators had a significant influence on Indian affairs policies throughout the treaty-making era. In many cases, however, they were not the first Europeans to interact with indigenous people in an area. Traders, especially fur traders, had prepared the way, and their business was equally important to treaty making.

■ Traders

Trade was the initial point of contact between the United States and indigenous nations. It was a field marked by rivalries. Colonialist nations and indigenous nations looked for material advantages over their neighbors, and diplomacy in North America often focused on treaties that would increase those advantages. The United States used trade to build alliances with indigenous nations, and to weaken indigenous alliances with other colonialist powers.

The conscious intent of US trade policies was to make indigenous nations dependent on trade goods and generate debt among indigenous people. As a result, land cession treaties would be easier to negotiate. Traders, then, became key players in US–Indian relations. Through commercial and family ties, white traders built such trust among indigenous nations that, in many cases, only they could broker land cessions. Once land was transferred to US control, traders invented new ways to profit from US–Indian relations.

The use of trade as an economic weapon against indigenous people was intentional and planned from the very start of US expansion. Thomas Jefferson knew that the fur trade would devastate traditional indigenous economies. He laid out the plan when he wrote in 1803: "The decrease of game rendering their subsistence by hunting insufficient, we wish to draw them to agriculture. . . . They will perceive how useless to them are their extensive forests, and will be willing to pare them off from time to time. . . . They will in time either incorporate with us as citizens of the United States, or remove beyond the Mississippi. The former is certainly the termination of their history."[1]

TERRITORY: 1800–1812

In 1800, a forest surrounded the village of Vincennes. The main road into the capital of Indiana Territory had been made by buffalo— which still lived in the area. A thousand-year history of local human

Grand Seal of the Territory of Oklahoma (1893), detail.

habitation was written in the landscape, where naturally formed mounds had been used as burial sites. When French traders had arrived in the area in the early 1700s, local Piankeshaw people had welcomed them, helped them build a fort, and gave them land on which to live. Though the British later claimed dominion over the place, and George Rogers Clark captured the fort for the United States during the Revolution, the Piankeshaw and French still lived and traded there when William Henry Harrison arrived as the new American governor.

Enthusiastic in his role, Harrison soon devised a territorial seal that he could use to stamp official documents. The image on the seal reflected Harrison's first-things-first approach to business: a farmer chopping down a tree and, in the foreground, a buffalo exiting stage left. Harrison's job was to clear the way for the westward expansion of the United States.[2]

One hundred fifty miles due west of Vincennes and just across the Mississippi, another thousand people of French descent lived in the village of St. Louis. Auguste and Jean Pierre Chouteau were leaders of the community; Auguste had founded the town as a trading post nearly forty years earlier. By 1800, the brothers held a monopoly on trade with the Osage, and their employees traveled far up the Missouri River to trade with distant nations. Their sisters had married rival fur traders, bringing more business into the family fold. This intricate network of personal and business connections positioned the Chouteaus as the unchallenged intermediaries between colonialist nations and indigenous nations. They were equipped to handle any regime change, and they knew all about William Henry Harrison.

To regulate trade between the United States and indigenous nations, Congress set up government trading houses, called factories, in the 1790s. Private traders continued to operate among indigenous nations for a profit, but the factory system was intended to undercut them; its only purpose was to create a dependence on trade goods, so prices at the factory trading posts were kept low. The first factories were opened in the Southeast, where unscrupulous private fur traders had created conflict. By 1803, the system moved west, to sites along the eastern bank of the Mississippi and to Detroit and Fort Wayne in Indiana Territory. Thomas Jefferson wrote to William Henry Harrison in February 1803, outlining how trade was connected to treaty making: "To promote this disposition to exchange lands which they have to spare and we want . . . we shall push our trading houses, and be glad to see the good and influential individuals among them run in debt, because we observe that when these debts get beyond what the individuals can pay, they become willing to lop them off by a cession of lands."[3]

Three months later, Harrison began his treaty-making career. In a period of five weeks, he negotiated three treaties—compared to the single abortive treaty by Arthur St. Clair in thirteen years as a territorial governor. True to his vainglorious nature, Harrison signed these treaties using his full title: "Governor of the said territory, superintendent of Indian affairs, and commissioner plenipotentiary of the United States, for concluding any treaty or treaties which may be found necessary with any of the Indian tribes north west of the Ohio."

Yet the conditions of the first two treaties were modest (from a colonialist point of view). The Delaware, Shawnee, and members of the Miami Confederacy—now actively engaged in diplomacy with the United States—ceded a salt mine, the right to build "houses of entertainment" and ferries on roads leading to Vincennes, a military bounty for George Rogers Clark, and the land on which Vincennes, the territorial capital, was located. In exchange, the indigenous nations would receive regular payments of salt and free rides on the ferries.

The third treaty was negotiated with tribes in Illinois country known collectively as the Kaskaskia, a group that "from a variety of unfortunate circumstances" (in treaty language) were "reduced to a very small number." Virtually powerless, they ceded their right to the soil covering more than a third of the present-day state of Illinois (though they retained the right to hunt there). In exchange, the United States offered to cover the salary of a Catholic priest and help establish a farming community near the Mississippi River.[4]

During the weeks when Harrison was signing treaties, Thomas Jefferson announced the Louisiana Purchase. Again the United States "doubled in size," but only in its claim to dominion, not in its all-important ability to distribute real estate. Scores of indigenous nations occupied those 828,000 square miles.

While the federal government figured out what to do with its vast dominion, the area was placed under the military control of Captain Amos Stoddard. The Chouteau brothers of St. Louis quickly charmed him. Within three months, Stoddard asked Jean Pierre Chouteau to accompany Osage leaders to a meeting with Thomas Jefferson.

The delegation arrived in Washington on July 11, the day that Aaron Burr killed Alexander Hamilton. Jefferson would meet the Osage, but treasury secretary Albert Gallatin had to deal with Chouteau. "He seems well disposed," Gallatin reported, "but what he wants is power and money. He proposed that he should have a negative [veto power] on all the Indian trading licenses, and the direction and all the profits of the trade carried on by the government with all the Indians of Louisiana. . . . I told him this was inadmissible; and his last demand was the exclusive trade with the Osages. . . . As he may be either useful or dangerous, I gave no flat denial to his last request."[5]

The Chouteaus did get their American monopoly on trade with the Osage. And Jean Pierre, who had operated as "Pedro" under the Spanish, was appointed under the name of "Peter" to be the sole US Indian agent west of the Mississippi.

Harrison negotiated several more treaties in 1804, and in September his power as a territorial governor reached its apex. The United States created the District of Louisiana and, pending the formal establishment of a territorial government, attached the huge district temporarily to Indiana Territory. For six months, William Henry Harrison controlled treaty making, land distribution, and trade throughout an area of more than a million square miles.

It took only weeks for Harrison and Jean Pierre Chouteau to manage the first US–Indian treaty west of the Mississippi. A Sauk and Meskwaki (Fox) delegation to St. Louis, not authorized by their nation to make a treaty and hoping only to retrieve an imprisoned member of their tribe, was cajoled into signing a document that would poison the US–Sauk relationship for years. The enormous ceded area—thirty-five thousand square miles—started just north of St. Louis on the west side of the Mississippi and included the northwestern third of Illinois and part of Wisconsin.[6]

The Louisiana Purchase—far from giving the United States outright ownership of the Midwest—bound the United States to respect aboriginal title to the land there. It required the United States to "execute Such treaties and articles as may have been agreed between Spain and the tribes and nations of Indians until by mutual consent of the United States and the said tribes or nations other Suitable articles Shall have been agreed upon."[7]

The fact that *France* insisted that the *United States* abide by *Spanish* treaties with *indigenous* nations indicates how complicated land tenure was along the Mississippi at the time. Some tribes over the years had

1804: Treaty with the Sauk and Fox

In 1804, William Henry Harrison and Jean Pierre Chouteau "negotiated" a treaty with the Sauk and Fox. Four tribal members were in St. Louis to inquire about a compatriot who had been arrested by US authorities. Though they were not authorized by their people to cede land, Harrison and Chouteau provided them with alcohol and pressed them into signing the treaty. The outrageous terms of the treaty—a land cession of thirty-five thousand square miles in exchange for an annual payment of $1,000—led directly to the Black Hawk War twenty-eight years later. And beyond that scandalous land grab, other motivations were also active in the engineering of the treaty.

One of these motivations was the US interest in wresting control of trade from the British. The treaty stipulated that "no person shall reside as a trader in the Indian country without a license under the hand [and] seal of the superintendent of Indian affairs. . . . [The] said tribes do promise and agree that they will not suffer any trader to reside amongst them without such license; and that they will from time to time give notice to the superintendent or to the agent for their tribes of all the traders that may be in their country."[1]

As a further means of gaining control of trade, the United States would "at a convenient time establish a trading house or factory where the individuals of the said tribes can be supplied with goods at a more reasonable rate than they have been accustomed to procure them."

A more personal motivation on the part of Jean Pierre Chouteau was also in play. The significance of an article included in the treaty would become apparent only later: "It is agreed that nothing in this treaty contained, shall affect the claim of any individual or individuals who may have obtained grants of land from the Spanish government, and which are not included within the general boundary line laid down in this treaty, provided that such grant have at any time been made known to the said tribes and recognized by them."

The Chouteaus and other French merchants in St. Louis had two major concerns about the new American regime. The first was a question of whether land grants recognized by the Spanish regime would be recognized also by the United States. The second was a question of slavery, which was illegal in Indiana Territory. Jean Pierre Chouteau had a personal stake in both questions. As a US official, Chouteau was the voice of local interests who held land and slaves.

The US property system was crossing the Mississippi River, and all of these aspects of life in 1805 St. Louis—the transfer of indigenous land to US control, US recognition of French land claims established under Spanish administrators, and slavery—were issues related to property.

given land to individuals—often to French and Spanish fur traders—and some of these gifts were recognized in land titles validated by French or Spanish administrations but not yet by the United States. Some tribes had ceded to colonialist nations land that other tribes also occupied, and some of those tribes had on occasion ceded the same land to a different colonialist nation. The colonialist governments, in turn, had sold and granted land to corporations and individuals, and only some of those titles survived regime change. Plus, some colonialists had squatted on indigenous-controlled land for generations without permission from anyone, and others had fabricated fraudulent titles.

The federal government set up a commission to examine land titles in Indiana Territory, even while Harrison aggressively engineered more disquieting land cessions.

In 1805, Harrison's domain was diminished by the creation of two new territories. Harrison, focusing on land along the Mississippi, had overlooked six hundred Americans living in distant Detroit and a few traders in Michilimackinac. These were important trading centers, and residents there felt keenly the lack of attention from distant Vincennes. In 1805, elections for an Indiana territorial legislature were held, but the election was over before Detroit residents learned it was happening. In outrage, they petitioned for the formation of their own government. Michigan was incorporated as a territory on June 30, 1805, and General William Hull was appointed governor.

The hapless Hull arrived in Detroit a few weeks early, on June 11, 1805. The day before he arrived, every building in town burned to the ground. In December, Hull was still writing to Washington, asking for permission to cut wood for house construction. During his twelve-year tenure as governor, Hull would negotiate two official treaties. The Council of Three Fires and the Wyandot ceded a tract that reached from Detroit into Ohio for two cents per acre. The same groups plus the Shawnee gave permission for the United States to build a road in northern Ohio. These treaties fueled a growing, grassroots resentment to continued US expansion among indigenous nations throughout the old Northwest Territory.[8]

Louisiana Territory was incorporated on July 4, 1805, five days after Michigan Territory. James Wilkinson's constant self-aggrandizement and criticism of Anthony Wayne had paid off: for the seven years since Wayne's death, Wilkinson had been commanding general of the US Army, and now he simultaneously would be governor of the largest of all US territories. He had traveled the lower Mississippi region for fifteen years, since first visiting New Orleans to become a spy for Spain, and arrived in St. Louis a month early, ready to start a new adventure.

One of his first official activities was to write the secretary of war about British influence in the fur trade: "The privation we Suffer from this diversion of our rightful commerce, is a trifling ill, when compared to the transcendent influence, which is thus acquired and perpetuated by a foreign power, over the aborigines within our national limits."[9]

This antipathy toward the British marked a rare convergence of Wilkinson's interest as a high-ranking American and his interest as a Spanish spy. As the Chouteau family received information on the progress of Lewis and Clark from their extensive network of traders on the Upper Missouri, they genially passed it on to Wilkinson, who passed it on to Spain. Nonetheless, within weeks of taking charge, Wilkinson sent Lieutenant Zebulon Pike to assess relations with indigenous nations, locate sites for fort construction, and assert American dominance among the British fur traders of the Upper Mississippi. While on this trip, Pike would negotiate the first treaty between the United States and Dakota people.

When Pike returned, he was immediately sent on a more ambitious expedition toward Santa Fe, though the origins of this excursion remain murky. Even while taking his pay from Spain, Wilkinson was also intimately connected to Aaron Burr, who was gathering men and supplies to attack Spanish territory in the Southwest. The second Pike trip may have been part of this conspiracy, intended to locate Spanish military installations (though Pike was apparently unaware of that purpose).

Burr's brother-in-law, Joseph Browne, was secretary of the territory, and Wilkinson appointed other Burr supporters to key offices. One focal point for his machinations was the territorial militia, a potential source of military support for Burr. The Chouteaus controlled the local St. Louis militia but were too politically astute to get involved in the Burr plot, and most of the officers in other areas of the territory actively disliked Wilkinson. But in St. Genevieve, just to the south of St. Louis, politics had fractured over control of the lucrative lead mines, and Wilkinson found a powerful ally there. John Smith T, the "land thief" of Tennessee, had raised a private army to take over the St. Genevieve lead mines. Wilkinson—never afraid to stir up trouble—put him in charge of the local militia and made him a territorial judge. Another lead miner, Henry Dodge, was appointed a militia lieutenant. Both Smith T and Dodge were deeply immersed in Burr's plans.[10]

Zealous factionalism in the territory—over the lead mines, over control of the militia, over support of Burr—was inevitable in a Wilkinson administration, and Thomas Jefferson soon decided to remove the governor from the political scene. In March 1806, as tensions grew between the United States and Spain, General Wilkinson was ordered to take charge of US troops in New Orleans.

Burr's plans had progressed by then to the point where an armed force was gathering in Natchez, and concerns about the conspiracy became acute in Washington. The treacherous Wilkinson chose that moment to blow the whistle on the scheme. John Smith T and Henry Dodge were moving six tons of lead and other supplies down the Mississippi to Natchez when news of the betrayal broke. They quietly sold their goods and returned home to St. Genevieve to find that a grand jury had indicted them for treason. Smith T threatened to kill the writ server who showed up with his indictment. Dodge posted bail before the grand jury, then whipped nine of its members.[11]

In the spring of 1807, Thomas Jefferson cleaned house in Louisiana Territory. Wilkinson's own role in the Burr conspiracy became too prominent to be ignored, and he was dismissed as governor after twenty contentious months in office. Burr's brother-in-law was replaced as secretary by Frederick Gates, a territorial supreme court judge from Detroit. William Clark was named an Indian agent (joining Jean Pierre Chouteau in the job) and the brigadier general of the militia. The new governor was Meriwether Lewis.

Lewis's mental health may have begun deteriorating already at that point. It took him a year to report to his new job. In his absence, Clark and territorial secretary Frederick Bates began a political purge of Burr supporters. Smith T was out as both judge and militia officer; the "Military School," an anti-Wilkinson association, replaced the St. Genevieve militia unit.[12]

When Lewis finally arrived in the territory, one of his first acts was to organize a Masonic Lodge in St. Louis. The founding members included Clark and the next generation of the Chouteau family: Pierre Chouteau Jr. and the brothers Gabriel and Rene Paul, who were married to daughters of Auguste Chouteau.[13]

Near the end of 1808, Clark attempted to negotiate a treaty with the Osage: a massive land cession covering much of present-day Arkansas and Missouri. Attained for minimal compensation and the promise of a trading post, the treaty demonstrated the efficacy of Jefferson's trade policy. Lewis reported to Jefferson that, by cutting off credit and supplies, "the Osage nations . . . were reduced in the course of a few months to a state of perfect submission without bloodshed; this has in my opinion very fairly proven the superiority which the policy of withholding merchandize from the Indians has over the chastizement of the swoard."[14]

But Lewis and Clark made the mistake of negotiating the treaty without the Chouteau family. Jean Pierre and Auguste Chouteau held the trust of the Osage, and they could make a treaty work or sabotage it. The Osage soon objected to Clark's handling of the treaty, and Lewis was compelled to send Jean Pierre Chouteau to renegotiate it.

Clark learned his lesson: diplomacy and the fur trade were inseparable. In March 1809, the St. Louis Missouri Fur Trading Company (later the Missouri Fur Company) was incorporated in St. Louis. Formed "for the purposes of trading and hunting up the river Missouri and to the head waters thereof," the company obliterated the lines between political power and commercial power. William Clark was one of the founders. Still only three years removed from his own famous trip up the Missouri, he now controlled which traders would get a license to operate anywhere on the river. The other partners included Clark's brother-in-law, Denis Fitzhugh; Jean Pierre Chouteau, his son Augustin, and his brother-in-law Sylvestre Labadie; Pierre Menard, a prominent fur trader from just across the Mississippi in Kaskaskia, who had wisely married the sister of Jean Pierre Chouteau's wife; the Chouteaus' greatest rival in the western fur trade, Manuel Lisa, co-opted as company director, and two other powerful traders; and just for good measure, relatives of both James Wilkinson and Meriwether Lewis. For the next forty years, this marriage of political and economic power would never lose its grip on the fur trade or on US–Indian relations west of the Mississippi River.[15]

Meriwether Lewis witnessed the incorporation of the company, but his days as governor of Missouri Territory were numbered. As he was stressed by debt and impaired by drink, his mental stability deteriorated during the year. In October, on his way to Washington to plead his case in several pressing territorial concerns, he met a violent death, presumably at his own hand. Six months later, a Kentucky congressman named Benjamin Howard replaced Lewis as governor.

In the same week in March 1809 that the Missouri Fur Company was created, William Henry Harrison saw his domain reduced again. Residents along the Mississippi succeeded in forming Illinois Territory; the capital was Kaskaskia, only fifty miles from St. Louis, and the

1808: Treaty with the Osage

When Osage representatives met Thomas Jefferson in 1804, the president promised to encourage trade by building a trading post in their territory. Within days of the promise, Meriwether Lewis and William Clark—ascending the Missouri River on their famous trip west—noted a location on the bluffs that had "many advantages for a fort and trading-house with the Indians."[1]

In 1808, Clark met Osage leaders at this spot for a treaty that reads like a commercial: "The United States being also anxious that the Great and Little Osage . . . should be regularly supplied with every species of merchandise, which their comfort may hereafter require, do engage to establish at this place, and permanently to continue at all seasons of the year, a well assorted store of goods, for the purpose of bartering with them on moderate terms for their peltries and furs."[2]

Through its factory system of trade, the United States was undercutting private traders. It was a situation in some ways analogous to the arrival of a big-box store in a small community. Locals could get anything they wanted at incredible prices, but the social fabric of the community would be frayed. In exchange for the trading post and other minor considerations—$1,500, a blacksmith, a water mill—the Osage ceded a territory covering half of present-day Arkansas and two-thirds of Missouri, "a country nearly equal in extent to the state of Virginia and much more fertile."[3]

Problems with the treaty arose immediately. Lewis was forced to admit to President Jefferson that, within days of the signing, he had been "informed by Mr. P. Chouteau, Agt. of the Osages, that the Indians complained of having been deceived. . . . [T]he chiefs who had signed it had no right to dispose of their lands."

In the face of Osage objections to the treaty, Lewis "dispatched Mr. Peter Chouteau . . . to obtain from them as general an assent to it as possible." Only Chouteau had the intimate connections required to carry the treaty through. On November 10, he accomplished his mission.

As a quid pro quo, Chouteau wanted Lewis to secure his title to twenty-five thousand acres that he claimed as a gift from the Osage. "The doubts and suspicions which overshadowed these transactions," Lewis explained to Jefferson, led to "a want of cordiality and confidence" between Chouteau and Clark: "I must from these considerations beg leave to recommend that Genl. Clark should be invested with some general power of control over all the Agents and Sub Agents in the territory."

It was an authority that Clark would hold for the rest of his life. But the involvement of the Chouteau family in treaty making did not end there. Jean Pierre remained an agent (and treaty signer) under Clark's supervision; his brother Auguste would enter the picture to negotiate twenty-eight treaties in the next ten years, and soon the next generation of Chouteaus would grow into their own major role in diplomacy with indigenous nations.

governor was Ninian Edwards, a Kentucky supreme court justice. Edwards would not jump into treaty making immediately. He was wedged between the powerhouses of William Henry Harrison and the Chouteau family, resentment over the fraudulent Sauk and Meskwaki treaty of 1804 still festered in his territory, and Tecumseh's resistance to US expansion was growing. When Edwards did start making treaties—eventually nineteen treaties, most of them just after the War of 1812—every one of them was cosigned by Auguste Chouteau.[16]

✕✕✕✕ ♦ ✕✕✕✕

In the six years after Jefferson wrote to Harrison to explain the connection between trade and treaties, the United States negotiated an average of three land cessions per year. These treaties extinguished aboriginal title to more than 125,000 square miles, most of it along the Mississippi River. After December 1809, the United States would not sign another treaty with any indigenous nation for four and a half years. At the beginning of 1810, the commission charged with examining land titles in Kaskaskia (now in Illinois Territory) completed its five-year investigation. Commission members described the situation there as "a melancholy picture of human depravity." Afraid of violent retribution for their report, the members also expressed their gratitude that "it has as yet, pleased that Divine Providence which rules over the affairs of men, to preserve us both from legal murder and private assassination."[17]

The methods used to secure and distribute land titles had also generated one of the most famous instances of indigenous resistance to US expansion: the multinational coalition led by Shawnee mystic Tenskwatawa ("Open Door," or "The Prophet") and his military-minded brother Tecumseh ("Shooting Star," or "Comet"). In October 1811, the brightest comet of the nineteenth century, with a tail a million miles long, appeared in the sky, an omen that people throughout the world took as a sign of conflict to come. The next month, Harrison led US forces in a military victory over Tecumseh's coalition at the Battle of Tippecanoe, driving Tecumseh to seek an alliance with the British.[18]

In the first ten years of the 1800s, the organization of US territories went through a rapid transformation. The old Northwest Territory was divided into the state of Ohio and Indiana Territory, from which Illinois and Michigan Territories were formed. In 1812, Louisiana Territory was also reconfigured: to avoid confusion upon the admission of Louisiana as a state, the area was renamed Missouri Territory.

Two weeks later, the United States declared war on Great Britain, and soon the governors of three territories had vacated their posts. In Indiana Territory, William Henry Harrison left office to lead the Army of the Northwest; Louisiana's US senator, Thomas Posey, replaced him. In Missouri Territory, Benjamin Howard left St. Louis to serve as a brigadier general. And the first governor to go—just ten weeks into the war—was William Hull of Michigan Territory. He surrendered Detroit without a fight, and even while being held prisoner by the British was fired from his position. Michigan Territory fell under the military rule of Great Britain.

SIGNERS: TRADE AND TRUST

My father had a great desire to go to Mississippi to get money. . . . They said that money grew on bushes! We got off and came into the Choctaw Nation.

Trader Nathaniel Folsom

In the westward expansion of the United States, trade preceded settlement. Before "pioneers" arrived at the borders of indigenous nations, traders had moved beyond those borders to live among, and make a living from, indigenous people. The earliest traders often arrived in indigenous nations as immigrants. Intending to establish themselves in a new homeland, they learned the local languages, married into local societies, and, especially in matrilineal societies, raised their children to be leaders in their communities. Nathaniel Folsom arrived with his father at a village in what is now the middle of Mississippi in 1775; the area would not be ceded to the United States and open to settlement for another fifty-five years. When his father left, Nathaniel stayed among the Choctaw, eventually fathering more than twenty Choctaw children. Many of his children signed treaties with the United States as representatives of the Choctaw nation.[19]

Indigenous societies as nations: this identification is so often dismissed in the American myth. The myth focuses on the interactions of colonialist powers and their perfunctory claims of dominion and casts all aboriginal inhabitants of the western hemisphere as members of a single race rather than members of diverse nations. But indigenous people were often pursuing their own national interests in diplomacy and trade with each other and with colonialist nations. Especially in the early stages of intercourse with colonialist powers, indigenous nations played the interests of Spain, Great Britain, France, and the United States against one another to get the best goods at the best prices and strengthen their position in a Native-centric world of long-established rivalries and alliances.[20]

The dismissal of indigenous nationhood stems in part from an intellectual bait and switch. In legal documents, political theories, and general public discourse, terms such as "nation," "country," "nation-state," and "ethnic group" serve to cover an inherent contradiction in US Indian policy: the United States *needed* to define indigenous people as nations in land cession treaties, where they collectively ceded their territory; and the United States later *needed* a different label for indigenous people, to assert its absolute (or *plenary*) political control over them.[21]

Beyond the confusing nomenclature, people historically have derived a sense of common identity from where they were born, the people among whom they were born, and the customs prevailing among those people and places. In English, the word *nation* retains this sense of connection to birth; hence the common origin of the words *nation*, *nativity*, and *native*. But in the century or so before the United States was formed, a new concept arose in Europe, that of "nation-state." Nation-states are not people or places, but governments that define the territories they control and citizens they govern, and resist interference from other nation-states. This political entity has been so successful that the word *nation* has come to refer, in common usage, to the "nation-state."

To complicate things further, John Marshall fabricated a new term for indigenous collective identity in the 1831 Supreme Court case of *Cherokee Nation v. State of Georgia*: "Though the Indians are acknowledged to have an unquestionable . . . right to the lands they occupy until that right shall be extinguished . . . , yet it may well be doubted whether those tribes which reside within the acknowledged boundaries of the United States can, with strict accuracy, be denominated foreign nations. They may more correctly, perhaps, be denominated domestic dependent nations."[22]

In American public discourse (which is seldom characterized by attention to nuance), "dependent" often means "weak" or "inferior," as a child depends on a parent. Certainly, the United States consistently has been paternalistic toward indigenous nations. But as a legal term, "domestic dependent nation" does not necessarily imply weakness. In fact, the status is at least as strong, relative to the federal government, as that of individual states. The question is, "On what does that nation depend?" Indigenous people, in ceding their land and transforming their way of life through treaties, made the conscious decision to depend on "the utmost faith" of the US government. In today's political system, indigenous nationhood and the integrity of the United States are intertwined.

Forty years after *Cherokee Nation v. State of Georgia*, Congress reconfirmed the essential nationhood of indigenous people, even as it denied their ultimate independence as nations, in ending the treaty-making era: "No Indian nation or tribe within the territory of the United States shall be acknowledged or recognized as an independent nation, tribe, or power with whom the United States may contract by treaty; but no obligation of any treaty lawfully made and ratified with any such Indian nation or tribe prior to March 3, 1871, shall be hereby invalidated or impaired."[23]

One final wrinkle in the concept of nationhood: ethnologists and political theorists sometimes equate nations (in the original sense) with ethnic groups. The idea, in simplest terms, is that primitive ethnic groups evolve into states, which evolve into nation-states. But indigenous nations were never simply ethnic groups. They often—if not always—included people from a variety of cultural backgrounds; birth was not the exclusive path to citizenship. As sovereign entities, indigenous nations had mechanisms—adoption, marriage—for incorporating outsiders into their society.

This ability of indigenous nations to confer membership on "outsiders" complicated the identities of colonialist traders who lived among them, and of their children. Some traders became formal members of indigenous nations; others did not but maintained a high level of status because of their commercial and political connections. They often arrived in "Indian country" with official roles among the Spanish, British, French, or Americans, too: jobs as government agents or licenses that sanctioned their trade; they often had families in both indigenous and colonialist societies. So the traders were often navigating their own complicated set of allegiances: to their new homelands and their families there; to the societies in which they were born and their families there; and most often of all to the impulse that led them beyond the settled areas in the first place, their own material gain.

The earliest commercial relationship between indigenous and colonialist powers was the fur trade, but this common name for the enterprise in itself undercuts the perception of indigenous nationhood. Furs, after all, are what the United States and European nations received in the exchange. The business might as accurately be called the arms trade, or the drug trade, or the household goods trade. Indigenous nations were importers as well as exporters, and the white traders who lived among them initially were welcome suppliers of materiel.

The most powerful fur traders acquired more than furs: they became cultural brokers on whom the United States depended when negotiating treaties. Traders could help secure the neutrality or alliance of indigenous nations during times of war; negotiate peace in the aftermath of conflicts (often conflicts that fur traders themselves had originated); and most importantly to the United States, broker land cessions.

In exchange for exploiting the trust they enjoyed among indigenous nations, the owners of fur trade companies took a heavy hand in the affairs of federal, territorial, and state governments. John Jacob Astor, founder of the American Fur Company, successfully lobbied Congress to exclude his British competitors from the US fur trade. Private traders torpedoed the government-operated "factory" trading posts in 1822. And the most powerful fur traders directed territorial governors in the distribution of trading licenses and the appointment of the Indian agents who enforced those licenses—the surest way to eliminate their rivals.[24]

During the ninety-year history of US–Indian treaty making, traders signed three out of every four treaties, more than 280 of them. When Virginia and Pennsylvania regiments arrived at Fort Pitt for the first US–Indian treaty in 1778, Colonel John Gibson was already well known there; he had traded among the local Lenape Delaware for fifteen years. The first treaties between the United States and the Cherokee, Chickasaw, and Choctaw in 1785 and 1786 were signed at Hopewell, a trading post established by soldier and trader Samuel Pickens (now the site of Clemson University). US signers of the momentous Treaty of Greenville in 1795 included General Anthony Wayne, William Henry Harrison, ten other soldiers, and twelve fur traders. From these early agreements, the focus of both trade and treaty making moved west. At the Treaty of Fort Laramie in 1851—nearly a hundred years after Nathaniel Folsom arrived in "the Choctaw nation"—the United States negotiated a treaty with a half dozen nations who lived "south of the Missouri River, east of the Rocky Mountains, and north of . . . Texas and New Mexico." The treaty was signed by Robert Campbell and Alexander Culbertson, two of the most successful fur traders in the West, and by Edmond F. Chouteau, the grandson of Jean Pierre. In 1864, trader William Bent was put under arrest to keep him from warning his Cheyenne family about the impending Sand Creek massacre; he helped negotiate peace treaties the following year. From east to west, and throughout the treaty-making era, traders played a crucial role in US–Indian diplomacy.

✕✕✕✕✕ ◆ ✕✕✕✕✕

On the orders of Governor James Wilkinson, Zebulon Pike left St. Louis on August 9, 1805, "with one sergeant, two corporals, and 17 privates, in a keel-boat 70 feet long." Over the next nine months, he would travel the Mississippi, encountering indigenous people from many nations and the many traders who lived among them. Wilkinson had assigned to Pike some impossible tasks: make peace among the nations and assert US control over British fur traders. None of these people had any reason to listen to a twenty-six-year-old lieutenant who worked in logistics and payroll at Fort Belle Fontaine.[25]

But Pike pursued his quest with ferocious single-mindedness. Along the way, he would flog his men, work them until they suffered frostbite and vomited blood, and join them in pushing their boat through neck-deep icy water. On some days he marched thirty-five miles (by his own estimate) in addition to the distance his men traveled.

Pike was woefully ill equipped to make the journey. His lack of familiarity with any scientific instruments would have been a short-coming if Wilkinson had given him any; virtually all of his technical observations were calculated with a thermometer and a watch, and at one point he lost the watch. He and his men spoke no language but English. They hauled four months' worth of provisions through a land that was teeming with game and edible plants, and then depended on charity for sustenance during a long winter in the North.

In his own preface to the 1810 publication of his journals, Pike recalled that his mission was "to explore the then unknown wilds of our western country." The country was in fact well known. Everything he saw already had a name, or many names. His journal is replete with Menominee, Ho Chunk, Iowa, Dakota, Ojibwe, Sauk, and Meskwaki place names, and their French and English translations and alternatives. The baffling place names were merely an introduction to the cultural and political landscape through which Pike uncomprehendingly passed. As he navigated the currents and shoals of the Mississippi, and a complex, long-established network of personal relationships along the river, Pike was in over his head (at times literally) and managed to misread virtually every encounter.

Pike met with many prominent members of the cultural/trade network that directed life along the Upper Mississippi. Indigenous leaders seemed delighted with the novel idea of making peace with their neighbors. British and French traders promised to cooperate fully with the new American regime and had vital information to share about the illegal operations of their rivals. The British traders, in particular, befriended and beguiled the young American.

Near the end of September on an island (later called Pike Island) at the confluence of the Mississippi and Minnesota Rivers, Pike depended upon British traders—the same people he had been sent to control—to negotiate the first treaty between Dakota people and the United States. The central point of the treaty was a cession by the Dakota of two tracts of land totaling 160 square miles. It is a problematic treaty, beset by many internal inconsistencies (for instance, the land cession cannot be located from its description). In this strange document Pike, unlike any other treaty negotiator, intentionally left blank the amount to be paid for the cession. He claimed in a letter to Wilkinson that he told the Dakota, "I have drawn up a form of an agreement which we will both sign in the presence of the traders now present. After we know the terms we will fill it up, and have it read and interpreted to you."[26]

The "traders now present" included William Meyer, Murdoch Cameron, James Frazer, and Duncan Graham, British agents demonstrating how the "transcending influence" of a foreign power was put into action.

In forwarding the document to the secretary of war, Wilkinson wrote, "You have a copy of the agreement under cover, in which, for what reason I cannot divine, he omits the stipulation on the part of the United States. . . . I do not fairly comprehend this reasoning, but I dare say Mr. Pike will be able to explain it satisfactorily, tho' it is unquestionable he is a much abler soldier than negotiator."[27]

People from many backgrounds bestowed upon Pike astonishing acts of kindness and generosity, even while skillfully resisting any of his demands. Pike took that kindness as only his due, as a representative of the United States. When the eminent Dakota leader Wabasha, after waiting for three days for Pike to arrive in his village, sent word that he was ready to "receive" the expedition, Pike answered by messenger "that the season was advanced, time was pressing, and . . .

I must go on." He was induced to delay his departure by a few hours when emissaries explained that Wabasha was offering a pipe that would signal peaceful Dakota intentions toward the Ojibwe—a main objective of the entire excursion.[28]

Along the way, Pike noted that the colonialist traders whom he encountered (and upon whom he depended for treaty negotiations) had secured their position of trust through marriage with indigenous women. In a rare instance of insight, he noted that these marriages were often more than a matter of commercial advantage: "I can only account for the gentlemen of the N.W. Company contenting themselves in this wilderness for 10, 15, and some of them for 20 years, by the attachment they contract for the Indian women."[29]

What Pike missed was that these relationships, centered on the kinship structure of indigenous societies, formed the ruling regime of the Upper Mississippi. British traders were firmly implanted in that regime. If he had bothered to ask, he might have learned that trader Duncan Graham was married to the sister of Fils de Pinichon, one of two Dakota leaders who signed the treaty; trader Joseph Renville was married to a sister of Petit Corbeau, the other Dakota signer (and grandfather of the Little Crow who would lead the Dakota in 1862); trader Robert Dickson was an in-law of Red Thunder, a leader of the Yankton; and trader James Aird was the brother-in-law of Wabasha. The structure of the regime was there for Pike to see, among the people he met, but the structure was more intimate than the political connections that underlay the US regime.

The connections were well established before Pike arrived and would continue after Pike was gone. Broken Tooth and White Fisher of the Ojibwe, who hosted Pike during his winter in the North, would have descendants named Aitkin and Beaulieu who were still prominent in treaty making two generations later. Pike paddled through these relationships without making a ripple. The one entry in Pike's journal that is most emblematic of his experience was recorded on August 19, 1805, after one of the party's frequent stops for repair: "Whilst we were at work at our boat on the sand beach, three canoes with Indians passed on the opposite shore. They cried, 'How-do-you-do?' wishing us to give them an invitation to come over; but receiving no answer they passed on."[30]

Still, at the time of Pike's excursion, French and British traders and their indigenous trading partners along the Mississippi were arriving at an accommodation of the new American regime. Scottish-born Robert Dickson, who controlled the fur trade in what is now Minnesota when he met Pike, was by then already an American justice of the peace to the south in Prairie du Chien. The Chouteau family was managing a similar transfer of allegiance in St. Louis. The pursuit of fortune trumped fidelity to colonialist nation.[31]

The most prominent trading firms of the time were family-owned empires. They operated dynastically, maintaining their influence over the course of generations: members of these families not only attended treaties; they often ran the negotiations. The Connor family asserted their influence on US–Indian affairs in Indiana; the Godfroy family, from Michigan to Vincennes; the Kinzies and Forsyths in Chicago, Detroit, and Toledo. The Ewings began their enterprise in Fort Wayne and extended it to the Rockies. These owners and their sons witnessed treaties one hundred times, and their other family members and business associates also signed treaties.

West of the Mississippi, the Chouteaus continually acquired more prestige and power in diplomacy for as long as the fur trade flourished. By 1815, Pierre Chouteau Jr. was moving into a leadership role in his family's fur trade empire. Under the direction of "Cadet" (as Chouteau Jr. was called), the family would secure an enviable position in the fur trade west of the Mississippi. While his father and his uncle Auguste maintained their positions in diplomacy and Indian affairs administration, Cadet held controlling interest in Bernard Pratte and Company. (Pratte was married to Cadet's cousin; like their indigenous counterparts, the Chouteaus kept the fur trade in the family.) All of the family-owned and family-related fur trading companies bought their supplies from Bernard Pratte and Company.[32]

Supplying the trade was the key to building a fortune. To every fur trade transaction at the time, indigenous traders brought pelts that they had acquired by their own initiative. The colonialist traders, on the other hand, brought manufactured goods: utensils and other household items, blankets and clothing, weaponry, and many other products. Where did they get these items? They purchased them on credit from a supplier. Companies such as Bernard Pratte and Company made money from both sides of every fur trade transaction. They acquired the furs and sold them at a profit on the East Coast or in Europe or China, and they marked up the price of goods that were exchanged for furs by traders in the field. Few companies other than Astor had the capital to supply an extensive trade in furs. Bernard Pratte and Company did, and it would help them withstand the commercial tidal wave that was the American Fur Company (AFC).

John Astor's intentions in starting the AFC were ambitious from the start. Incorporated in 1808, the company would compete with the giants of the British fur trade, both in the Pacific Northwest and in the Great Lakes region; with the family dynasties of the Ewings and Conners and Godfroys east of the Mississippi; and with the Chouteau family and other companies along the Upper Missouri and Upper Mississippi.

Through a subsidiary, the Pacific Fur Company, Astor initiated his grand plan by establishing the post of Astoria in 1811 at the mouth of the Columbia River. The venture was short-lived. Soon after the War of 1812 began, British fur traders seized the post. Most of Astor's employees returned to the East on an arduous overland journey through the Rockies. But several left by ship, carrying the cash. One of these employees, Russell Farnham, was dropped off in Kamchatka, Russia, with $40,000 and business correspondence, and ordered to deliver it to Astor. Farnham walked across Siberia, at one point eating part of his boots to stay alive, sailed from Europe, and reached New York in 1816. For his dedication, Farnham received the dubious reward of leading the AFC advance into the territory of the Chouteaus.[33]

Though Astor became famous for buying out or burning out his competitors, he met his match in Pierre Chouteau Jr. By 1815, the Chouteau family had traders in place far up the Mississippi and Missouri Rivers, they had the capital to supply their traders, and they had political connections that rivaled Astor's. On one of Farnham's first trading trips along the Mississippi, he was arrested in Prairie du Chien. To Colonel Chambers at Fort Crawford (where William Clark's nephew was the Indian agent), Farnham and his companions "appeared to be hardened rascals." Their imprisonment down the river at Fort Armstrong led eventually to a $5,000 settlement against Chambers, but the Chouteaus had demonstrated their clout.[34]

As increased American settlement east of the Mississippi disrupted the fur trade there, Chouteau territory became the focal point for competition. By 1826, the two titan firms had fought to a draw. They merged, and the American Fur Company was reorganized. A Northern Department would trade in the old Northwest Territory and

the northern reaches of what would become Minnesota. Pierre Chou-
teau Jr. would head a Western Department, operating as far as the
Rockies. The next year, the combine put an end to its last major com-
petitor; the Columbia Fur Company was divided between the AFC's
Northern Department (operating around the Great Lakes) and a new
Upper Missouri Outfit.

By 1834, Astor was ready to cash out. He sold the Northern Department to Ramsay Crooks, who had been with him from the establishment of Astoria, and two newcomers: Henry Sibley and Hercules
Dousman. The new owners retained the name of the American Fur
Company and rode out the decline of the fur trade around the Great
Lakes. Pierre Chouteau Jr.'s company purchased the Western Department. Just as importantly, he received a contract to supply the newly
reconfigured AFC in the North. Chouteau was more powerful than ever
in the fur trade.[35]

As long as the fur trade flourished, companies needed the collective
labor of functioning, cohesive indigenous nations. This often put the
fur trade at odds with land speculators, whose fortunes depended upon
the separation of indigenous people from their homeland. But as the
fur trade fell off, the interests of the colonialist fur trade companies
pivoted. Eventually, in location after location from east to west, the
local fur trade ended. Indigenous nations ceded the territory needed
to hunt a dwindling population of animals and were pressured to adopt
agriculture rather than hunting as their livelihood. For indigenous
people, the land cession treaties marked a wrenching transition to a
new way of life. For the fur trade companies, treaties were the door-
ways to new fortunes, and they became the active agents of enormous
land cessions.

In 1837, during the season when the Dakota and Ojibwe were hunting game, the AFC raised its prices by 300 percent. The hunters returned from the hunt intending to exchange their furs for the material
necessities of the coming year; instead, they found those necessities
priced beyond their ability to pay for them. In a seemingly counter-
intuitive move, the fur trade companies—even though they knew
that each succeeding year would produce fewer furs—offered virtually
unlimited credit, encouraging indigenous traders to secure whatever
their families needed. The result was a spiraling debt cycle from which
indigenous nations could not recover.

As the fur trade collapsed, the trading companies waited for the most opportune time to cut off credit, suddenly and completely. Indigenous nations, unable to survive in their traditional economy because hunting was impossible, and crippled with too much debt to maneuver in a colonialist economy, were forced to cede their land. Jefferson's plan from decades earlier proved to be an effective one.

Such was the power asserted by fur trade companies that government payments for land cessions were earmarked to cover the debts that indigenous nations owed to traders. For a huge 1842 cession of land in present-day Minnesota and Wisconsin, for instance, the United States promised to pay the Ojibwe $36,000 per year in cash and goods for twenty-five years. In addition, "the sum of seventy-five thousand (75,000) dollars, shall be allowed for the full satisfaction of their debts within the ceded district, which shall be examined by the commissioner to this treaty, and the amount to be allowed decided upon by him, which shall appear in a schedule hereunto annexed."[36]

The attached schedule of debt payments listed tens of thousands of dollars for the AFC, its local traders, its lawyers, and even the retired John Astor. Treaty after treaty became a bailout of the fading fur trade companies.

By 1851, when the Dakota ceded virtually all of their homeland, traders engaged in a feeding frenzy during treaty negotiations. The Ewing family faced off against Pierre Chouteau Jr., Henry Sibley, and Hercules Dousman of the AFC, maneuvering to get their allies appointed as treaty commissioner, the position that would lead the negotiations. Knowing that all of the inflated debt they carried could not be paid in a single treaty, they competed for distribution of $250,000 in treaty funds that would be allocated specifically to the trading companies. Other traders tried to cut side deals with the bigger players. As the result, a fortune went into the pockets of the fur traders.[37]

Traders were very aggressive about capturing debt payments. After signing an Ojibwe land cession treaty in 1837, trader Lyman Warren was "entitled" to $25,000 in debt payments. He pressed the Indian agent at Fort Snelling for these payments so forcefully that the agent, Lawrence Taliaferro, felt compelled to brandish a handgun (and Hole-in-the-Day, a prominent Ojibwe leader in attendance, urged him to use it).[38]

In 1836, the Ewing brothers (who signed Potawatomi land cession treaties in the 1820s and 1830s) attended an annuity payment in Logansport, Indiana. As many as four hundred other traders also attended to present claims for debt payments. The Indian agent in charge of distributing the payments, John Tipton, was a sometime business partner with the Ewings, and at the suggestion of some of the Potawatomi leaders he appointed the brothers to be his assistants. George and William Ewing locked themselves in a cabin and disbursed to themselves and their associates $34,000 of the $48,000 available for payments of trader debts. During the ensuing trader riot, a rival trader (Jean Baptiste Chandonnai, who served as interpreter for several treaties) climbed onto the cabin and began to dismantle the roof. Meanwhile, a Potawatomi man climbed onto another cabin roof and suggested that the Potawatomi attack all the traders and take the gold that should by rights belong to them. After being threatened with lynching, the Ewings and their associates returned the money.[39]

The government-sponsored retirement of debt was only the beginning of the windfall that fur trade companies found in treaty making. Land cessions forced indigenous people into a new, unfamiliar economy in which they were dependent upon annuity payments—annual disbursements of money, goods, and services. Traders found ways to capture these resources for themselves.

The government did not trust indigenous people with large amounts of money, so the millions of dollars promised for their land were put in trust (theoretically). The interest on these funds was paid in cash annuities, small amounts of money that seldom lifted indigenous people out of poverty. This cash was needed to buy necessities such as food and clothing—items sold by the same companies that had once accepted furs in payment. Known as the "Indian trade," it was a guaranteed source of income for traders, who planned their enterprises around the dates when annuities were disbursed.

Payments for land were also made in the form of merchandise that was intended to support a new agriculture-based life for indigenous people: plows, for instance. The well-supplied fur trade companies sold this merchandise to the government. And treaties often stipulated that, in order to ease the transition to a new economy, services would be provided to indigenous people at government expense. Their new life would be supported by teachers and blacksmiths and farming instructors. The service providers, as it turned out, were often former fur traders. So every form of payment benefited the fur trade companies.

Another trade-related business that was often extremely lucrative was that of the army sutler. Soldiers posted at forts formed communities with material needs that had to be brought in from somewhere. Sutlers were often fur traders and/or ex-soldiers who used their connections (and kickbacks) to secure contracts to provide goods at the forts, and many became wealthy enough to enter land speculation, mining, and other ventures. About twenty-five men who received these lucrative contracts signed treaties at some point in careers spent navigating the connecting doors between private and public money handling.

Seth Ward, for instance, joined the dwindling Rocky Mountain fur trade in 1834, at the age of fourteen. He began selling merchandise to local ranchers and other settlers in present-day Wyoming and Colorado and on the Arkansas River. In 1857, his appointment as sutler at Fort Laramie gave him a monopoly on trade at the major commercial hub in the West. A year later he hired a manager and, with the income from his sutler business, became a major real estate holder and bank president in Kansas City. He signed the 1868 Treaty of Fort Laramie.

W. A. Carter, who signed a Shoshoni treaty in 1888, retired as a soldier in the 1830s and received sutler contracts, first in Florida, then at Fort Bridger in Wyoming. In 1862, he was placed in charge of moving the fort's property to Denver, where he organized a vigilante group of settlers and stagecoach employees. His position was profitable enough to allow him to branch out into other enterprises. He was the first person to process lumber in western Wyoming and was also an early cattleman, and he began splitting his time between Wyoming and New York.

At seventeen, John Dougherty ran away from home and joined an expedition of the Missouri Fur Company. In 1821, he began a career as an Indian agent. He signed six treaties before he was fired when William Clark died in 1838. He then became a sutler at Fort Kearny and Fort Laramie, and he amassed enough wealth to buy thousands of acres in Missouri and nearly seventy slaves.

Charles Oakes moved to Chicago in 1821 and was employed in the sutler's department of Fort Dearborn. In 1822, he moved to Sault Ste. Marie and ran a mercantile business before starting in the Indian trade. He hired his own voyageurs and ran an independent operation until joining forces with the AFC. From 1834 to 1838, Oakes used his fur trade earnings to engage in land speculation in Michigan. In 1838, he returned to the AFC. He worked for a time in La Pointe, Wisconsin, and in northern Minnesota before moving to St. Paul. In 1853, he opened a bank with his brother-in-law, Charles Borup, and became an important player in the development of St. Paul. His business interests included investment in the Saint Paul Fuller House Company. Oakes signed Ojibwe treaties in 1842 and 1847.

Samuel Stambaugh signed the first of eight treaties as an Indian agent at Green Bay. In 1835, he received a four-year appointment as sutler at Fort Snelling. While there, he illegally negotiated with the AFC to split profits and control the Indian trade. The treaties that Stambaugh negotiated included several with the Menominee nation that exacerbated tensions leading to the Black Hawk War, and an Ojibwe land cession treaty of 1837. Lawrence Taliaferro, the US agent at Fort Snelling, accused Stambaugh and other government officials of manipulating provisions of the 1837 Ojibwe treaty for their own ends.[40]

Henry Rice and Henry Sibley, two of the most prominent traders and politicians in Minnesota, started their careers as sutlers. Rice became a US senator and Sibley became a governor. They signed sixteen treaties over the course of thirty years and became wealthy from their position at the center of US–Indian relations in the Midwest.

The large land cession treaties, such as that of the Ojibwe in 1842 or that of the Dakota in 1851, marked a sudden change wherever they occurred. Before the cessions, indigenous people had become dependent on the fur trade, and fur traders had become wealthy. After the cessions, indigenous people were dependent on government payments, and fur traders, wealthier still because of the treaties they signed, diversified their portfolios.

When those vast tracts—tens of millions of acres in some treaties—went up for sale, the fur trade companies had more resources than anyone else on the scene to buy the land in large quantities. They enthusiastically transformed themselves into land speculators. And the fur traders exploited every emerging opportunity to wring a profit from the new, treaty-generated economy.

The Godfroys, Kinzies, Forsyths, Connors, and Ewings went into real estate. Charles Oakes and Charles Borup, who married sisters from the Ojibwe Beaulieu family, became prominent bankers in Minnesota. Henry Connor, in addition to townsite development, raised livestock and opened stores and mills and distilleries in Indiana. Gurdon Hubbard started with the AFC in its infancy, as an indentured servant, and eventually purchased the Illinois trading posts of AFC; he signed treaties with the Potawatomi and Ojibwe in 1832 and 1833, and he opened the first meat-packing plant in Chicago in the 1840s.

Robert Stuart, director of the Northern Department of the AFC under Astor, invested in the Grand Haven Lumber Company, which started the town of Grand Haven, Michigan.[41]

Pierre Chouteau Jr., Hercules Dousman, and Henry Sibley—the men left standing at the end of the fur trade era along the Mississippi—remained partners in townsite development. The capital of South Dakota is named for Chouteau; Hastings, Minnesota, is named for Sibley. They also went into banking, developed water-power facilities for milling, and invested in gaslight companies, timber, gold mining, and railroads.

Because fur traders had intimate knowledge of the land, they were particularly well positioned to profit from other sources of land wealth in the treaty-making era: timber, mining, and transportation opportunities. As the United States expanded westward, the exploitation of natural resources came to rival land speculation and the fur trade as the foundation of private fortunes.

Men of Industry

After the War of 1812, the United States pursued treaty making with increased intensity. New territorial leaders enlisted key personnel from business, politics, and the military to streamline the treaty-making process. In the thirty years before the war, the United States signed a total of fifty-two official treaties with indigenous nations; that number was surpassed in the first six years after the war.

As US treaty making became more machine-like, the objectives of treaty making expanded. Land acquisition remained a primary motivation for US Indian policy, and trade continued to play an important role in diplomacy. But natural resources such as minerals and timber, in addition to furs, became the targets of treaty making. The movement of goods and people led to a growth in roads, canals, railroads, and river navigation; building this transportation infrastructure required treaties with the indigenous nations that controlled the lands it crossed. Consequently, new corporate special interests in the fields of extraction and transportation arose to influence US Indian policy. Representatives of those interests increasingly engineered and attended treaties to serve their own economic ends.

By 1828, when the United States negotiated for control of lead mines in present-day Illinois and Wisconsin, minerals rivaled the fur trade and land speculation as the foundations for fortunes. At that treaty, the Ho Chunk representatives repeatedly used a new image to describe their white counterparts.[1]

> The Great Spirit . . . has put a pen in your hand.
>
> ◆————
>
> *White Crow*

> But the whites, when he [the Great Spirit] made them, he made them with a quill in one hand, and a paper in the other.
>
> ◆————
>
> *Snake Skin*

Top right: Great Seal of the State of Nebraska (1867), detail.

The Great Spirit made you with paper in one hand and pen in the other.

Little Priest

TERRITORY: 1813-1829

When William Clark became governor of Missouri Territory in July 1813, he had experience in two of the most important aspects of his new job. For six years, he had been both brigadier general of the territorial militia and superintendent of Indian Affairs. During the War of 1812, he led military campaigns as far north as Prairie du Chien, while his network of traders and agents, stationed in posts along the Mississippi and Missouri Rivers, tried to secure the neutrality if not the alliance of indigenous nations.

Lewis Cass, the new governor of Michigan Territory, was a New Hampshire native who moved to Ohio on his father's Revolutionary War bounty warrant and became wealthy there as a lawyer: he specialized in lawsuits over land titles. At the outbreak of the War of 1812, he organized a militia unit so quickly that it was captured during Hull's immediate surrender of Detroit to the British. Upon his release, Cass hurried to Washington to defend his own dubious role in that disaster; thanks to his testimony at a later court martial, Hull—who served as his own defense attorney—became the only US general ever sentenced to death. (The sentence was commuted.) Cass was rewarded for his political maneuvering with a brigadier generalship in the US Army, and weeks after the United States recaptured Detroit in October 1813, he was named the territory's governor.[2]

Cass and Clark would work together in US–Indian affairs for the next two decades. Directing their negotiating machines at full speed, these two men signed more treaties than anyone else in history, fifty-one treaties from 1814 to 1829 alone. These treaties secured peace accords, trade agreements, and land cessions that totaled twenty-five thousand square miles, an area about the size of present-day West Virginia. But by comparison, during the nine previous years in which Harrison was a governor, land cessions in the old Northwest and Louisiana Territories had amounted to five times as much. As the Mississippi River became the focal point of US expansion, location rather than quantity became the important aspect of land acquisition. The locations that mattered contained natural resources: copper, lead, salt, timber, and navigable bodies of water.

But the first order of business after the War of 1812 was reconciliation with indigenous nations. The United States was bound to this task by the 1814 Treaty of Ghent, which ended the war: "The United States of America engage to put an end immediately after the Ratification of the present Treaty to hostilities with all the Tribes or Nations of Indians with whom they may be at war at the time of such Ratification, and forthwith to restore to such Tribes or Nations respectively all the possessions, rights, and privileges which they may have enjoyed or been entitled to in one thousand eight hundred and eleven previous to such hostilities."[3]

Cass signed an 1815 peace treaty with a half dozen indigenous nations in Detroit that reflected the language of the Treaty of Ghent. Near the Mississippi, however, conciliation was a harder sell among white settlers. Indigenous nations had taken the lead in the West in prosecuting war against the United States, and many settlers wanted revenge. But the stakes of peace were high: the British were withdrawing militarily—and commercially—from Prairie du Chien and other trading sites along the river. With the prospect of a rejuvenated fur trade in sight, Secretary of State James Monroe implored the citizens there to engage indigenous nations in treaties with "the sole object of peace." He appointed three treaty commissioners who could be counted on to recognize the importance of restoring trade relations: Governor Clark of Missouri Territory, Governor Edwards of Illinois Territory, and Auguste Chouteau.[4]

Beginning in mid-July 1815, these commissioners signed twelve treaties in thirteen weeks at Portage des Sioux in Missouri. The treaties all contained identical clauses: all injuries were to be forgiven; peace and friendship were to be perpetual. Another five treaties were signed in the next ten months in St. Louis. By 1820, a total of twenty-six treaties had been negotiated in the St. Louis region by Clark and/or Chouteau, and more had been signed in Illinois by Chouteau and Edwards. Tribal representatives from throughout the Midwest traveled to the St. Louis area for the earliest treaties to establish a new status quo in the fur trade; the Dakota and Yankton sent four delegations from the distant North.

Scores of Indian agents, military officers, and politicians were engaged in these treaties in Missouri. But to accomplish such wholesale diplomacy, Clark pulled together a treaty-making machine of insiders: the commissioners and their relatives and business partners; local politicians; a few trusted interpreters and Indian agents; military officers

1815: War of 1812 Peace Treaties

From 1815 to the end of 1820, twenty-six treaties were signed in the vicinity of St. Louis. Negotiating so many treaties with so many nations required scores of Indian agents and interpreters. To streamline this wholesale diplomacy, Clark pulled together a treaty-making machine. While 110 men witnessed the treaties, fifteen men account for half of the witness signatures on the documents. This select group included the commissioners and their family members and business partners, trusted interpreters, and a few politically ambitious men involved in Indian affairs. The rest of the signers were other relatives and business associates of the commissioners. Among the treaty signers were:

- both of the Chouteau brothers, three of their sons, and two of their nephews.
- William Clark, two of his sons, two of his nephews, and two of his brothers-in-law.
- Ninian Edwards and his brother.
- Pierre Menard and Manuel Lisa, partners in the Missouri Fur Company.
- Thomas Forsyth, of Chicago's Forsyth/Kinzie clan, who moved to Prairie du Chien in the late 1700s.
- Eight other interpreters who each signed between five and fifteen treaties.

Involvement in the peace/trade treaties was part of the political landscape of Missouri and Illinois, though several members of the Clark political machine arrived at the treaties at the insistence of the federal government. Colonel John Miller was ordered to the site with a military contingent to address local concerns about the continued hostility of the Sauk and Meskwaki. Colonel Alexander McNair was recommended by James Monroe: "Should any opportunity occur to enable the commissioners to avail themselves of his services with advantage in the proposed treaty with the Indians, it is desired you should do it." McNair in turn suggested the involvement of attorney Robert Wash as secretary to the commissioners.[1]

Many of the men who signed these treaties were, or went on to become, prominent politicians. Indian agent John W. Johnson was later elected mayor of St. Louis. Richard Graham, an Indian agent, married Catherine Mullanphy, daughter of the first millionaire in St. Louis. (This made him a brother-in-law of Thomas Biddle—Clark's secretary—and of General William S. Harney.) Henry S. Geyer was elected to the US Senate. Henry Dodge (who redeemed himself from the Burr scandal as a general in the militia during the war) became governor and congressional delegate of Wisconsin Territory and a Wisconsin US senator.

And the outsiders stayed around after the treaty making to become major players in Missouri politics. Robert Wash, who signed twenty-three treaties as secretary to the commissioners, went on to serve on the Missouri Supreme Court and amassed a fortune in real estate. Alexander McNair was elected governor of Missouri. John Miller became both governor and US representative.

with political ambitions. The twenty-six treaties negotiated from 1815 to 1820 bear nearly four hundred signatures of US representatives; fifteen men provided more than half of those signatures.

While making peace made sound political and economic sense, the Clark machine did not neglect to acquire indigenous resources at opportune times. In 1811, the Indian agent at Prairie du Chien, Nicholas Boilvin, had reported to the secretary of war on the strategic importance of a local deposit of lead, without knowing precisely where it was. During the frenzy of treaty making in 1815, Clark engineered treaties with the Sauk and Meskwaki in which the United States acquired rights to an apparently insignificant 240-square-mile tract just south of Prairie du Chien. It was a shot in the dark, an attempt to secure the lead mines.[5]

In 1818, Clark signed treaties with the Quapaw and with the Osage in which those nations ceded a large tract of land in Arkansas and further west. The area was about to become a separate political entity, Arkansas Territory.

At the end of 1818, Illinois became a state, and Michigan Territory expanded to include all of the current states of Michigan and Wisconsin, plus Minnesota east of the Mississippi. Suddenly, Lewis Cass was a political powerhouse. By 1821, he had negotiated thirteen treaties in his tenure as governor. Like William Clark, he depended on a cadre of intimate associates to get this job done, adroitly exploiting his family members and well-established connections between indigenous people and fur traders in the territory—the Kinzies and Forsyths, Godfroys and Connors and Ewings. Many of these treaties involved land cessions, and one negotiated by Cass in October 1818 is notable, not for the size of the land cession it engineered, or the resources it transferred to US control, but for the content of its first two articles:

Article 1: The Delaware nation of Indians cede to the United States all their claim to land in the state of Indiana.

Article 2: In consideration of the aforesaid cession, the United States agree to provide for the Delawares a country to reside in, upon the west side of the Mississippi, and to guaranty to them the peaceable possession of the same.

"Indian removal" from the eastern United States had begun.

In the Panic of 1819, land prices in the United States collapsed. Land speculation—the great economic machine that drove early US expansion—would be out of operation for years. But that year, a twenty-six-year-old mineralogist named Henry Schoolcraft published the results of an exploratory excursion in the Ozarks. In his book, entitled *A View of the Lead Mines of Missouri*, Schoolcraft outlined the location of lead deposits. Suddenly, American interest in mining the West exploded and drove the acquisition of indigenous land. In Missouri and Wisconsin, the focus was lead. Around the Great Lakes, Michigan Territory was rich in both lead and copper.

In 1820, Lewis Cass organized an excursion through his recently enlarged domain. Cass intended to find the headwaters of the Mississippi. At the suggestion of the secretary of war, he added Henry Schoolcraft to the party. The goals of the excursion came to include explorations "at the bed of copper ore on Lake Superior," "at Prairie du Chien," and "each side of the Fox and Ouisconsin Rivers," all places important to the mining of copper and lead. While on the journey, Schoolcraft took a side trip to explore the lead mines around Prairie du Chien. He received information about the mines from local traders, but when he sought to examine the mines himself, he found that the local indigenous people "manifested a great jealousy of the whites—were afraid they would encroach upon their rights . . . and did not make it a practice even to allow strangers to view their diggings." He distributed whiskey and "two guides were furnished" for a brief tour of the mines.[6]

The Cass expedition was in part an outing for members of his treaty-making machine. Robert Forsyth went along as his secretary. James Duane Doty, the Wisconsin land speculator, also performed secretarial duties. Chicago Indian agent Alexander Wolcott Jr. (married to a Kinzie) was the company physician. The group made two treaties along the way, acquiring islands from the Ojibwe and Ottawa that contained a deposit of gypsum (plaster of Paris), and took a side trip to see the Ontonagan Boulder, a multi-ton mass of copper. The interest in minerals was reflected in the choice of David Bates Douglass, an engineer who taught at West Point, to lead the military escort. Charles C. Trowbridge, deputy marshal in Detroit and son-in-law of one of Cass's best friends, kept a journal on the trip. At St. Peters (now Mendota, Minnesota) he noted, "St. Peters may boast of many curiosities. M' Schoolcraft has procured some handsome specimens of native copper from the cliffs on the east side of the river; and we have seen curiosities in natural history. The Gopher is one of them."[7]

The source of the Mississippi was not one of those curiosities, but the excursion came close. The water was too low to get through a body of water that the Ojibwe called Red Cedar Lake (now also called Cass Lake), so Cass identified the lake as the headwaters of the river.

In 1820, William Clark suffered two losses: his wife, Julia Hancock, died in June. A month later, in the run-up to Missouri statehood, Clark was defeated by Alexander McNair in the race for governor. After Missouri was officially admitted to the Union in 1821, Clark resumed his duties as superintendent of Indian Affairs west of the Mississippi (and married his first wife's cousin).

Upon Missouri statehood, everything in the territory north and west of that state "fell unorganized." That is, it remained an incorporated area of the United States, where citizens would be protected by the Constitution, but it would have no territorial government. Regardless of the statehood or territorial status west of the Mississippi, however, William Clark was still in charge of Indian affairs. In 1824, treaties with the Sauk and Meskwaki and Iowa nations extinguished their title to all lands in Missouri. (Osage title had been extinguished to much of this land in the Clark/Chouteau treaty of 1808.) A treaty with the Quapaw extinguished their title to half of Arkansas, which had become a separate territory in 1819.

In 1825, Clark extended his treaty making into the "unorganized" region of US territory: the Osage and the Kansas nations ceded western Missouri, most of present-day Kansas, the northern half of present-day Oklahoma, and part of present-day Nebraska. These cessions included important deposits of gypsum and salt, including one salt deposit in what is now Oklahoma that was thirty-five miles in circumference and hills that "might be ranked as mountains" from which salt flowed in springs. They had been examined by treaty signer George Sibley, under the direction of Osage guides, in 1811. Thomas Jefferson once had been ridiculed for instructing Lewis and Clark, on their trip to the Pacific, to look for a fabled mountain of salt. In 1825, Clark in effect delivered it through treaty making.[8]

Late in the summer of 1825, Lewis Cass and William Clark, with their respective treaty-making machines, met in Prairie du Chien for a multinational treaty. As many as four thousand indigenous people were in attendance, including delegations of Ho Chunk, Iowa, Menominee, Sauk and Meskwaki, Ottawa, Ojibwe, Potawatomi, and Dakota peoples. It was the only US treaty ever signed by both Cass and Clark and the only signed by both the Dakota and the Ojibwe.

They were meeting, ostensibly, to broker peace among all the nations of the Upper Midwest. Negotiations opened in early August, as Clark stated the purpose of the gathering: "Your great Father has not sent us here to ask any thing from you. We want nothing, not the smallest piece of your land, not a single article of your property—we

1825: Treaty of Prairie du Chien

Lewis Cass and William Clark, members of their treaty-making machines and their military escorts, and thousands of indigenous people from eleven nations arrived in Prairie du Chien in the summer of 1825 for a treaty. Cass and Clark opened the proceedings by emphasizing that the objective of the meeting was to broker an international peace accord: Cass said, with a straight face, "We tell you again, your Great Father does not want your land. He wants to establish boundaries and peace among you." The boundaries, to Cass and Clark, were key to the peace. "Fixed boundaries for your country . . . will allow you to live in peace and harmony."[1]

Indigenous representatives expressed their reservations about the idea. The young men of their nations would not be restrained within boundaries; hunting required pursuit of game that was not contained by lines on a map. During the discussion, the indigenous leaders shared a variety of attitudes and positions in relation to land ownership.

I call the Great Spirit to witness that what I claim is my own.
Wabasha, The Leaf, Dakota

I never yet heard from my ancestors that anyone had an exclusive right to the soil.
Chamblis, Ottawa

I claim no land in particular. The land I live on is enough to furnish my woman and children.
Mahoska, White Cloud, Iowa

I have a small section of country of which I wish to tell you. It is where I was born and now live. . . . The lands I claim are mine and the nations here know it is not only claimed by us but by our brothers the Sacs and Foxes, Menominee, . . . and Sioux. . . . It belongs as much to one as the other. I did not know that any of my relations had any particular lands. It is true everyone owns his own lodge and the ground he may cultivate. I had thought the rivers were the common property of all . . . and not used exclusively by any particular nation.
Coramonee or Carimine, The Turtle that Walks, Winnebago

have come a great way to meet you for your own good and not for our benefit. . . . We propose to you to make peace."[9]

The US proposal was to set boundaries among indigenous nations for the first time. Over the course of a contentious week, the indigenous nations reluctantly drew boundary lines with Cass and Clark, predicting every day that the process would end in disaster. Traditional indigenous land use did not conform to lines on a map.

By the end of the week, a reluctant agreement to boundaries was reached. The Ojibwe representatives, always politically astute, showed up one morning with a map of the land they claimed, and everyone else presented their counterclaims. They insisted, however, on the addition of a clause to the treaty that would ameliorate the contradiction between traditional land use and set borders.

Article 13. It is understood by all the tribes, parties hereto, that no tribe shall hunt within the acknowledged limits of any other without their assent, but it being the sole object of this arrangement to perpetuate a peace among them, and amicable relations being now restored, the Chiefs of all the tribes have expressed a determination, cheerfully to allow a reciprocal right of hunting on the lands of one another, permission being first asked and obtained, as before provided for.[2]

While the indigenous nations looked for ways to work around the boundaries, the United States was intent on enforcing them—and not necessarily out of an interest in peace. Perfecting the US title to land was difficult when many nations claimed that land; establishing specific boundaries among indigenous nations had the effect of associating aboriginal title with a single tribe, facilitating future negotiations. Scores of subsequent treaties refer to the borders set at Prairie du Chien to demark land cessions. Cass and Clark apparently never acknowledged that aspect of boundaries, preferring to emphasize, when they reported to the secretary of war on their proceedings, the promise of a change the treaty would make in international relations: "We had nothing to ask of them, neither the confirmation of old nor the grant of new cessions. Such a spectacle has not been witnessed since the white and the red man have been brought into contact with each other. The effect of this paternal interposition on the part of the United States is most favorable and will be permanent."[3]

"Permanent" lasted about eighteen months. It took several years and subsequent treaties for bands of indigenous nations to sign on to the boundaries set at Prairie du Chien, and by then the United States was already acquiring land from within those boundaries. Eventually, Hercules Dousman—Henry Sibley's partner in running the American Fur Company—purchased Fort Crawford, the very site where a permanent homeland for so many nations had been guaranteed, and built a mansion for his family there.

Many bands and nations with an interest in the Upper Midwest were absent at Prairie du Chien. Subsequent treaties would be needed to secure their agreement to the boundaries. By then, an ulterior motive to the US "peacemaking" effort emerged.

Article 10 of the Treaty of Prairie du Chien stated that, once the boundaries were drawn, "the reservations at Fever River, at the Ouisconsin, and St. Peters, and the ancient settlements at Prairie des Chiens and Green Bay" would not be claimed by any indigenous nations. Cass negotiated a follow-up treaty with additional bands of Ojibwe the following year. The Ojibwe agreed to the borders, and to "grant to the government of the United States the right to search for, and carry away, any metals or minerals from any part of their country. But this grant is not to affect the title of the land, nor the existing jurisdiction over it."[10]

Thousands of lead miners moved to Prairie du Chien in the next four years, ignoring the boundaries set at the treaty and squatting on unceded land where the Ho Chunk had once guarded the location of their mineral resources from Americans. Several attacks by the Ho Chunk on American miners and boats caused immediate and widespread alarm from St. Louis to Green Bay. In response to the attacks, the United States tweaked the peacekeeping process it had started at Prairie du Chien. First, several thousand troops invaded Ho Chunk land, including the US Army and many militia members from Illinois, Missouri, Kentucky, and elsewhere. The leader of a militia unit organized in Galena, Illinois, was Henry Dodge, who, having gone bankrupt in Missouri, had just moved his mining operations across the Mississippi River. And second, Cass—who wanted nothing from indigenous nations in 1825—forced a Ho Chunk land cession that included their lead mines in 1828.[11]

The lead mining rush that was kicked off with the publication of Schoolcraft's book continued throughout the treaty-making era. Mining interests engineered and appeared at treaties more frequently after 1820. The focus on lead mining expanded to include other minerals, grew from minerals to include timber and other natural resources, and enlarged from the acquisition of natural resources to the creation of a transportation infrastructure—railroads, canals, steamships, and roads—that depended on treaties for its construction. As the US property system spread, it put everything in the natural world up for sale.

1828: Treaty with the Winnebago, etc.

At an 1828 treaty with the Ho Chunk nation and members of the Council of Three Fires, Lewis Cass announced that he had something personal to share. "Spotted Arm was about to tell us his dream," Cass said. "I will now tell him mine. I dreamed I was going along by the prairie and I saw a great many shining things on the ground. I did not know what they were. As I travelled along, I came to the foot of a hill where I met a red man on a fine horse. I asked him where he came from. He said he came from the Great Spirit. I was glad to hear it, for I was lost and he would put me right."

Cass was an orator, proud of his ability to hold an audience spellbound, but surely his audience in this case was wondering where he might be going with this subject. "I asked him what country this was," Cass continued. "He said it belonged to the red man. I told him I wondered, for there was no game. He said that the red man had killed it all. I asked what that shining stuff was that I saw. He said it was what the white people called lead. I asked him if that was made for the red people. He said no." And the unspoken question of the audience was answered.

> I asked him what the Great Spirit did make for the red man. He said, game, corn and wild rice, but this he made for the white people. I asked him why he put that stuff on the land of the red man for? He said it was put there, so that when the red men had killed all the game, they might sell the land to the whites and buy themselves whatever else they wanted. I said that I was very glad he told me, for I would tell my red children the first time I saw them. This is my dream. You see by this that the Great Spirit did not make this land for you but for us, & you must ask a good price.

The response was, predictably, one of mistrust. "One of our nieces is living with this man ([Henry] Gratiot)," said one Ho Chunk representative. "We want to give her a piece of land. We want to put her where we can talk to her. We can then hear your words through our nephew."

Snake Skin asked Cass to consider what it would cost to buy the lead, rather than the land, from the Ho Chunk: "You know you do not take what belongs to another without his permission. And your young men have done so to us. They are working on our land where we need to hunt. Now we see so many on it that there are no game. . . . If we did as you did, if we weighed the lead [to set a price for it in trade goods], we think you would want goods enough to cover the whole Winnebago nation."

And Little Priest said, "You think nothing of the land, because the Great Spirit made you with paper in one hand and pen in the other, and although he made us at the same time, he did not make us like you."[1]

SIGNERS: THE MACHINES

The copper mines of Lake Superior, the lead mines of Prairie
du Chien . . . and other minerals which abound in this country,
are also destined to accelerate its march to wealth, civilization,
and refinement.

◆———

Henry Schoolcraft, A View of the Lead Mines of Missouri, 1819

Southeastern Missouri has the world's highest concentration of
galena, a valuable lead ore. This mineral was mined long before the
American regime arrived there, first by indigenous people, and later
under license by the Spanish government. By 1770—six years after
they founded St. Louis—the Chouteau family was already engaged in
mining in the town of St. Genevieve.[12]

In the 1790s, Moses Austin arrived in the area that would become
Missouri. He was already known in Virginia as the "Lead King" and
had introduced several British innovations into the mining, smelting,
and application process. But a contract to sheath the dome of the state
capitol in lead helped bankrupt him, so he skipped out on his debts
there and arrived near St. Genevieve in 1797. With a Spanish license
to operate the "Mines of Breton," Austin produced millions of pounds
of lead.

In 1805, John Smith T relocated to Missouri after monitoring the
value of lead there for several years. He claimed ten thousand square
miles with dubious land title and began mining in Shibboleth, near
Austin's operation. By 1807, the federal government was regulating
lead mining in Missouri through the issuance of licenses, just as the
Spanish regime had done. Austin and Smith T held two of those rare
licenses. Over the next ten years, the two men employed thousands of
workers in mining and processing lead and engaged in a vicious rivalry
for the title of "Lead King of Missouri." Austin, who referred to Smith
T by the title "God of Darkness," secured a cannon to protect his home
from armed attack. Smith T devoted the labor of two of his slaves to
manufacturing weaponry, and he walked around armed with several
handguns and knives and a rifle he called "Hark from the Tombs." The
weaponry of the dueling kings discouraged wildcat miners who might
squat on land in Missouri and start digging.[13]

〉〉〉〉〉 ◆ 〈〈〈〈〈

Before Moses Austin arrived in St. Genevieve, Julien Dubuque was already operating a large-scale mining operation to the north, at the confluence of the Fever (later, Galena) River and the Mississippi. He first leased a lead mine from the Meskwaki in 1788, and ten years later, he received a license to operate "the Mines of Spain." He eventually traded with indigenous miners in present-day Iowa, Wisconsin, and Illinois, processing two thousand tons of lead per year.

Zebulon Pike visited the Mines of Spain in 1805 and was determined to report to his superiors in St. Louis on the extent of those operations. Following the pattern of so many of Pike's encounters, Dubuque gave him a hospitable welcome with a gunfire salute, fed his men, and handsomely introduced them to the locals. He then stonewalled Pike on information about the mines, providing only the barest information in response to a written questionnaire:

QUESTION 1: What is the date of your grant of the mines from the savages?

ANS. The copy of the grant is in Mr. Soulard's office in St. Louis.

QUESTION 2: What is the date of the confirmation by the Spanish?

ANS. The same as to query first.

As Pike was preparing to leave the mines that afternoon, an alternative source of information appeared, but Pike failed to recognize it. A week before arriving at the Mines of Spain, Pike had lost his two favorite dogs. Two of his men volunteered to look for them, but as they headed into the tall grass, Pike abandoned the scene: "They knew my boat never waited for any person on shore." The men were still missing as Pike said good-bye to Dubuque. That afternoon, Pike recalled, "I had now given up all hopes of my two men, and was about to embark when a peroque arrived, in which they were, with a Mr. Blondeau, and two Indians."[14]

Maurice Blondeau, described frequently and dismissively in the historical record as a "Fox half breed," hopped out of his boat and into that of the impatient Pike. "I immediately discharged the hire of the Indians," Pike wrote, "and gave Mr. Blondeau a passage to the Prairie des Chiens. Left the lead mines at four o'clock." If Pike had understood that everyone he met moved in an indigenous-centric network of personal relationships, he might have learned about the lead mines from Blondeau. The passenger had a relative (presumably an uncle), also named Maurice Blondeau, who was one of the most powerful fur traders in North America at the end of the 1700s. The elder Blondeau was a cofounder of the Beaver Club of business titans in Montreal, but so great was his reach into the interior of the continent that he convinced the Sauk and Meskwaki along the Mississippi to grant exclusive mining rights to Dubuque. He also helped Dubuque secure confirmation of the grant from the Spanish authorities in New Orleans in 1796. The younger Maurice Blondeau, who hitched a ride with Pike to Prairie du Chien, who spoke the languages of many nations along the Mississippi, became one of the trusted members of the Clark treaty-making machine, serving as interpreter at sixteen treaties.

With the coming of the American regime, however, Dubuque's Spanish title to the mines was called into question. In 1804, he took the prudent course of selling half the enterprise—seventy thousand acres—to Auguste Chouteau. Their title would wind its way through the US courts for decades, until it reached Congress and the Supreme Court long after both men were dead.[15]

In 1816, the United States was still trying to clear the title to land ceded by the Sauk and Meskwaki in the exploitive treaty of 1804. Ottawa, Ojibwe, and Potawatomi who lived in Illinois also claimed much of this area. In an unusual negotiation, they ceded the southern stretch, and in return the United States "relinquished" to them the remainder of the territory, from Rock Island, Illinois, north to Prairie du Chien. As it turned out, this very tract of land was the Fever River lead district—the second-richest deposit of lead in the United States, after the Missouri deposit around St. Genevieve.

In 1819, Henry Schoolcraft published *A View of the Lead Mines of Missouri*. In his book, Schoolcraft listed the many uses of lead that made it such a valuable commodity: pigments and paints, solder and pewter, lead shot for ammunition, sheet metal for construction, printer's type, and—number twenty-two on his list—toys. Schoolcraft also stated: "Every day is developing to us the vast resources of this country in minerals, and particularly in lead; and we cannot resist the belief that in riches and extent, the mines of Missouri are paralleled by no other mineral district in the world. . . . The earth has not yet been penetrated over 80 feet! We know not what may be found in the lower strata of the soil. There is reason to believe that the main bodies of ore have not yet been hit upon."[16]

His language was tailor-made to launch the first major mineral rush in US history. And he mentioned specifically that "galena is also found at Prairie du Chien . . . where it is worked by the savages." By 1822, scores of wildcat lead mines were in operation near present-day Galena, Illinois—the southern tip of the Fever River lead district. The US Army tightened its control there by issuing and enforcing licenses to operate mines. The idea was, in part, to restrict squatters and avoid antagonizing the Ojibwe by permitting mining only with a license from the American government.[17]

Among the early licensed lead miners were Henry Gratiot, the nephew of Auguste and Jean Pierre Chouteau, and his brother-in-law, William Hempstead, who arrived near Galena in 1825. Gratiot started a smelting furnace to process the ore that he and his neighbors mined; he became a local community leader and signed treaties with the Ho Chunk and Ojibwe in 1828 and 1829. Hempstead's mines produced thirty-five thousand tons of lead before 1830, when he signed a treaty with the Sauk and Meskwaki. The mines in current-day Illinois and Wisconsin were so successful that the fortunes of Henry Dodge were pinched in Missouri. In 1827, Dodge moved to the Fever River area himself but did not bother with a license. He started mining on Ho Chunk land in violation of treaty stipulations and US law and attracted an army of miners—literally, an army of fifty men prepared to do battle with anyone who threatened their illegal claims. (His biographer, treaty signer Addison Phileo, rightly called Dodge the "Captain of Aggressive Civilization.") By January 1828, Dodge and his allies were producing a ton of ore per day. Despite threats of military force from Indian agent Joseph Street, Dodge stayed in place until the land upon which he squatted was ceded by the Ho Chunk in 1829, in a treaty he himself signed. He was part of the flood of miners who invaded Ho Chunk, Ojibwe, and Sauk and Meskwaki lands in Wisconsin, eventually sparking the Black Hawk War of 1833.[18]

The United States continued to acquire through land cession treaties the lead deposits that indigenous people controlled until, by the end of the 1830s, the Fever River lead district (from Galena to Prairie du Chien and to the east along the Fox, Galena, and Wisconsin Rivers) was in US hands.

XXXXX ◆ XXXXX

After publishing his book on lead and accompanying the Cass expedition in 1820, Henry Schoolcraft became the head Indian agent in

Michigan Territory. With Lewis Cass, he began engineering targeted land cession treaties: to save the cost of Indian removal, Cass and Schoolcraft concentrated on mining locations. In most of Michigan Territory, copper was a larger draw than was lead. Deposits were found all along the southern shore of the Great Lakes, from Michigan to Minnesota. As a result, treaty making related to copper focused primarily on US relations with the Ojibwe. By the 1840s, copper mining and US–Indian affairs, including treaty making, were inextricably linked.

Copper mining at rare times served as a brake on Indian removal in Michigan. The Ojibwe knew where the deposits were, and their labor was needed in the mines. Cyrus Mendenhall worked for the American Fur Company (AFC) in the 1830s, as a trader and in the transport of furs and fish. In 1842, he witnessed the Ojibwe cession of lands in Wisconsin and Michigan. By the 1850s, he was both a mining entrepreneur—owning and operating mines along the north shore of Lake Superior—and a missionary. He spearheaded a public interest campaign that led one newspaper to charge that a removal order against the Ojibwe was "uncalled for by any interest of the government—uncalled for by any interest of the Indians."[19]

But for the most part, copper mining in Michigan developed after Indian removal. In 1841, the Michigan state geologist released a report on the vast extent of copper deposits around the Great Lakes. Douglass Houghton, the geologist, had been a member of Lewis Cass's 1820 exploratory expedition and became a real estate developer. Because Houghton had conducted an extensive survey of copper deposits, Henry Schoolcraft, his companion on the Cass expedition, recommended him for the geologist job. His explosive report earned him the nickname "Father of Copper Mining" and set off the "Lake Superior Copper Fever." Scores of ambitious mining operations sprang up, attracting capital from the East Coast. Prominent among the new mining operators were men who had been present at the removal of the Ojibwe and other nations from the copper mining region.[20]

Chauncy Bush signed treaties in the 1830s; John H. Kinzie (second generation of the Kinzie-Forsyth clan) signed an Ojibwe treaty in 1829. Years later, in 1848, they were cofounders of the Lake Superior Mining Company of Eagle River in Michigan's Upper Peninsula; Bush was also an incorporator of the Albion Mining Company and the Medora Mining Company, and Kinzie was incorporator of the Ontonagon Mining Company. Also in 1848, Samuel Abbot (who earlier signed a Menominee treaty) and other employees of the AFC incorporated the Mackinaw and Lake Superior Mining Company.

As the political and economic power of copper mining interests grew, the mining companies began exploring the Great Lakes for potential sites of new mines and became a force in negotiating new treaties. J. Logan Chipman graduated from the University of Michigan at Ann Arbor in 1845 and took a job as explorer in the Lake Superior region for the Montreal Mining Company. He represented mining interests at three Michigan treaties with the Ojibwe in the 1850s. Reuben Carlton and J. W. Lynde signed separate treaties in 1847 by which the Ojibwe ceded land in the middle of present-day Minnesota. Part of the payment for that land was the creation of a blacksmith position, and Carlton took the job. But he immediately began exploring locations for copper mines by trespassing in the Minnesota Arrowhead Region. When the Ojibwe ceded the territory in 1854, Carlton and his business partners were ready to start mining.[21]

Copper and lead were the minerals that most often engaged the treaty-making interests of the United States. But two other minerals captured the interest of many treaty signers. They were the least romantic and the most romantic of minerals: salt and gold.

Salt production was the first major industry in the state of Illinois. The first governor, Shadrach Bond, secured ownership of the valuable Gallatin Saline for the state in 1818. He had advocated for the introduction of slave labor to work the salt deposit for five years, since serving as the territorial delegate to Congress, when he wrote that his introduction of a bill "respecting the partial introduction of negroes to carry on the salt-works will, I suppose, make a fuss with some." A slaveholder himself, Bond pushed through an exemption to the state constitution allowing slave labor in salt production. Salt was an important commodity, and numerous treaty signers worked in salt production at some point in their lives.[22]

While Henry Dodge was mining for lead and signing treaties in Missouri in 1815, he also took an interest in salt production. With treaty signer Edward Hempstead he purchased Peyroux's Saline, a salt spring near St. Genevieve that had been exploited for generations by the Spanish. (Edward was the brother of treaty signer Charles Hempstead, the Galena lead miner.) This enterprise gave Dodge another nickname:

"Salt Boiler." When river navigation made cheaper salt from Illinois available, Dodge's salt empire crumbled.[23]

In 1811, George Sibley, the Indian agent near present-day Kansas City, led an expedition to improve relations with the Osage—and to find the legendary mountain of salt that Thomas Jefferson believed to exist somewhere in the Midwest. He did locate the "Rock Saline deposit" in present-day Oklahoma on this expedition and, remaining in the area, signed treaties with the Osage in the 1820s.[24]

William P. Rathbone witnessed treaties with the Wyandot and Miami in 1818–19 while in the army. Years later, after being elected to the New York city council and then getting involved in bank fraud, he bought land in West Virginia; by 1848, he owned twenty-one thousand acres. Drilling for salt brine, he found a product that he sold as "Rathbone's Rock Oil—Nature's Wonder Cure" and was "partly responsible" for coining the term *petroleum* to name the substance. In 1860, his son drilled the first oil well south of the Mason-Dixon Line.[25]

The most direct connection between treaty making and salt, however, was the profit made by Robert P. Currin. He was one of the negotiators of the first Choctaw and Chickasaw removal treaties in 1830, in which indigenous leaders—as an inducement to move west—were given the title to "reserved" lands in the Southeast that they could sell personally. Currin helped locate those "reservations" near salt springs, then bought them. A salt reserve that he purchased for $500, for instance, he later sold for $10,240. In 1841 he became the head of public education in Tennessee.[26]

Like members of the general population, many treaty signers were attracted by the 1849 California gold rush, either before or after their involvement in treaty making. William Coriell was the first lawyer to locate permanently at Dubuque. He moved there in 1835 and in the next two years founded the Miners' Bank of Dubuque and the *Dubuque Visitor* newspaper. In 1837, he signed a treaty with the Ojibwe in which they ceded the first of their territory in present-day Minnesota. He was investigated for illegal acts as a commissioner to survey and plat the town of Dubuque, but he beat the charge and was elected alderman. Then, in 1849, he left Dubuque for California.[27]

Clark Thompson was a forty-niner before becoming an Indian agent in Minnesota in the 1860s, signing treaties with the Dakota and overseeing their removal to Nebraska. "California is a grand humbug!" was his summary of the mining experience. Charles White returned to Wisconsin after the gold rush and received a contract in 1854 related to Menominee removal from the state. Robert Biddle was a tailor who formed a partnership to ship supplies to miners in California during the gold rush, and he went to California himself in 1849, then convinced his family to emigrate to Oregon by wagon train. His youngest daughter, Alice, was one of the first three graduates of Oregon State University in 1870.

Other treaty signers looked for gold elsewhere. Thomas Adams arrived in the Pacific Northwest with Washington territorial governor Isaac Stevens in 1853 and took an active role in treaty making as an Indian agent; he later made the first gold strike in Montana. Robert Campbell, a famous mountain man and immensely successful trader, signed the Treaty of Fort Laramie in 1851, and with the proceeds from his trading invested in gold mines in New Mexico.[28]

But two treaty signers were involved in gold rushes in a location not famous for its gold: Minnesota. In 1856, Reuben Ottman, a newspaper editor, cofounded the Oronoco (Minnesota) Mining Company to capitalize on a short-lived local belief that gold had been discovered outside of town. (He signed a treaty with the Red Lake Ojibwe in 1863.) And the 1866 treaty with the Bois Fort band of the Ojibwe was negotiated for no reason other than gold.[29]

The Bois Fort band had occupied an area near Lake Vermilion in Minnesota since being promised, in an 1854 treaty, a reserved land base and annuity payments that never materialized. In 1865, geologists reported a vein of gold near the reservation. St. Paul residents began forming gold-mining corporations, and speculative capital began pouring into the coffers of these companies from throughout the country: $300,000 to the Vermilion Falls Gold Mining Company, $500,000 to the Minnesota Gold Mining Company cofounded by Henry Sibley.

In April 1866, the United States convinced the Bois Fort that the onslaught of gold-mining squatters in their vicinity was uncontrollable. The band agreed to relocate to another location, specified by treaty. The state invested in road construction from St. Paul north to Lake Vermilion as the trek to the gold fields began. Six months later, the miners began their return to St. Paul. The geologists had been wrong; there was no gold at Lake Vermilion.[30]

The first Ojibwe cession within the current boundaries of the state of Minnesota occurred in 1837. (Most of the large cession lay in Wisconsin, but a triangle of land along the Mississippi is now within Minnesota's

borders.) The ceded area and the treaty itself were a mother lode of resources from which capitalists—fur traders, miners, land speculators—
could extract their fortunes. But the event is known as the White Pine
Treaty, because the ceded area included millions of acres of valuable
timber. And the new markets for that timber were conveniently located
downstream, in Illinois and Missouri.

One of the signers was Hercules Dousman, co-owner of the AFC. In
1837, he was busily diversifying the wealth he had accumulated from
furs, and within a few years he would own extensive timberland in
Wisconsin—in the heart of the land that was ceded in 1837. Other signers included Samuel C. Stambaugh, who sold supplies at Fort Snelling;
Indian agent Daniel Bushnell; and Dr. John Emerson, surgeon at Fort
Snelling. Two days after the treaty, they cofounded the St. Croix Falls
Lumber Company. And fur trader Lyman Warren, who also signed the
treaty, moved to the Chippewa River the next year, where he served as
an Indian agent and started processing lumber.[31]

The US acquisition of timberland was a relatively late development
in treaty making with indigenous nations. As late as 1830, Bangor,
Maine, was the world's largest exporter of timber; the densest population of the United States, along the Eastern Seaboard, was well supplied with lumber. Early in the history of the Northwest Territory,
settlers saw forests such as those in Indiana more as an impediment
to agriculture than a source of income. In the north and along the Mississippi, harvesting timber was not the avenue to great fortunes until
closer to the end of the 1800s.

But one of the most stable and profitable ventures in any location
was the operation of a sawmill that would process lumber for local use.
It might sound like an unassuming enterprise, but sawmills were the
springboards to minor fortunes, on which larger fortunes were sometimes built. And as might be expected in an undertaking associated
with treaty making, many of the men who signed treaties on behalf of
the United States were at some point sawmill owners.

In Michigan, Wisconsin, and Iowa, sawmill owners featured in the
early histories of the counties in which they started their enterprises.
Henry Whiting (who signed a treaty with the Ojibwe in 1837) and his
father-in-law, Justin Rice (who signed an Ojibwe treaty in 1842), established the first sawmill on Michigan's St. Croix River in 1848; Rice
had earlier co-owned the Detroit & Black River Steam Saw-mill Company with Edmund Brush (who signed Ojibwe treaties in the 1820s
and 1830s). Brothers Ephraim and Gardner Williams started the first

steam-powered sawmill on the Saginaw River in 1834; both signed treaties with the Ojibwe during the next four years. John P. Arndt, the founder of townsites in Wisconsin, began his career in the family lumber, milling, and shipbuilding business in Pennsylvania. He moved to Green Bay in 1824 and shortly thereafter build the first sawmill in the area, through an agreement with the Menominee nation; he later built additional sawmills. Joseph Renshaw Brown was one of many prominent Minnesotans who owned sawmills, including one established by his Dakota Land Company in Sioux Falls.[32]

Processing lumber at sawmills evolved over time into harvesting and transporting timber, and treaty signers were among the earliest men to enter those fields. John P. Arndt claimed that he was the first person to export lumber from Green Bay. Joseph R. Brown was the first to raft logs down the St. Croix River. In 1833, Charles Trowbridge, the brother-in-law of Henry Sibley and part of the Cass treaty-making machine, invested in the Boston Company, a lumber company that created the town of Allegan, Michigan. As noted earlier, Robert Stuart left the AFC in 1834, after receiving $17,000 in debt payments at the Treaty of Chicago, and became a partner in the Grand Haven Company, which purchased pinelands and erected lumber mills in Michigan. Joel Bassett moved from Bangor, where he worked in the lumber manufacturing industry, to Minnesota in 1852. By 1859 he was president of the J. B. Bassett Lumber Company, and organized the Mississippi & Rum River Boom Company to move logs by river to market. He simultaneously served as an Indian agent to the Ojibwe, living at the White Earth reservation when it was created in the 1860s. He secured a contract to collect dead wood on the reservation, but years later was found liable by the US Supreme Court of illegally harvesting seven million board feet of lumber. By then, Bassett had moved into flour milling and the purchase of pinelands.[33]

But it was in the Pacific Northwest where a few treaty signers, appearing on the scene just before land cession treaties were negotiated, made the most money directly from the harvesting of timber. Benjamin Shaw arrived in 1844 and started sawmills at Tumwater, Washington, with entrepreneur M. T. Simmons. In 1849, they built the first boat to ship timber out of Puget Sound, an immensely profitable business that supplied San Francisco during the gold rush. In the 1850s, they signed many of the coercive treaties that confined tribes of the new Northwest to reservations. Josiah P. Keller also signed one of those treaties in 1855; he had arrived at Puget Sound two years earlier with equipment and workers from Maine to start a lumber mill. Keller cofounded the Puget Mill Company at Teeklat and founded the town of Port Gamble on the site. By 1862, the mill was the largest business in Washington Territory and made Kitsap County the richest county in the country for a quarter century.[34]

Shipping and boom companies were natural ancillaries to the timber industry. Product had to move, and extraction of natural resources—furs, minerals, timber—required the development of a transportation infrastructure. The beginning of this infrastructure can be found in numerous treaties where the United States secured permission to build roads within or through indigenous nations. These treaty stipulations—which often included the construction of trading posts—were, in effect, a government investment in the fur trade. Trade alliances were stronger if products could be moved more easily and cheaply, and, as noted earlier, trade was a strategy for obtaining Indian land cessions. In order to carry goods and facilitate westward migration, the United States also secured the right to build ferries across rivers. As might be predicted, treaty signers received contracts to build roads and operate ferries, undertakings that either resulted from their participation in treaty making or gave them the standing in local societies that led to their presence at treaties.

The first US–Indian treaty to mention transportation was in 1791, when the Cherokee, as part of a land cession in present-day Tennessee, "stipulated and agreed, that the citizens and inhabitants of the United States, shall have a free and unmolested use of a road from Washington district to Mero district, and of the navigation of the Tennessee river."[35]

Robert King witnessed this treaty. He had already built a road in Virginia and already owned six thousand acres in Tennessee. When a fort was built at the treaty site on the Holston River in 1798, he was stationed there as a major, possibly an indication that he was an Indian agent. By the next year, he founded the town of Kingston with partners John Smith T, William Lovely, and Thomas N. Clark. When the road that was stipulated in the treaty was finally built, Thomas Clark represented the partnership in cofounding the Cumberland Turnpike Company. The company was authorized to maintain a toll road connecting Kingston and Knoxville and charge "$1.50 for four-wheeled carriages . . . 12-1/2 cents for a man and a horse . . . Indians exempt."

This was the road that immigrants to the West took when they passed through the Cumberland Gap. In 1804, Clark was licensed by the National Council of Cherokee Chiefs to operate six "houses of entertainment" on the Cumberland Road.[36]

John Shelby received a contract to build a road after attending a Seneca treaty in Ohio in 1831. Elisha Smith Lee graduated from Union College and "became the first judge of Monroe County, NY"; in 1840, he moved to Detroit as a lawyer and invested in the Detroit and Birmingham Plank Road Company. Later, he secured a position in the War Department, where he signed a treaty with the Ojibwe in 1854.

Rivers were barriers for the overland transportation of goods, and ferries were a lucrative component of a burgeoning transportation system. In the early 1800s, Samuel Solomon had one of the choicest licenses: to run a ferry on the Mississippi River at St. Louis. He became one of the interpreters of the William Clark treaty-making machine. Edmund Hogan, who signed a treaty with the Quapaw in 1824, was the first ferry operator in Little Rock. Daniel Vanderslice was captain of a company of vigilante riflemen in the Fever River lead district in the 1830s, signed treaties as an Indian agent in the 1850s at the Great Nemaha Indian Agency in Kansas, and in 1860 was licensed to operate a ferry across the Great Nemaha River. D. T. Sloan signed a land cession treaty with the Ojibwe in 1847 and later received a license to operate a ferry in Benton County, Minnesota. William Brewster received $2,000 as a provider of dry goods in the 1842 treaty with the Ojibwe and opened a ferry on the Minnesota River. Henry Sibley and Martin McLeod, fur traders and politicians, also operated ferries on the Minnesota River.[37]

While small fortunes could be made in moving goods across rivers, much larger fortunes grew from river navigation. Pierre Chouteau Jr. was the driving force behind the construction of the first steamship to travel up the Missouri River from St. Louis to a point beyond Omaha; on its maiden voyage, it reached Fort Union in present-day North Dakota, twelve hundred miles upriver from St. Louis, and revolutionized the transportation of furs and trade goods in the West. Along the way, the initial group of passengers, including Chouteau, renamed a trading post Fort Pierre, which gave its name to the capital of South Dakota. The Chouteaus added more steamships to a fleet that traveled both the Missouri and the Mississippi over the next thirty years. In 1863, they owned the steamships on which the Dakota people were transported into exile on a Nebraska reservation.

Merchandise was not the only cargo on these ships. In 1837, a Chouteau-owned steamship named the *St. Peters* brought smallpox up the Missouri. From infected passengers, including a Chouteau clerk named Jacob Halsey (who had signed an 1830 treaty), the disease spread among indigenous populations, killing twenty thousand people in a year.[38]

As in the case of the Chouteaus, the most successful owners of fur trade, mining, and timber companies developed their own resources for transporting what they extracted from the natural world. Hercules Dousman and Henry Sibley added steamboats to their many other enterprises by the 1840s. Gurdon Hubbard, the fur trader and Chicago meatpacking plant owner, also owned a steamboat line. R. R. Thompson, signer of treaties with tribes in the Pacific Northwest in 1855, channeled the fortune he made in the California gold rush into trade with settlers who were migrating west; he built the largest wagons ever seen on the Oregon Trail to carry freight to his fifty-ton steamboat and eventually added a railroad to his portfolio.

Edmund Lockwood, who signed an 1837 Ojibwe land cession treaty, owned the Adventure (copper) Mine in Michigan, sold stock in mining companies, and made more money transporting copper on a ship he commissioned with his uncle, treaty signer Daniel S. Cash. In addition to his work as a copper mine owner and missionary, Cyrus Mendenhall transported furs and fish for the AFC in the 1830s and signed an 1842 treaty with the Ojibwe. David D. Mitchell signed treaties with the Sauk as superintendent of Indian Affairs in St. Louis in 1830, signed another treaty at Fort Laramie in 1851, and started the Missouri and California Overland Mail and Transportation Company in 1855. Auguste Chouteau's son Henry Pierre signed a treaty with the Kickapoo as a teenager and started the company of Chouteau and Valle, which transported metals and ammunition, three decades later.

One of the greatest fortunes made by a treaty signer at the intersection of extraction, transportation, and land speculation was Augustus Kountze. After working in his father's grocery store, Kountze moved to Omaha just as the Omaha nation was ceding much of its homeland to the United States. Kountze entered the real estate business, acquiring with his brothers land along the Missouri that became the towns of Brownville, Nebraska City, Tekamah, and Dakota City in Nebraska and Sioux City in Iowa. Eventually, the Kountze brothers expanded their empire to include real estate in Minnesota, Chicago, and Denver, tens of thousands of acres of farmland in western Nebraska, 250,000 acres of timber in eastern Texas, and more. In 1856, the brothers began opening banks: First National Bank of Omaha, the Colorado National Bank, the Kountze Brothers Bank of New York City. Augustus Kountze also became an important railroad financier as president of the Boston, Hoosac Tunnel and Western Railway and as investor in the Omaha and Northwestern Railroad, the Denver and South Park Railroad, and the Sabine and East Texas Railway. In the 1860s, he was one of the original organizers, and the government director, of the Union Pacific Railroad, and he managed to place its world headquarters in Omaha.[39]

Just as land speculation companies engineered treaties in the 1700s, and companies in fur trade, mining, and timber later engineered treaties in their turn, by the 1860s, railroads were driving the treaty-making process in Kansas. The language in these treaties approaches the absurd. Indigenous nations are presented as railroad boosters, railroads are given the right of public domain over any land they want, and the treaties virtually serve as advertisements for specific railroads. In 1860, for instance, Indian agent and railroad promoter Thomas Sykes engineered a treaty with the Delaware: "The Delaware tribe of Indians, entertaining the belief that the value of their lands will be enhanced by having a railroad passing through their present reservation, and being of the opinion that the Leavenworth, Pawnee, and Western Railroad Company, incorporated by an act of the legislative assembly of Kansas Territory, will have the advantage of travel and general transportation over every other company proposed to be formed, which will run through their lands, have expressed a desire that the said Leavenworth, Pawnee, and Western railroad Company shall have the preference of purchasing the remainder of their lands."

In 1862, Indian agent Charles Keith engineered a treaty with the Kickapoo that was also signed by his father-in-law, John E. Badger (a railroad booster):

The Kickapoo tribe of Indians, . . . believing that it will greatly enhance the value of their lands . . . by having a railroad built . . . ; and entertaining the opinion that the Atchison and Pike's Peak Railroad Company, incorporated by an act of the legislative assembly of the Territory of Kansas, approved February 11, 1859, has advantages for travel and transportation over all other companies, it is therefore provided that the Atchison and Pike's Peak Railroad Company shall have the privilege of buying the remainder of their land. . . . And said company shall have the perpetual right of way over the lands of the

Kickapoos not sold to it for the construction and operation of said railroad, not exceeding one hundred feet in width, and the right to enter on said lands and take and use such gravel, stone, earth, water, and other material, except timber, as may be necessary for the construction and operation of the said road.

And in 1863, the railroads entered Shoshone country, in a treaty signed under the auspices of Utah territorial governor James Doty:

The telegraph and overland stage lines having been established and operated through a part of the Shoshonee country, it is expressly agreed that the same may be continued without hindrance, molestation, or injury from the people of said nation; and that their property, and the lives of passengers in the stages, and of the employees of the respective companies, shall be protected by them. And further, it being understood that provision has been made by the Government of the United States for the construction of a railway from the plains west to the Pacific ocean, it is stipulated by said nation that said railway, or its branches, may be located, constructed, and operated, without molestation from them, through any portion of the country claimed by them.

"Transportation" is a euphemism that was used for both the transatlantic slave trade and Indian removal. Many of the treaty signers who were engaged in the "transportation" of indigenous people were soldiers and bureaucrats; others were private citizens who engaged in the enterprise for personal profit. John Schermerhorn, for instance, was a member of the Society for the Propagation of the Gospel and the pastor for a Reformed church in New York. He was a personal friend of Andrew Jackson, and in 1832 he was appointed by Jackson to remove the Cherokee and Chickasaw past the Mississippi River. While conducting this work, he managed to acquire about four hundred thousand acres of land.[40]

In 1835, Luther Blake and Alfred Iverson (editor of the Columbus-based *Sentinel*) formed a company to secure a contract to remove Creeks from Florida for profit. They were notorious land speculators, and they saw the Indian removal as an opportunity to acquire more land. Blake had signed a Creek removal treaty in 1827. Iverson was in Washington to discuss "Alabama emigration" in 1838, when he signed a treaty with the Oneida. He was later elected to the US Senate, and on the occasion of his resignation due to Alabama secession, he gave a speech proclaiming that the South "will rise again."[41]

James Gardiner was an Ohio state legislator and newspaper publisher who supported the policies of Andrew Jackson. Jackson nominated him for a post in the US land office at Xenia, but frequent intoxication was used as grounds for denying him the job. He was, however, appointed to a position in Indian Affairs. In negotiating five removal treaties in 1831, "his character and methods were so open to question," the *Congressional Edition* noted, "that Ewing, of Ohio, moved in the Senate for an inquiry into the genuineness of the documents presented for ratification." Yet in 1832, Gardiner was appointed to conduct the Ottawa, Seneca, and Shawnee from Ohio to new homes across the Mississippi River. He was dismissed several months later for drunkenness and incompetence (the emigration party had traveled only as far as central Illinois). Four men who had signed Shawnee and Seneca removal treaties—John Shelby, Martin Lane, James McPherson, and David Robb—found jobs as conductors, assistant conductors, and interpreters in charge of tasks such as "collecting Indians."[42]

Benjamin Reynolds, a Tennessee state legislator, was appointed agent to the Chickasaw in 1830. After signing four treaties, he was placed in charge of their removal. He formed a partnership with fellow treaty signers R. P. Currin and John Davis to speculate in Choctaw land and found the Mississippi Texas Land Company.[43]

Verplanck Van Antwerp was a lawyer with connections to the railroad industry and to President Martin Van Buren. In 1837, he was appointed to serve as recording secretary at an Ojibwe land cession treaty in present-day Minnesota and as disbursal agent for removal of Cherokee. Consequently, he was positioned to start a newspaper and become "Receiver of Public Moneys" in Iowa.[44]

Politician, trader, and treaty signer Henry Rice received a contract to manage the removal of Ho Chunk people from Wisconsin in the 1840s. He selected a location in present-day Minnesota for their new home, at a spot so isolated from other traders that they would depend on his business for all the necessities of life.[45]

The men who signed US–Indian treaties represented a network of business interests: extraction and transportation, land speculation and trade. The network that connected signers to one another, however, depended upon more than business ties. Political connections also were an important part of the network. And to strengthen this network, a connective tissue of family ties, racial identity, and voluntary associations reinforced the cultural assumptions that treaty signers almost universally shared: the superiority of "civilization" over "savagery" and the primacy of private property over any other relationship to the natural world. The presence of so many newspaper owners among the treaty signers (such as Van Antwerp, Gardiner, and Iverson) was no accident. Treaty signers were interested in promulgating the assumptions that they shared, controlling the public narrative about treaty making and westward expansion.

Daniel Vanderslice exemplified the convergence of business, family, race, and mythmaking in the lives of treaty signers. Vanderslice moved to the Fever River lead district in the 1820s and cofounded a vigilante rifle company of squatters to maintain an illegal presence on indigenous land. In the 1830s, he moved to Kentucky and published a newspaper, and in 1837, he was appointed an agent for Chickasaw emigration. He moved west and became an Indian agent in Kansas and Nebraska, signing treaties beginning in the 1850s. Near the start of the Civil War, Abraham Lincoln fired Vanderslice for his belligerent proslavery politics, but by then he had amassed a fortune and commissioned a sculpture that presented his own family in mythic terms. "Pioneer Mother," the statue of the Vanderslice family, still stands in Kansas City.[46]

Political and
Personal Boundaries

I n the 1830s, political borders in the Midwest assumed a new, intense significance. At Prairie du Chien, indigenous nations had agreed, for the first time, to define their homelands with permanent boundaries drawn on a map. American squatters soon violated these boundaries, sparking the Black Hawk War. By the end of the decade, the United States redrew its own political boundaries by creating Iowa and Wisconsin Territories on the banks of the Mississippi.

This situation created an interesting map: the borders of indigenous nations, created at the insistence of the United States, and a completely different set of US territorial borders, all written on the same land. But US mapmakers generally ignored the borders of indigenous nations, and so did lead miners who flooded past them to spark the Black Hawk War.

One border that nobody could ignore, however, was drawn west of the Mississippi. A line on the western edge of what is now Missouri marked the official limits of US settlement and organized territory.

While changing *political* boundaries shaped US–Indian relations, *social* boundaries also made an impact. The financial windfall of treaty making was distributed through networks built on political, business, social, and family connections. And the modern formation of race, created by people of European descent to justify their actions toward people of indigenous and African descent, spread with the US property system beyond the Mississippi.

Political borders and racial boundaries: these abstract inventions converged in the ethnic cleansing of organized US territory, as indigenous nations from the east were moved beyond the western limits of US settlement. Andrew Jackson, in his 1830 address to Congress, dismissed the traumas that Indian removal inflicted on indigenous nations by comparing their forced relocation to the experience of a nation of immigrants:

Top right: Seal of the Commonwealth of Kentucky (1792), detail.

To better their condition in an unknown land, our forefathers left all that was dear in earthly objects. . . . Does humanity weep at these painful separations from every thing, animate and inanimate, with which the young heart has become entwined? Far from it. . . . And is it supposed that the wandering savage has a stronger attachment to his home, than the settled, civilized Christian? Is it more afflicting to him to leave the graves of his fathers, than it is to our brothers and children? Rightly considered, the policy of the General Government towards the red man is not only liberal but generous.[1]

TERRITORY: 1830–1838

John Adams and Thomas Jefferson both died on the Fourth of July, 1826, the fiftieth anniversary of the Declaration of Independence. In that first fifty years, the United States extinguished aboriginal title to territory from the Atlantic to well beyond the Mississippi. Anthony Wayne and territorial governors such as Hull, Harrison, and Cass had negotiated treaties north of the Ohio River; indigenous nations still held land around Lake Michigan. Clark and the Chouteau family had led treaty making west of the Mississippi, where the United States held title to Louisiana, 98 percent of present-day Arkansas, and all of Missouri but the northwestern corner. Andrew Jackson had negotiated treaties (often at gunpoint) with the Choctaw, Muscogee, Chickasaw, and Cherokee nations, and he had illegally invaded Florida, single-mindedly pursuing land cessions of tens of millions of acres. So on the day that Jefferson and Adams died, the United States held title to 30 percent of the area that would become the forty-eight contiguous states.

After the 1825 treaty at Prairie du Chien set "permanent" borders among indigenous nations in the Upper Midwest, William Clark and the Chouteau family took a hiatus from treaty making. Auguste Chouteau, founder of St. Louis, died in February 1829, marking the end of an era in the city's history and in treaty making west of the Mississippi.

A new era in US–Indian relations began on May 28, 1830, when Congress passed "An Act to provide for an exchange of lands with the Indians residing in any of the states or territories, and for the removal west of the river Mississippi." This was the famous Indian Removal Act, the United States' most extensive campaign of ethnic cleansing. Despite vigorous opposition organized by missionaries among indigenous nations, the bill passed the House of Representatives by five votes.

Section 3 of the act bound the United States to "forever secure and guaranty [for indigenous nations] . . . the country so exchanged . . . *Provided always,* That such lands shall revert to the United States if the Indians become extinct."[2]

By December, Jackson could say in his second annual message to Congress: "It gives me pleasure to announce to Congress that the benevolent policy of the Government, steadily pursued for nearly thirty years, in relation to the removal of the Indians beyond the white settlements is approaching to a happy consummation."[3]

Jackson and his allies believed that the identity of indigenous nations—so often structured on kinship ties to a specific place—could be simply reformulated in a different location. But the onerous burden that indigenous nations faced in maintaining their identity in a new homeland could not have been that incomprehensible even to Jackson. Forced removal was part of the European experience, too—an experience reflected in the English word *exterminate*. Originally meaning "to drive beyond one's borders," the word quickly came to mean "to utterly destroy." (And so language embodies human relationships. For this reason, indigenous languages have been central to maintaining indigenous cultural identity—and so became a target for extinction by the United States.) Use of the word *exterminate* would burgeon quickly after the Indian Removal Act, during the Black Hawk War.[4]

By 1830, political conditions were rapidly deteriorating in the Upper Midwest. The Sauk and Meskwaki had been driven west into territory of the Dakota people to hunt, causing a war that threatened to escalate into a region-wide conflict. Many Sauk and Meskwaki people had moved into Iowa, and they were apprehensive about US reprisals when a group led by Black Hawk refused to relocate. Thousands of white settlers—farmers and miners—had moved to the east bank of the Mississippi from Galena to Prairie du Chien, sparking incidents of violence. The Upper Mississippi was a tinderbox, and in this tense situation, William Clark returned to Prairie du Chien to negotiate the first treaty of the Indian removal era.

As with the 1825 treaty there, the ostensible purpose of this meeting was to broker peace. But as the indigenous delegations moved cautiously toward a formal truce, they were convinced by Clark to cede the western quarter of present-day Iowa, a tract that Clark intended as a landing place for tribes being removed from the East. As a contribution to Indian removal, the treaty was a success; as a peace agreement, it was a dismal failure.

✕✕✕✕ ◆ ✕✕✕✕

In May 1830, John Thomson Mason arrived in Detroit as secretary of Michigan Territory, instigating a series of strange episodes in territorial government that would unfold over the next six years. By October, Mason's interests had drifted to Mexico; he became a shareholder in a scheme to sell twenty million acres there and relied on his precocious

1830: Treaty with the Sauk and Fox, etc.

The 1825 peace treaty at Prairie du Chien was a failure. By 1830, international relations had deteriorated into open warfare among indigenous nations and increasing tensions with settlers. So William Clark called for another treaty at Prairie du Chien, and brought along the US Army as a show of force.

Leaders of all four Dakota bands attended; Wabasha and Petit Corbeau had been engaged in diplomacy since before Pike met them in 1805. Big Elk of the Omaha and leaders of the Iowa, Oto, and Missouri were also there. Keokuk, who was leading some Sauk and Fox to relocate into Iowa, attended the treaty; Black Hawk, who was resisting removal, did not.

Willoughby Morgan, Clark's co-commissioner, set the tone for the meeting with his opening remarks: "Your Great Father the President commands me to say to you, if you continue your wars he will march an army into your country . . . and more especially will he do this if in your wars your young men should kill any of his white children. Your Great Father warns you beforehand of your danger."[1]

As tribal representatives moved cautiously to end their disputes, Clark and Morgan introduced a proposition for building a lasting peace: the Dakota and the Sauk and Meskwaki would cede a strip through northeast Iowa to serve as a buffer zone between them; and all the tribes would cede land along the Missouri River—the western quarter of present-day Iowa. Central to the negotiations was the idea that the United States would maintain the land cessions as common hunting ground, rather than open them to white settlement.

Clark expended the trust he had built over a quarter century to secure this land cession. "If I had not attended the treaty meeting," he wrote, "[neither] Sauks nor Foxes would have attended." But the establishment of shared hunting grounds was a cynical move on the part of the United States. In reporting on the treaty to the secretary of war, Clark and Morgan mentioned the peace-making effort but emphasized the value of the land cession, describing portions of it as "fully timbered . . . a fine farming and grazing country . . . well adapted to agriculture. We are also informed it contains lead ores." The land would be used for hunting only temporarily, and then for Indian removal and settlement. On the day the treaty was signed, Clark and Morgan wrote that eastern Iowa soon could be "assigned to such tribes as are now, or may be located hereafter upon it by the President of the U. States. . . . Hunting will be nearly at an end in this tract of Country in the course of two or three years and it will not then be necessary to retain it for that purpose."[2]

nineteen-year-old son, Stevens T. Mason, to help perform territorial duties. In July 1831, Jackson accommodatingly sent the distracted father on a mission to Mexico and named the son—who was still too young to vote—to the position of secretary.[5]

The next month, Lewis Cass became secretary of war. In eighteen years as governor of Michigan Territory, he had extinguished aboriginal title to millions of acres; in his new position, he would be in charge of US–Indian relations during the "removal" era. George Bryan Porter, leader of a machine called the Lancaster Regency that controlled elections in Pennsylvania, replaced Cass in Michigan, but he was often absent from Detroit, leaving young Stevens T. Mason in charge of Michigan Territory.[6]

When Cass arrived in Washington, a panicked letter from the recently elected governor of Illinois awaited him. A large party of Sauk and Meskwaki families led by sixty-five-year-old Black Hawk had returned from hunting to re-occupy their villages in Illinois, alarming many new white settlers in the state. "I consider the State to be actually invaded," Reynolds wrote to Cass, "and the country in 'imminent danger.'" He continued, "A sufficient force of mounted men . . . was immediately called into the field. This efficient and bold movement intimidated the Indians. . . . I do assure you, that if I am again compeled to call on the militia of this State, I will place in the field such force, as will exterminate all Indians, who will not let us alone."[7]

Thousands of white settlers throughout the Midwest were primed to take the field against Black Hawk. In July, Reynolds received a typical letter from a volunteer in Kentucky, offering "a cavalry company say of one hundred men, but if five hundred I have no doubt it will be attended to" and promising to "meet you with out delay in the Prairie or in the wood to chastise or exterminate as may seam the most advisable, those hostile tribes now infesting the Young but flourishing state of Illinois."[8]

When Black Hawk's group—about a thousand men, women, and children—returned the next year, Reynolds did in fact call out the militia, and a skirmish sparked full-scale war. As many as six thousand militia members from throughout the Midwest—plus the Dakota and Menominee, longtime enemies of the Sauk and Meskwaki—volunteered to fight Black Hawk's band. On June 7, the Indian agent in Chicago wrote to acting governor Stevens T. Mason, "Sir. Within you have a letter from the citizens of Chicago requesting a force from our territory to exterminate those vile savages that are devastating our frontiers. I hope the call on the patriotism of the people of Michigan will not be made in vain."[9]

The next day, an outraged William Clark, in his official capacity as superintendent of Indian Affairs, wrote about the Black Hawk band to his old treaty-making partner, the secretary of war: "As they have afforded sufficient evidence not only of their entire disregard of Treaties, but also of their deep-rooted hostility, in shedding the blood of our women & children, a War of Extermination should be waged against them. The honor & respectability of the Government requires this:— the peace & quiet of the frontier, the lives & safety of its inhabitants demands it."[10]

The war was over by September. Black Hawk and his allies had killed about seventy-five people, including noncombatants. Between 450 and 800 members of Black Hawk's band were killed, including noncombatants trying to escape across the Mississippi into Iowa. It was the last military resistance to Indian removal in the old Northwest Territory.[11]

In 1833, Governor George B. Porter of Michigan Territory was the commissioner for a momentous treaty in Chicago. The Council of Three Fires ceded the last of their land in Illinois and Indiana in exchange for five million acres in present-day western Iowa (part of the 1830 land cession at Prairie du Chien). The treaty established a three-year timeline for their removal. During that period, the history of Michigan Territory would ravel toward its strange conclusion. In the spring of 1833, an act of the Michigan territorial legislature demanded statehood: "Resolved, That this Council cannot believe that Congress will be so far regardless of the wishes and rights of the people of this territory, as to refuse their present application for admission into the Union, and also deny them the means of placing the justice of their application and their rights to admission fully before the National Legislature."[12]

So the legislators were shocked when Congress tabled the matter in May 1834, in large part because Michigan still claimed a strip of land in the state of Ohio. On June 30, instead of joining the Union, Michigan Territory was enlarged to its greatest extent ever. With the addition of unorganized territory from west of the Mississippi, the boundaries of Michigan Territory came to include all of present-day Michigan, Wisconsin, Minnesota, and Iowa, and half of North and South Dakota. For the first time, a US territory spanned the Mississippi.

A week later, Governor Porter died of cholera, and young Stevens T.

Mason was in charge of the entire territory. Despite the lack of authorization from Congress, Mason called for a state constitution and the election of legislators and a governor. Because this apparatus would operate only within the proposed borders of the state of Michigan, he also established a separate "rump council," a legislature to oversee operations in the western portion of the territory.

Mason's aggressive pursuit of Michigan's statehood, and its territorial claim against Ohio (which came to be known as the Toledo War), cost him his job. His replacement as secretary, John S. "Little Jack" Horner, arrived in Detroit in September 1835—only weeks before the "statewide" election that Mason had organized. For the next year, Horner would be in charge of a territory that had no governor, and Mason would be the governor of a state that did not exist.[13]

Henry Dodge and the dangerous John Smith T, impresarios of lead mining in Missouri and coconspirators with Aaron Burr, became bitter enemies as the years unfolded. After the 1825 Treaty of Prairie du Chien, Dodge moved his enterprise to the recently opened lead region of Illinois and became a leading citizen of Galena. During the Black Hawk War, he was one of several enthusiastic militia commanders, but through the efforts of a shady character named Dr. Addison Philleo, Dodge became a legend.[14]

Philleo, a man described by his peers as "disgusting and cruel," operated the local newspaper in Galena. At the outbreak of the war, he embedded himself in Henry Dodge's militia battalion. Because the *Galenian* was the only newspaper in northern Illinois, and Philleo was the only journalist reporting on events as they happened, his dispatches were widely circulated. By aggrandizing the role of Dodge and ignoring the role of any other commander, Philleo turned Galena's new favorite son into a national celebrity. Dodge—the Salt Boiler—also became known as "Hero of the Black Hawk War" and "Captain of Aggressive Civilization."[15]

In 1836, when Michigan was admitted to statehood, it lost Toledo to the state of Ohio but gained the Upper Peninsula. The remainder of the territory was reincorporated, and Dodge received a new title: Governor of Wisconsin Territory. As governor, he immediately became involved in an important aspect of Indian removal: clearing aboriginal title in the West to make room for indigenous people from the East. An early, complicated target for US acquisition was the area of northwestern Missouri and western Iowa—promised to so many nations in 1830 as their common hunting ground—and the United States approached the problem from several directions. Dodge negotiated the extinguishment of Sauk and Meskwaki claims to the area; Lawrence Taliaferro, agent at Fort Snelling, negotiated a treaty with the Dakota; and William Clark negotiated a treaty with the Iowa—the last of the thirty-seven treaties that he signed in his long career.

In 1837, the forced exodus of the Cherokee began. By then, so much indigenous land had been acquired and sold by the United States under the Indian Removal Act that, for the only time in its history, the country was debt-free. But much of that land had been purchased with currency issued by fly-by-night wildcat banks in an economically fragile, speculative bubble. The bubble burst in the Panic of 1837, a financial collapse that would grip the United States for nearly a decade.

As this collapse began, both the Dakota and the Ojibwe ceded land east of the Mississippi. It was an area rich in resources, but it would be exploited only fitfully in the following few years because of the economic downturn in the United States and the continual shifting of US territorial boundaries.

For seventeen years, from the statehood of Missouri to 1838, US territory "beyond the Mississippi" was either unorganized or administered from the East. During that period, William Clark retained his position of superintendent of Indian Affairs, interacting with successive governors of territories and states that touched the eastern bank of the river: Lewis Cass, Ninian Edwards, John Reynolds, George Porter, Henry Dodge. On July 4, 1838, Iowa Territory was formed west of the Mississippi, including the present-day state of Iowa, most of Minnesota, and part of the Dakotas. Wisconsin Territory was reduced to an area east of the river, composed of the current state, recent Dakota and Ojibwe land cessions, and the yet-unceded Arrowhead Region in Minnesota.

On the day that Iowa Territory was formed, a Mormon orator gave a Fourth of July address in a town called Far West, Missouri. Responding to growing violence between Mormons and their neighbors, Sidney Rigdon said, "That mob that comes on us to disturb us, it shall be between us and them a war of extermination." William Clark died on September 1 as the conflict escalated, and on October 27, Governor Lilburn Boggs issued Missouri Executive Order 44, in which he commanded that "the Mormons must be treated as enemies, and must be exterminated or driven from the state."[16]

It was a sentiment that would be directed to the Dakota, in virtually the same words, twenty-four years later.

1837: Treaties with the Ojibwe and Dakota

With the collapse of the fur trade in the upper Mississippi during the 1830s, the Ojibwe and Dakota became willing to cede land along the river. In July 1837, the Ojibwe signed a treaty at St. Peters (the present site of Mendota, Minnesota). Henry Dodge, the US commissioner, described the cession as "nine to ten millions of acres of land, and abounding in Pine Timber. A part of it is presented as being well suited to Agricultural purposes, and discoveries are reported to have been made of copper on the St. Croix and Rum Rivers and near Lake Couterille [Lac Courte Oreilles, Wisconsin]."[1]

During the treaty negotiations, Ojibwe leaders were explicit in their reservation of deciduous forests from the land cession and of their right to continue using the resources of the ceded territory. La Trappe of Leech Lake used a visual aid to explain their position: "Of all the country that we grant you we wish to hold on to a tree where we get our living, and to reserve the streams where we drink the waters that give us life. . . . This is it (placing an oak sprig upon the table near the map). It is a different kind of tree from the one you wish to get from us."

The representatives also spelled out their "wish to reserve the privilege of making sugar from the trees, and getting their living from the Lakes and Rivers." With these stipulations clarified, Dodge offered annuity payments, a payout to relatives of tribal members, and $70,000 for debt payments to traders. Some Ojibwe objected to the debt payments, because traders had taken so much fish and wood from the territory over the years without paying for it, but the treaty was signed.

In Washington two months later, commissioner Joel R. Poinsett tried a power play at the beginning of negotiations with a Dakota treaty delegation: "You have passed through some of our great towns . . . you have seen enough to be aware of the power of the nation."

The method backfired. Big Thunder of the Dakota responded, "We did not come here to learn the strength of your nation. Our friends have been here and have told us of your power." Contrasting the situation of the Americans who had requested their land with that of his own people, Big Thunder added, "Since I have been here I have been looking around, I see all of your people are well dressed."

The Dakota negotiators requested $1.6 million for an area east of the Mississippi, about evenly divided between the present-day states of Minnesota and Wisconsin. The United States offered a million dollars but pointed out that the Dakota would have blacksmiths and other assistance in adapting to a new way of life. A Dakota negotiator named He Who Comes Last said, "I wish to enquire where the Black Smiths are that were promised us in the Treaty of 1830," and Morning Shadow added, "I suppose you have heard of the treaty made some years since, 1830. I suppose you have it in a book."

At the beginning of negotiations, Poinsett promised that the power of the United States "will in no event be exerted to do you evil. It will always be used to protect you and defend you."

Days later, Good Road summed up the proceedings by saying, "I think you love money."[2]

SIGNERS: WHO ARE YOUR PEOPLE?

Henry Sibley signed the 1837 treaty in which the Ojibwe ceded part of present-day Minnesota and Wisconsin. But he was not the first member of his family to sign a treaty. His father, Solomon, the Michigan territorial delegate to Congress, signed a land cession treaty with the Ojibwe, Ottawa, and Potawatomi in 1821. Henry Sibley's brother-in-law Charles C. Trowbridge, while on the Lewis Cass expedition in 1820, signed a treaty with the Ojibwe in Michigan. And the family involvement in US–Indian relations began even earlier: Henry Sibley's grandfather was Ebenezer "Buckeye" Sproat of the Ohio Company.

Henry, as head of the American Fur Company (AFC) in present-day Minnesota, traded with the Dakota for decades, and after the War of 1862, he was a leader of the punitive military expedition that chased them into Canada, though he never signed a treaty with the Dakota. But his brother Frederick did—in 1851, when the Dakota ceded most of their land in Minnesota. Henry himself signed treaties with the Lakota toward the end of the western Indian Wars in 1865—more than seventy-five years after Grandpa Sproat arrived in Marietta, Ohio.

The Sibley family's involvement in US–Indian affairs—especially treaty making—was not a unique situation. Of the 2,300 men who signed treaties on behalf of the United States, at least one-third were related by blood or marriage to other treaty signers. These family connections can be traced to long before the Revolution, and they continued throughout the treaty-making era in every region of the United States.

In the 1740s, John Lewis, an Irishman who fled to North America after killing his landlord, received one of the largest of the early Virginia land grants. The British Proclamation of 1763 frustrated his family's ambitions. So it is not surprising that his sons, keeping alive the dream of land speculation, negotiated the very first official treaty that the United States signed with an indigenous nation—the Lenape Delaware in 1778. (The treaty was also signed by their nephew Joseph L. Finley and by Washington's western land agent, William Crawford.)

In 1868, at the other end of the treaty-making timeline, a "peace commission" traveled the West by train, making treaties as they went. Members of this group had relatives who signed earlier treaties. John Sanborn was the brother-in-law of Henry Rice, trader and former senator of Minnesota. William Tecumseh Sherman was the brother-in-law of treaty signer and future US congressman Thomas Ewing Jr. General William S. Harney, recently retired after a long army career, was the brother of Benjamin Harney, who signed the 1825 Treaty of Prairie du Chien, and he was the brother-in-law of Thomas Biddle and Richard Graham, members of the Clark treaty-making machine at the end of the War of 1812.[17]

Family groups among the treaty signers ranged in size. At one end of the scale, small family units signed treaties together or, as with the Sibleys, at different times and locations. In other cases, however, large kinship groups included scores of men who signed as many as a hundred treaties and shaped the course of US–Indian relations.

Along with business and political connections, kinship connected the US treaty signers to a remarkably intimate degree. This is a story that has been submerged in the historical record because of several factors. First, the American myth is an egalitarian dream, in which any concentration of wealth and power is downplayed. Second, the treaty signers as a group seldom have received much attention, and their names are spread over hundreds of documents. One might be aware that lead miner and US senator George W. Jones was the son of lead miner and Missouri supreme court justice John Rice Jones, or even that George Jones and Indian agent Felix St. Vrain married sisters, but though these men signed seven treaties, they never signed *the same* treaty. A family connection among treaty signers never rises to daylight.

Even when multiple members of a single family signed the same treaty, the family connection is not always readily apparent. Looking at the twenty-one US signatures on a treaty with the Kickapoo in 1820, one might surmise that signers Henry P. Chouteau and Gabriel Chouteau were related to commissioner Auguste Chouteau (and they were his sons), but the connections don't end there. Signers Pascal Cerre and G. P. Cerre were Auguste's brother-in-law and nephew; signers Gabriel Paul and his brother Rene were married to sisters—Marie Louise and Pelagie Chouteau—who were Auguste's daughters.

The identities of women are often overlooked in nineteenth-century history and biography, so those family connections are submerged in the historical record. The connections among William Harney, who married Mary Mullanphy; Thomas Biddle, who married Ann Mullanphy; and Richard Graham, who married Catherine Mullanphy, are relatively well known in large part because the Mullanphy sisters were members of one of the two wealthiest families in St. Louis at the time. But the astounding extent of family ties among the men who signed US–Indian treaties is relatively unknown. These kinship groups were built through marriages, mentioned in passing and left unconnected to other historical events, that involved women whose names are more obscure today. The Saucier sisters, Brigitte and Angelique, married Pierre Chouteau and Pierre Menard, men who signed treaties eighteen times; Brigitte and Angelique had sons (Pierre Chouteau Jr. and Pierre Menard Jr.) who signed five treaties. That in itself is a significant family connection, including the most powerful family west of the Mississippi and the lieutenant governor of Illinois. But Angelique's daughter Alzira Menard, seldom mentioned today outside of genealogical charts, married George Kennerly, who signed eighteen treaties himself, and George's sister Harriet married William Clark, who signed more treaties than anyone.

Genealogy can be a seductive subject. Any American with an ancestor who arrived in Virginia from England before 1650 might be fascinated to learn that he or she is related to five US presidents, Elvis Presley, and Charlemagne. But in practical terms, these connections do not always make a large impact on the day-to-day lives of family members. Among treaty signers, though, family connections—even relatively distant ones—mattered. Menard and Clark and Chouteau, for instance—connected familially only by a string of marriages and births—cofounded the Missouri Fur Company and continued their involvement with each other and with other relatives for decades to their own personal benefit.

One might expect to find family relations among treaty signers who lived in the small and isolated settler communities where treaties were often signed. But the size of some of the family groups among treaty signers far exceeds what might be expected. George Rogers Clark signed a treaty near Pittsburgh in 1785. Edmond Chouteau signed a treaty at Fort Laramie in 1851, fifteen hundred miles and ninety-six years removed. The two men were connected by family relationships that included scores of other treaty signers.[18]

Alice Forsyth was not a treaty signer—all of the US treaty signers were men—but she had relatives who signed treaties. Her father, Robert, had three half brothers in a complicated family structure; they were named Thomas Forsyth, James Forsyth, and John Kinzie. These three uncles of Alice were among the earliest American fur traders at the site of Chicago, and they signed treaties thirty-nine times. Alice's three fur trading cousins—Robert, James, and John H.

Kinzie—signed six treaties. Her sister Jane married Charles Brush, from a family that owned a lot of Detroit real estate and many Detroit businesses; Charles, his brother Edmund, and his father, Elijah, signed seven treaties. Alice's sister Maria married Benjamin Kercheval, an Indian agent in Detroit who moved into the Chicago fur trade; Benjamin and his brother Gholson signed six treaties. And Alice's brother Robert Forsyth signed seventeen treaties as Lewis Cass's private secretary.[19]

When Alice Forsyth was ten years old, the British attacked Detroit. Fleeing to safety with her father and siblings, she arrived at the local fort just as a cannonball took the head off a soldier. She later told her daughter that General Hull had surrendered the fort without a fight because of his "sense of responsibility for the lives of the women and children committed to him. At the time, Hull was ill and confined to bed." In fact, Hull was drunk and eventually sentenced to death for cowardice, but Alice apparently never shook the belief that her presence affected the outcome of the War of 1812. In 1820, she married Lieutenant Thomas Hunt.

Thomas Hunt was not a treaty signer, either, but his relatives were. Thomas and his brother George were sent to Detroit as small boys when their father—one of the few survivors of St. Clair's Defeat—was posted to Fort Wayne as an army major. They arrived at about the same time as William Hull to find Detroit in ashes, and according to the family story told by the daughter of Thomas and Alice, "the boys sat down on the river bank with their arms around each other's necks and cried." Their older brother Henry quickly found them, and they grew up in his home. Henry Hunt was already a well-established fur trader; he would later become a partner of Lewis Cass in buying Detroit real estate and sign four US–Indian treaties. George lived in Detroit for the rest of his life and signed two treaties. Their brother Charles wound up in Toledo running a fur trade post for Henry and also signed a treaty. Sister Ruth married Abraham Edwards, a doctor who ran the Detroit militia with Cass, went into local politics, and signed four treaties. Sister Abigail married Colonel Josiah Snelling, who built the fort in Minnesota that became the epicenter for treaty making in that region. And brother John E. Hunt, a Detroit fur trader and politician, was also a treaty signer; he married the sister of Lewis Cass's wife.

Thomas Hunt was taken prisoner in Hull's surrender of Detroit when he was twenty and contracted illnesses while in captivity. Because of the effects of his captivity, Hunt was assigned to a desk job in Washington, and he and Alice lived a life of privilege among the upper echelons of society. They attended parties with Lewis Cass, who by then was secretary of war, and with Alexander Macomb (son of the land speculator), who signed treaties as commanding general of the US Army. They sampled a new invention, ice cream, at the home of the French ambassador. Thomas played cards with Henry Clay and Daniel Webster. Their son ran a wheelbarrow into Andrew Jackson's legs, and their daughter was the model for a character in the painting *Baptism of Pocahontas* in the US Capitol rotunda.

And the family network extended from Washington beyond Detroit and beyond Chicago, all the way to the Mississippi: Kinzies and Forsyths married into the Whistler military family, who in turn married into the Bailly and Faribault families that ran fur trading posts in present-day Minnesota.

Many members of this family attended the signing of the Treaty of Chicago, a famous treaty with the Ojibwe, Ottawa, and Potawatomi in 1833. In fact, ten of the US signers were close relatives of Alice Forsyth. The treaty is notable for the land cession made there—it included the site of Chicago—and for the amount of money that was distributed. One hundred thousand dollars was paid "to individuals in lieu of Reservations," with dollar amounts attached to specific names. In a second list, $175,000 was distributed "to individuals, on claims admitted to be justly due." Charles Trowbridge, Henry Gratiot, and Pierre Menard Jr. received payments, as did members of several treaty-signing families in the fur trade such as the Bourassas, the Beaubiens, and the Grignons. The extended Connor and Godfroy families each received about $4,500; the Ewings received $8,200. And through direct payments and money for which they were trustees, members of the Kinzie/Forsyth/Hunt clan walked away in control of nearly $70,000, one-fourth of all the money handed out there. George Hunt, for instance, received $750, Robert Forsyth $3,000, and James Kinzie $5,000 in the first category of payments, though it was inconceivable that any of them would be entitled to a reservation. For no discernible reason, Alice Forsyth Hunt and her sister Jane Forsyth Brush each received $3,000 in debt payments, and her brother Robert received $10,000. Alice's daughter suggested that they had been "adopted members of this particular [unspecified] tribe." Alice and her husband used the largesse to move from Washington back to Detroit, where Thomas Hunt had been appointed the register of the land office.[20]

XXXXX ◆ XXXXX

Marie Therese Bourgeois, the daughter of a French father and a Spanish mother, married a New Orleans baker in 1748, when she was fifteen. Within a year, she escaped that abusive relationship by fleeing to a convent with her infant son, who had been named after his father: Auguste Chouteau. The elder Auguste left for France shortly thereafter, and Marie pretended he was dead. Wives had no property rights in New Orleans, but widows did, and Marie Chouteau wanted property.

In 1758, Marie had the first of her children with Pierre Laclede, a businessman who would secure a Spanish monopoly on trade west of the Mississippi. She and Laclede did not marry; she was listed as "Widow Chouteau" in census records, and all of her children with Laclede carried the surname of her husband. In February 1764, Laclede and fourteen-year-old Auguste founded a fur trading outpost at the confluence of the Missouri and Mississippi Rivers. In June, Marie boarded a raft in New Orleans to join them with her other children—six-year-old Jean Pierre, four-year-old Marie Pelagie, two-year-old Marie Louise, and three-month-old Victoire. It was a grueling twelve-hundred-mile trip that took three months.

By the time Marie arrived in the settlement—already called St. Louis—more than forty French families were living there. The French had withdrawn their claims to dominion east of the Mississippi, and many of the fur traders from "the Illinois country" were gravitating to the confluence of rivers. Marie became "the mother of St. Louis," and with Laclede's backing, she accumulated assets and enterprises: a large house that she owned in her own name, "a farm lot, three black slaves and two Indian slaves," a beekeeping business.[21]

Three years later, her husband returned from France and demanded all of her property. Marie successfully challenged an extradition order that would have returned her to New Orleans, and, still only thirty-four years old, she settled into her role of running St. Louis for the next half century. Before she died in 1814, St. Louis became part of the United States, and her offspring expanded Laclede's fur trade business throughout the Midwest.

The family that thrived with Marie as a matriarch also played an enduring role in US treaty making with indigenous nations. Their extensive involvement illustrates how closely connected the US representatives at treaties were, through business and political ties but also, to a surprising extent, through family ties.

Marie's sons, Auguste and Jean Pierre Chouteau, accounted for thirty-five signatures on thirty-one different treaties. As noted earlier,

Auguste married Marie Therese Cerre, the sister and aunt of treaty signers; Jean Pierre married Brigitte Saucier, the sister-in-law of Pierre Menard, who would become the lieutenant governor of Illinois. Menard signed eleven treaties, and his son signed two.

Nine of Marie Chouteau's grandsons placed twenty-nine signatures on twenty-three treaties. They included Henry Gratiot, one of the most successful lead miners in Illinois.

Marie Chouteau's granddaughters married owners of fur trade companies that formed partnerships with the Chouteaus—Bernard Pratte and J. B. Cabanne. They did not sign treaties, but other granddaughters did marry treaty signers, including John Honey and the Paul brothers. Gabriel and Rene Paul arrived in St. Louis after their father, the lieutenant governor of St. Domingo (now Haiti), fled the slave revolt in 1791; they and their sons signed twenty-five treaties as interpreters, although it is unclear how, from St. Domingo, they had learned the languages of the Meskwaki, Pawnee, Iowa, Kansa, Kickapoo, Omaha, Osage, Piankeshaw, Potawatomi, Quapaw, Dakota, and Ho Chunk.

Marie Chouteau's great-grandsons also included treaty signers J. B. Sarpy and Edmond Chouteau. Her great-granddaughters married Lewis Bogy, who signed five treaties as US commissioner of Indian Affairs; J. F. A. Sanford, who signed four treaties; and James Wilkinson Kingsbury, who signed ten treaties as a young West Point graduate on an expedition to the Yellowstone River. Kingsbury was in command of the steamship that fired on Black Hawk's band as it fled from Illinois across the Mississippi River; he later left the military to become "keeper of U.S. military stores in St. Louis," where he acquired "a large landed estate."[22]

Several women in the Chouteau kinship group served a function like that played by Alice Forsyth, forming a lateral connection among treaty-signing families. Henry Gratiot's wife, Susan Hempstead, had three brothers who signed treaties: Charles, who moved to Galena as a lawyer in 1829 to capitalize on the lead mining rush and signed treaties with the Ojibwe and Ho Chunk that year; Edward, another lawyer who became attorney general for Upper Louisiana, a territorial delegate to Congress, and a partner in Henry Dodge's salt-making operation; and William, a very successful lead miner in Galena who also owned steamboats—including the one commanded in the Black Hawk War by his brother-in-law's nephew, James Wilkinson Kingsbury. Susan's sister Mary married Manuel Lisa, a managing director of the Missouri Fur Company.[23]

Alzira Menard and her sister-in-law Harriet Kennerly connected the Chouteaus to the other powerhouse family of Missouri Territory, that of William Clark. Kennerly had two children before she married Clark. Her son William Radford became a rear admiral in the US Navy after signing three treaties; her daughter Mary Radford married Stephen Watts Kearny, who signed nine treaties and became the military governor of California and, later, of Mexico City. In her second marriage, to Clark, Harriet Kennerly became the sister, mother, mother-in-law, wife, stepmother, sister-in-law, grandmother, and aunt of men who added ninety-nine signatures to sixty-nine treaties. These men included her stepson Meriwether Lewis Clark, who designed the first theater west of the Mississippi and became a Confederate major (and whose son started the Kentucky Derby), and her nephews, the O'Fallon brothers. John O'Fallon, thanks in part to government contracts steered his way by his uncle William, became the richest man in St. Louis.

This kinship group also typifies another situation in which family connections are submerged in the historical record: they include ties forged through relationships with indigenous women. The narrative that fur traders entered these relationships only for commercial advantage in indigenous communities is so strong that intimate and advantageous connections *among white treaty signers*, forged through these marriages, go largely unacknowledged. In the case of the Chouteau extended kinship group, one set of such connections centers on Omaha and Ponca families.

Big Elk, the primary leader of the Omaha, had two daughters. One, Mitane, married Manuel Lisa (while he was still married to his first wife in St. Louis); another, Meumbane, married Lucien Fontannelle. Big Elk also formally adopted as his son the child of a Ponca woman and a white trader named Joseph LaFlesch. This child was known as Joseph LaFlesch Jr. and as Estamaza (Iron Eyes). Through his adoption, he became the hereditary primary leader of the Omaha. Estamaza married Mary Gale, the daughter of an Iowa woman and John Gale, an army doctor. Gale, Joseph LaFlesch Sr., Henry Fontenelle, and Manuel Lisa signed twenty-four treaties on behalf of the United States. Estamaza and Logan Fontenelle signed three treaties as representatives of the Omaha. The Omaha land cession of 1854 affected all of their lives because of their kinship with Black Elk.[24]

Henry Dodge, who negotiated the 1837 Ojibwe land cession in Minnesota, was initiated into Western Star Lodge No. 109 in Kaskaskia, Illinois, in 1806. He went on to become a founding member of Freemasonry west of the Mississippi, helping to create Louisiana Lodge 109 in St. Genevieve, Missouri.[25]

The Masons were one of a number of voluntary associations that connected treaty signers to one another and distinguished them from their peers. The Society of the Cincinnati, patrician and hereditary, began as an exclusive group that was focused on securing western land; scores of the Continental Army officers who joined it went on to sign treaties. The Aztec Club was another military organization, more social in nature, formed immediately after the war between the United States and Mexico, while the United States still occupied Mexico City. All of its members were officers serving in Mexico, and many of them had been involved in Indian removal and/or "frontier duty" at western posts in the United States or in indigenous-held territory. More than thirty members of the Aztec Club were treaty signers.[26]

Before the start of the American Revolution, Irish Americans formed the Friendly Sons of St. Patrick, which evolved into the Hibernian Society just after the war. Many of the early members went on to sign treaties: Anthony Wayne, Richard Butler, Robert Morris, Henry Knox, and Francis Johnston. Later members included treaty signers Andrew Jackson, Mahlon Dickinson, Henry Toland, and Andrew Porter.[27]

The voluntary association that attracted the most treaty signers, however, was the Freemasons. With more than a hundred Masons among the 2,300 signers, the rate of membership in this group was as much as four times higher than among the American male population as a whole. As an early historian of Indiana remarked, "The Ancient Order of Free and Accepted Masons, for centuries past, has been the handmaid of civilization, her members carrying with them into the unbroken wilderness the fraternizing influences which have been found to be of such momentous value, even in the habitations of the unlettered. . . . The first settlers here [in Logansport] were all, or nearly all, of them members of this honorable fraternity."[28]

The remarkable aspect of this membership was not the number of Freemasons among the treaty signers, however, but the status they held in the organization. Treaty signers originated many local lodges and were cofounders of the first lodges in areas that became Indiana (1807, John Gibson and Henry Vanderburg); Missouri (1807, Henry

Dodge and John Smith T.); Arkansas (1819, Richard Mentor Johnson); Wisconsin (1824, John McNeil); and Florida (1825, William Duval).

When a state was admitted to the Union, lodges in that area were organized under a Grand Lodge. Treaty signers co-organized these more powerful, statewide Grand Lodges in Missouri (1821, James Kennerly, Archibald Gamble); Florida (1830, Richard Call, William Duval); Minnesota (1853, Charles Borup); and Kansas (1855, Daniel Vanderslice). A Grand Master presides over each Grand Lodge, serving as the most powerful Mason in each state. A surprising number of treaty signers held that position. Shadrach Bond was Grand Master in Illinois at the state's inception in 1818; Richard Keith Call was a Grand Master in Florida in 1850. Elisha Smith Lee and Levi Cook were Grand Masters in Michigan (1841), Elihu Stout in Indiana (1827), Robert Furnas in Nebraska (1865–67). Lewis Cass was a Grand Master in Ohio (1804–07) before starting Freemasonry in Michigan, and he became the first Grand Master there.[29]

Membership in groups and exclusive clubs no doubt reinforced the leadership status of select treaty signers and strengthened the business and social ties among US representatives on the front line of US–Indian relations. The term *voluntary association* resonates also in some modern considerations of indigenous property rights. Some political philosophers in recent times have found it difficult to conceive of a nation that is not based on the concept of private property. Libertarians in particular are interested in identifying an organizational model that might more comfortably describe the identity of indigenous people. As one Libertarian author has put it, "Were the tribes, in effect, voluntary associations of individuals who consented to their collective ownership of the land? The fact that no form of tribute or taxes was ever collected among the Indian tribes inhabiting what is now the United States lends some credence to the view that the tribes were voluntary organizations."[30]

Stephen Bonga, like Henry Sibley, signed the 1837 treaty in which the Ojibwe ceded part of present-day Minnesota and Wisconsin. He was born in the area of present-day Duluth, at the southern tip of Lake Superior, in 1799; his brother George Bonga was born there in 1805 and went on to sign treaties with the Ojibwe in 1847 and 1867. The

Bonga brothers were children and grandchildren of enslaved people of African descent who had been emancipated by a white military officer. Their father, Pierre, entered the fur trade and married an Ojibwe woman, as each of the Bonga brothers did. As adults, Stephen and George—though they shared no European biological heritage at all—referred to themselves as the "first white children" born in what is now Minnesota.[31]

The brothers were certainly aware that they could not have made that statement if they had been born in Virginia instead of at Lake Superior. And today it is difficult to imagine any world in which their statement might be true: society in the United States is shaped fundamentally by a particular formation of race. But in the place and time where the Bongas were born, that formation had not yet arrived to define human relationships. Unlike today, where at least in much public discourse the dominant identity is presented as "white" and everyone else is a "person of color," the Bongas were born in a world where the local dominant cultures were indigenous and everyone else was white. And in that world, "white" was not a racial term in our contemporary sense. It might be considered more of an economic term, arising from a negotiating position in the fur trade. Sellers were indigenous, and buyers were white, and each side was backed by its own system of culture, language, and history. The Bongas arrived at the fur trade exchange from the "white" side, yet they could take an active role in Ojibwe culture. In the indigenous-centered world where the Bongas lived, racial/cultural identity was still fluid.

That peculiar formation of race that twists American society today—and makes the Bongas' identity confusing—was already in place on the Atlantic seaboard when the Bongas were born. But it was not always there. Race in the modern sense of the word emerged only in the hundred years before the American Revolution. It was a sick response to the idea that private property is a universal right. Those two concepts—private property and race—evolved together and spread across the continent together.[32]

In 1689, near the midpoint between the first British settlement in North America and the Declaration of Independence, John Locke presented an idea that was revolutionary in Europe. He claimed that private ownership of land was a natural right. At a time when European monarchs claimed this right for themselves, the idea was an assault on the social order; Locke from the beginning equated private property rights with personal liberty.

In proposing this idea, though, Locke had to answer several questions. First, who made John Locke king? By what authority was he challenging the authority of monarchs? Locke argued that if one started with some basic principles and applied human reason, one would inevitably arrive at his conclusion; it was the answer of the Enlightenment. He found his basic principles in the biblical book of Genesis and explained: "God, who hath given the world to men in common, hath also given them reason to make use of it to the best advantage of life, and convenience. The earth, and all that is therein, is given to men."[33]

If the right to property sprang from the mind of God *and* of John Locke, it must be universal, a right that every person holds. This stance raised more questions. How and why, then, do indigenous societies in North America operate with neither monarchs nor private property? And how can taking their land be justified? These were not idle questions. The colonialist enterprise was already underway, and Locke himself was on the British Board of Trade, in charge of the colonies in North America. So the Enlightenment philosophers of property rights became obsessed with indigenous people of North America as the difficult test case for refining their theories. Locke mentioned indigenous societies *in the same paragraph* as the sentences above: "[Y]et being given for the use of men, there must of necessity be a means to appropriate them some way or other, before they can be of any use, or at all beneficial to any particular man. The fruit, or venison, which nourishes the wild Indian . . . must be his, and so his . . . that another can no longer have any right to it, before it can do him any good for the support of his life."

And here Locke had to answer another question: How exactly do resources given by God to "men in common" become the private property of an individual? If there "must of necessity be a means to appropriate them," what might that means be? The answer was labor. One transforms an element of the natural world into private property by working on it: "Though men as a whole own the earth and all inferior creatures, every individual man has a property in his own person; this is something that nobody else has any right to. The labour of his body and the work of his hands, we may say, are strictly his. So when he takes something from the state that nature has provided and left it in, he mixes his labour with it, thus joining to it something that is his own; and in that way he makes it his property."[34]

And this, in Locke's eyes, was justification for acquiring land in North America: indigenous people did not work hard enough: "Several

nations of the Americans . . . are rich in land, and poor in all the com-
forts of life; whom nature having furnished as liberally as any other
people, with the materials of plenty . . . yet for want of improving it by
labour, have not one hundredth part of the conveniencies we enjoy."

The problem here, of course, is that in providing a spurious justification for taking indigenous land—it needs to be worked—Locke wiped
out any justification for slavery. The acquisition of territory, and slavery in different forms, had been part of the human social landscape
throughout the world and throughout history; Locke's attempt to
equate private property with personal liberty called this history into
question. As historian Barbara Fields has put it, "Bondage does not
need justifying as long as it seems to be the natural order of things. You
need a radical affirmation of bondage only where you have a radical
affirmation of freedom."[35]

And many Enlightenment philosophers, from Locke (who was an investor in the first British slave trading monopoly) to Jefferson, wanted
that justification. Slavery and acquisition of indigenous land were the
ways they made their money. They could follow the light of what they
arrogantly called pure human reason so far as to challenge the authority of kings, an act that required physical and intellectual courage. But
with that light in their hands, they faltered at the threshold of some
dark places; they abandoned reason where their own livelihoods were
threatened.

But their justification was on the way. In the years that Locke was
composing his thoughts on private property, Francois Bernier published an article entitled "New division of Earth by the different species or races which inhabit it." It was the first attempt to divide the
human population into the races in the modern sense of the word:
"Geographers up to this time have only divided the earth according to
its different countries or regions. . . . Still I have remarked that there
are four or five species or races of man in particular whose difference
is so remarkable that it may be properly made use of as the foundation
for a new division of the earth."[36]

Bernier proposed dividing humans into species based on physical
characteristics, though not on skin color. "Colour is only an accident,"
he wrote. One of his divisions included people in Europe, North Africa,
North America, and parts of Asia including India. "As to the Americans," he wrote to his European audience, meaning indigenous people
of the hemisphere, "I do not find the difference sufficiently great to

make of them a peculiar species different from ours." His other divisions included people in China and the rest of Asia, people in sub-Saharan Africa, and Laplanders. He included a long passage on what makes women beautiful and concluded, "A Negro will always be a Negro, carry him to Greenland, give him chalk, feed and manage him never so many ways."

From this dubious beginning, the "natural philosophers" (scientists) of Europe and America began an academic debate about the boundaries and origins of the newly proposed races, using their own imaginations and the Bible as a biology textbook. Racial categories would be refined over the next seventy years. As late as 1744, the Virginia doctor and mapmaker John Mitchell could argue, in "An Essay upon the Causes of the Different Colours of People in Different Climates," that complexions of "Asiatics and Native Amerindians" retained the original color of all mankind, although how he identified a uniform skin color for all of the individuals in these groups went unstated. More Eurocentric points of view came to dominate the field, however, and by 1758 the influential Swedish scientist Carl Linneaus, in evolving editions of his *System Naturae*, had divided the human race into four varieties:

- The *Americanus*: red, choleraic, righteous; stubborn, zealous, free;
- The *Europeanus*: white, sanguine, browny; gentle, acute, inventive;
- The *Asiaticus*: yellow, melancholic, stiff; severe, haughty, greedy;
- The *Afer* or *Africanus*: black, phlegmatic, relaxed; crafty, sly, careless.[37]

Over the next hundred years, scientific racism calcified into a debate in Europe and America between academics who believed that people of all races originated in the Garden of Eden, though some devolved into inferior species, and academics who believed that only the white race was created in the Garden of Eden.

For the philosophers of private property, the formation of race solved an inherent contradiction in their thought. Every human might have a right to property and labor, but Europeans could claim indigenous land and African labor because only Europeans were fully human. So as the US property system spread across the continent, that sense of racial superiority necessarily traveled with it. It informed John Marshall in *Johnson v. M'Intosh*, bolstering his confidence in proposing the Doctrine of Discovery.

On the discovery of this immense continent, the great nations of Europe were eager to appropriate to themselves so much of it as they could respectively acquire. Its vast extent offered ample field to the ambition and enterprise of all, and the character and religion of its inhabitants afforded an apology for considering them as a people over whom the superior genius of Europe might claim an ascendency. The potentates of the old world found no difficulty in convincing themselves that they made ample compensation to the inhabitants of the new by bestowing on them civilization and Christianity in exchange for unlimited independence.

The widely diverse national identities of indigenous people were subsumed, in colonialist eyes, into a distinctive, monolithic racial identity.[38]

One effect of this switch was to insulate the American psyche from charges of committing genocide. The forced removal of a race of people from the territory of the United States rises only to the level of ethnic cleansing; the American public finds consolation in a hierarchy of human rights violations, in which deplorable incidents from an incomprehensible, distant past fall short of the utter extinction of a race composed of all aboriginal people on the continent. If indigenous identity is perceived as national rather than racial, though, the defenses are weakened and require the invention of conditional categories. It was certainly the conscious policy of the United States to destroy indigenous cultures: their relationships to land, their languages, their ways of life. This is "cultural genocide," or "ethnocide." More problematic, though, are instances in which representatives of the government ordered or sanctioned the extermination of nations.

In 1862, Kit Carson (who lived among, fought against, and signed treaties with the Comanche, Arapaho, Kowa, and Apache people) refused to follow the direct orders of General James Carleton, commander of the army's Department of New Mexico: "All Indian men of that tribe [the Apache] are to be killed whenever and wherever you find them. The women and children will not be harmed but you will take them prisoners." Carson did lead the expedition, but he imprisoned some Apache men rather than killing them.[39]

The same year, Governor Alexander Ramsey, in a special session of the Minnesota legislature held during the US–Dakota War, applied to the Dakota the same words that Missouri Governor Boggs once directed toward the Mormons: "The Sioux Indians of Minnesota must be exterminated or driven forever beyond the borders of Minnesota." The state attorney general and local governments then offered cash bounties to anyone who killed a Dakota person, and in a follow-up military campaign, General John Pope announced, "It is my purpose to utterly exterminate the Sioux if I have the power to do so, and even if it requires a campaign lasting the whole next year. Destroy everything belonging to them and force them out on to the plains, unless, as I suggest, you can capture them. They are to be treated as maniacs or wild beasts, and by no means as people with whom treaties or compromises can be made."[40]

The argument continues to this day in Minnesota: does that conciously stated policy against the Dakota constitute genocide, or does the failure of the policy outweigh the sentiment behind it?[41]

In 1824, the year after *Johnson v. M'Intosh*, a new racial division was introduced into land cession treaties: "The small tract of land lying between the rivers Desmoin and the Mississippi, and the section of the above line between the Mississippi and the Desmoin, is intended for the use of the half-breeds belonging to the Sock and Fox nations; they holding it, however, by the same title, and in the same manner, that other Indian titles are held."[42]

Other "half-breed tracts" were created in subsequent treaties. At the 1830 treaty in Prairie du Chien, for instance, 320,000 acres were identified in present-day Minnesota for the children of white traders and indigenous women. As in several of these transactions, Dakota people wanted to take care of their relatives who were not officially members of the tribe and who would not receive annuity payments in exchange for a land cession. The half-breed tract was one option for accomplishing this. Other tribes at the treaty made the same request for a tract in present-day Nebraska. These requests were taken by the United States as an opportunity to extend the system of private property: "The President of the United States may hereafter assign to any of the said half-breeds, to be held by him or them in fee simple, any portion of said tract not exceeding a section, of six hundred and forty acres to each individual."[43]

The creation of these tracts also provided opportunities for more coercive and avaricious intentions by the United States and men who

represented it at treaties. The 1826 treaty in which Ojibwe bands recognized boundaries set in 1825 and ceded mineral rights to the United
States also included the following clause: "It being deemed important
that the half-breeds, scattered through this extensive country, should
be stimulated to exertion and improvement by the possession of permanent property and fixed residences, the Chippewa tribe, in consideration of the affection they bear to these persons, and of the interest
which they feel in their welfare, grant to each of the persons described
in the schedule hereunto annexed, being half-breeds and Chippewas by
descent . . . six hundred and forty acres of land."[44]

The attached schedule lists forty-four grantees, including relatives
of Henry Schoolcraft, Alan Morrison, Daniel Dingley, and Henry Connor, who represented the United States at the treaty. The half-breed
tracts became a way to circumvent laws prohibiting US citizens from
receiving land directly through treaties and another avenue for treaty
signers to profit from their positions of trust. Treaty signers and
other Americans, usually traders who had built trust among indigenous people, were often the legal guardians, if not the parents, of the
"half breeds" who received land titles in these tracts. The 1833 Treaty
of Chicago is an example of this principle in operation. Payments were
promised to the relatives of treaty signers "in lieu of reservations" but
wound up in the hands of Alice Forsyth and her relatives.

As soon as the tracts were established, white squatters typically
rushed to the area and treated it as if it were open to settlement. In
Minnesota, the squatter vigilantes posted themselves at the land office
and turned away legitimate land claimants by force. From this dire
situation, Henry Rice (Minnesota territorial delegate to Congress in
1854) created the greatest opportunity for US citizens to make money
from the tracts. He sponsored legislation to allow "half breeds" (and
their guardians, the treaty signers) to receive written scrip that eventually would entitle them to land anywhere in the US public domain.
This scrip entered the speculation market, and its possessors made
spectacular profits. It was used by speculators to purchase land for
silver mines in Nevada, near the Comstock Lode; timber land in Nevada and California; and land on Minnesota's Mesabi Iron Range.[45]

John Emerson and Lawrence Taliaferro signed the Treaty with the
Chippewa in 1837, along with Henry Sibley and Stephen Bonga. Em-

erson was an army surgeon with obscure origins in Pennsylvania. He recently had been transferred to Fort Snelling from Fort Armstrong in Illinois. Taliaferro, member of an aristocratic Virginia/Kentucky family, was the longtime Indian agent at Fort Snelling.

Taliaferro and Emerson had a family connection that also involved two other treaty signers. Taliaferro had accompanied the Dakota to the 1830 multinational treaty in Prairie du Chien. Strangely enough, two of Emerson's future brothers-in-law also signed that treaty: Henry Bainbridge and John F. A. Sanford. Bainbridge was a career soldier who later served in Florida, Texas, and Mexico. An Indian agent on the Upper Missouri in 1830, Sanford would soon marry Emilie Chouteau, become a partner in the Chouteau family law firm, and, after his wife's death, move to New York, where he amassed great wealth in attending to Chouteau business.

Emerson, Taliaferro, Sanford, and Bainbridge were connected not only by their own families but also by their involvement in one of the most noted families in American history. In 1836, when Emerson arrived at Fort Snelling, he brought an enslaved man named Dred Scott. Taliaferro owned a young enslaved woman named Harriet Robinson. Just before the Treaty of 1837, Taliaferro presided at the marriage of Scott and Robinson, and Emerson became her owner, too. Emerson was soon transferred again but left the Scotts at Fort Snelling. In Louisiana, he met the Sanford sisters, Irene and Mary, and Mary's husband, Henry Bainbridge. Emerson married Irene, but then he died suddenly in 1843; Irene then hired out her slaves, and Bainbridge "leased" Dred Scott. Dred and Harriet, brought to Missouri after living in a free state, sued for their freedom. By the time the tortuous legal battle over the Scotts' freedom reached the Supreme Court, Irene's brother J. F. A. Sanford owned Dred Scott. (His lawyer at the court was Senator Henry Geyer, who long before had signed the 1816 treaty with the Sauk.) That court decision, of course, ruled that the Northwest Ordinance, or any act that outlawed slavery, was unconstitutional. From 1857 until the Civil War, the United States was not divided into slave states and free states: the country itself was a slave state.

As members of commercial, political, social, and family networks, treaty signers worked to shape US Indian policy in their own interests. At the same time, the federal government created complex bureaucracies to prosecute its policies: territorial governments, the military, and eventually a department solely for Indian affairs. Bureaucracies are famous for being faceless, for diffusing responsibility among functionaries who are "just doing their jobs" without a personal stake in the outcome of their actions.

As it turns out, however, the officers and officeholders who carried out US policies in regard to indigenous nations were members of the networks that made treaty making personal.

Bureaucrats

A fter removing indigenous people from its borders, the United States turned its attention once again to expanding those borders. Through a combination of political will and military might, directed toward both indigenous nations and colonialist powers, the United States quickly extended its territory from the Mississippi to the Pacific.

To administer its westward expansion into Indian country, the United States developed a complex system of competing military and political bureaucracies. Officers and civilian leaders of these bureaucracies jockeyed for control of federal policy and for career advancement. Rival military factions—local militia led by politicians and federal troops that were answerable to the commander in chief—conducted campaigns against indigenous people. Treaties were negotiated by military personnel in some cases and by politicians in others. In the 1860s, as the end of the treaty-making era approached, representatives from both of these bureaucracies were assigned to peace commissions that wandered the West, trying to quell indigenous resistance to US expansion.

Many bureaucrats found that US Indian affairs provided ample opportunity for personal gain, through schemes that defrauded both indigenous nations and the federal government. Corrupt from top to bottom, the bureaucracies of US Indian affairs nonetheless are overshadowed by the rhetoric of the American myth. In 1845, a jingoist journalist suggested that any US excess could be excused by "our power, . . . our greatness and . . . our manifest destiny to overspread the continent allotted by Providence for the free development of our yearly multiplying millions."[1]

TERRITORY: 1838–1848

By 1838, Iowa, Wisconsin, and Florida were the only organized territories of the United States. Wisconsin Territory (covering the present

---

Top right: Great Seal of the State of Iowa (1847), detail.

state and eastern Minnesota) and Iowa Territory (covering the present state, western Minnesota, and part of the Dakotas) were the remnants of the enormous areas that Arthur St. Clair and James Wilkinson originally governed. Florida Territory had been a war zone for three years, as indigenous people there resisted removal to the West; General Zachary Taylor requested bloodhounds to use in tracking refugees through the swamps.[2]

In the eight years since the passage of the Indian Removal Act, the United States had negotiated or forced removal treaties throughout the East. In the old Northwest Territory, the Kaskaskia, Seneca, Shawnee, Ottawa, Wyandot, Ho Chunk, Kickapoo, Ojibwe, Ottawa, Potawatomi, Sauk, and Meskwaki peoples were resettled or en route to new homelands. Without a hint of irony, William Clark included in an 1832 treaty a clause in which "the Kaskaskia . . . do forever cede and release to the United States the lands granted to them forever by the first section of the treaty of Vincennes of 13 August 1803."[3]

West of the Mississippi, tribes including the Dakota had ceded their common hunting grounds in Iowa Territory, as William Clark had planned from the moment the land was set aside in 1830. Tribes in Missouri and Arkansas—many of whom had already been relocated once—signed removal treaties that expelled them to points even farther west. They included the Shawnee and Delaware, Pawnee, Piankashaw and Wea, Western Cherokee, Caddo, Oto, and Missouri. In the Southeast, many Choctaw, Chickasaw, Creeks, and Cherokee were moving or preparing to move. Tens of thousands of indigenous people were beginning their exile from traditional homelands, often under the "supervision" of US Indian Affairs agents and contractors, supported where necessary by the US Army.

Several of the removal treaties proved to be particularly problematic. The most famous example is the 1835 treaty at New Echota, where a faction of the Cherokee—unauthorized by their government—agreed to cede land and relocate; despite the treaty's obvious illegitimacy, the US Senate ratified it by one vote. As it became clear that a majority of Cherokee people refused to recognize the treaty, the US military was assigned to hunt, imprison, and move by force those indigenous people who had dispersed from their towns and plantations to avoid removal.

In May 1838, General Winfield Scott was "charged by the President to cause the Cherokee Indians . . . to remove to the West." Scott had led the US Army in the Black Hawk War and signed the original removal treaties with the Ho Chunk and the Sauk and Meskwaki in 1832.

His second-in-command was William J. Worth (for whom Fort Worth, Texas, is named), who had more recently signed the Dakota land cession treaty in 1837. In Scott's Order No. 25 to the troops under his command, he pledged "to carry out the general object with the greatest promptitude and certainty, and with the least possible distress to the Indians." He noted that "of the 15,000 of those people who are now to be removed . . . it is understood that about four fifths are opposed, or have become averse to a distant emigration; and altho' none are in actual hostilities with the United States, or threaten a resistance by arms, yet the troops will probably be obliged to cover the whole country they inhabit, in order to make prisoners and to march or to transport the prisoners, by families."[4]

By August, the *Vermont Telegraph* reported that "in most cases, the humane injunctions of the commanding General were disregarded" and described Cherokee families being herded across rivers "like cattle" and "driven promiscuously into one large pen." While en route, thousands of Cherokee, by some estimates, died in concentration camps from diseases that were exacerbated by "heat, overcrowding, poor food and lack of shelter."[5]

An 1837 treaty with the Ho Chunk was similarly questionable: even the indigenous representatives at the treaty denied that they had any authority to make it. And the Ho Chunk were particularly reluctant to relocate, because the site identified for their new home was the "neutral ground" between the Dakota and the Sauk and Meskwaki in present-day Iowa, a site that would leave them vulnerable to conflicts with traditional enemies. Ho Chunk (Winnebago) removal became an occasion for two titans in Wisconsin territorial government to stake out rival political positions.

Henry Dodge was the governor of Wisconsin Territory in 1840. As "Captain of an Aggressive Civilization," he had squatted illegally on Ho Chunk land in 1826 to mine for lead; he had been prominent among the military leaders that expelled the Sauk and Meskwaki from east of the Mississippi River in 1832, and he was a member of the Democratic Party of Andrew Jackson and his successor, Martin Van Buren. For all of these reasons, Dodge was an avid supporter of Indian removal. James Duane Doty, Wisconsin's premier land speculator, was at the time the territory's delegate to Congress. Although nominally a Democrat, he was aligning himself with the Whig Party of William Henry Harrison, hoping that a change in administration would net him Dodge's job.

So in August 1840, Dodge addressed the territorial legislature with an assurance that military force was available to help dislodge the Ho Chunk from their homeland: "I am advised by the Commanding General of the United States troops, charged with the removal of the Winnebago Indians, that, should any of them remain in the country east of the Mississippi, the dragoons will be detached to collect them, and form an escort for their removal from this Territory. . . . The removal of the Winnebagoes will enable our enterprising citizens to extend their settlements to a desirable and interesting country north of the Wisconsin river." And with a notable lack of irony, given his history as a squatter, he added, "The settlers on the public lands in this Territory form the best safeguard for the defence of our extended frontier from the encroachments of the Indians."[6]

Doty responded by printing a broadside that was widely reprinted in newspapers, in which he castigated President Van Buren for a list of offenses against Wisconsin Territory, including the removal of the Ho Chunk: "He has endangered the peace of the frontier by compelling by a military force the Winnebago Indians to remove from the country, and before the Government had fulfilled on its own part, the stipulations of the treaties with that tribe."[7]

That summer, General G. M. Brooke arrived in Green Bay with the Fifth US Infantry Regiment to follow the path advocated by Dodge. A settler remembered years later how the soldiers took a Ho Chunk woman from a farm near Madison: "Her pots and kettles, her blankets and her few other possessions were packed on two Indian ponies, and followed on the line of march, in company with numerous others of her tribe to their new home west of the Mississippi River. An eye witness related that as [she] bade adieu to her half civilized home, her white husband and to the beautiful site of the City of the Lakes, she gave vent to great weeping and wailing and to unutterable sorrow, as expressed in a manner peculiar to her race."[8]

Dodge had won, in a conditional fashion, his twenty-year war against the indigenous people of Wisconsin, but he lost one battle against Doty. William Henry Harrison was elected president later that year, and though he died in office before naming Doty to the territorial governorship, President John Tyler made the appointment. Harrison did manage, during his month in office, to name as secretary of war congressman John Bell, who had shepherded the Indian Removal Act through Congress.

But the Whigs, including Bell and Doty, late defectors from the

Democratic Party, held such deep animosity against Andrew Jackson and his legacy that they devised a shift in Indian policy. Doty was commissioned by Bell to negotiate a treaty with the Dakota that stemmed from a unique combination of paternalism, utopianism, and payola. In 1841, with little advance notice to politicians and lobbyists in Washington or in the Midwest, Doty arrived at Traverse des Sioux in Minnesota and secured a stunning land cession. The Dakota agreed to cede thirty million acres—virtually their entire homeland—to create an Indian Territory for northern tribes. After two years, indigenous people could become citizens of the United States and enter the path toward statehood. Traders, despite recent policy changes that prohibited the practice, would receive a large distribution of debt payments, and Henry Sibley would be recommended as the interim governor. The treaty—presenting the astonishing prospect of an "Indian State"—was signed at Traverse des Sioux and later at Mendota, then sent to the Senate for ratification.

There, the treaty died. The Whigs were furious that Tyler—termed "His Accidency" because of his unorthodox ascent to the presidency—was re-aligning himself with the Democrats. They refused to pass any new legislation at all; Bell, the champion of the treaty, resigned with the rest of Tyler's cabinet. And beyond the political machinations that stalled the treaty, the idea of a multicultural America was too much for Congress to digest.[9]

In 1905, a Minnesota historian stated the commonly accepted judgment on the abortive 1841 cession: that land was far better used for white settlement than for "Indian civilization": "The object of this treaty was not to open the country for settlement, but primarily to provide a location for the Winnebago Indians . . . and, secondarily, to furnish reservations for a number of other tribes similarly situated. In short, it was designed to create of the Sioux country a second Indian Territory, into which to dump all the odds and ends of Indian tribes still left east of the Mississippi. Fortunately, however, this treaty failed . . . and thus this vast and fertile territory was saved to a grander destiny."[10]

That destiny would be Minnesota Territory.

While Doty began a single contentious term as governor of Wisconsin Territory, his rival Henry Dodge won election as the territory's delegate to Congress: the two men simply switched positions. Both Dodge and Doty, however, proved ineffectual in their new jobs. Doty antagonized the territorial legislature at every petty opportunity, insisting, for instance, that the name of the territory should be spelled "Wiskonsan." Dodge, meanwhile, expended his efforts on trying to get Doty removed from the governorship. "You will perceive from the Documents I have inclosed You lately," he wrote to Iowa's territorial delegate, "that I have been Nailing Doty."[11]

James Polk replaced John Tyler as US president in 1845. He reappointed Henry Dodge to be governor of Wisconsin Territory. (Doty bowed out of Wisconsin territorial politics, but the new delegate to Congress would be his cousin and business partner, Morgan Lewis Martin.) The last presidential act of John Tyler was to leave on the desk of incoming President Polk an option to annex the Republic of Texas; administrations in both the United States and Texas had agreed to the arrangement. The topic of annexation, however, was highly contentious. It was widely understood as a formality needed to add the state of Texas to the Union and increase the power of the slaveholding states. Congress was therefore sharply divided on the issue. In the larger picture, the government of Mexico strongly disputed the boundaries of Texas, and annexation was likely to spark a war. Polk immediately dispatched Zachary Taylor and 3,500 troops to the Southwest and began to marshal support for military aggression by the United States.[12]

During the heated Congressional deliberations, journalist John O'Sullivan wrote an essay in which he dismissed opposition to annexation as avoidance of the inevitable. He coined the phrase that resonates even today as a label for the territorial expansion of the United States. He cast annexation as "the fulfillment of our manifest destiny to overspread the continent allotted by Providence for the free development of our yearly multiplying millions. . . . Already the advance guard of the irresistible army of Anglo-Saxon emigration has begun to pour down upon it."[13]

While O'Sullivan was writing his editorial—and Governor Dodge was returning to parades and welcoming speeches at his home in Mineral Point, Wisconsin—Andrew Jackson was dying in Tennessee. The deaths of Jackson and Harrison, two of the most famous "Indian fighters" in history, might be seen as a conclusion to the era of Indian removal from the East. From the Treaty of Greenville in 1795, these two men were among the leading architects of an America without indigenous people. The funerals of the two men—Harrison the patrician in 1841 and Jackson the radical democrat in 1845—were a study in contrasts. William Hawley—a Washington Episcopal pastor who had signed a treaty with the Dakota in 1837 and officiated at the marriages of the children of presidents—performed Harrison's funeral services at the White House to an invitation-only congregation before the casket was paraded solemnly to the Congressional Burial Ground. Jackson's funeral, on his front porch, was attended by thousands of Tennesseans and a parrot that screamed obscenities.[14]

When the United States declared war on Mexico in May 1846, the focus of the US military shifted from Indian removal. General G. M. Brooke, who had led the Ho Chunk removal from Wisconsin Territory, was placed in charge of military forces west of the Mississippi, and in fact, the entire military hierarchy of Indian removal—Generals Winfield Scott, William Worth, Zachary Taylor—became the hierarchy that led the invasion of Mexico. Harrison and Jackson were gone, but a new generation of military heroes, shaped by their experience in Indian affairs, rose to spectacular heights of national fame in the era of Manifest Destiny.[15]

During the short-lived war, however, Indian removal did continue. In 1846, the Ho Chunk ceded their untenable land in the "neutral ground" of present-day Iowa for "a tract of country north of St. Peter's and west of the Mississippi Rivers, of not less than eight hundred thousand acres." This was an unusual situation, because the United States was engineering Ho Chunk removal to land where the Ojibwe people still held aboriginal title. Ten months later the United States negotiated a cession of land on the Ojibwe/Dakota border (which had been established in 1825 at Prairie du Chien). The Ho Chunk were to move from a buffer zone between the Dakota and the Sauk and Meskwaki to a buffer zone between the Dakota and the Ojibwe. And in 1848, the Menominee ceded their land in Wisconsin in exchange for a new homeland next to that of the Ho Chunk.[16]

Between 1846 and 1848, the Mexican War ended with the Treaty of Guadalupe Hidalgo, and both Iowa Territory and Wisconsin Territory evolved into the present-day states of the same names. Iowa became a state first, in 1846. So great was the fervor of Iowans in support of US expansion that they eventually named eleven counties after veterans or battles from the US war with Mexico. With the admission of Iowa into the Union, the rest of Iowa Territory fell unorganized. Present-day Minnesota west of the Mississippi again had no government.

In his last address to the local legislature in February 1848, Henry Dodge summarized the history of the territory: "Twelve years ago, Wisconsin's fertile plains lay almost untouched by the hand of agriculture. . . . Where the wigwams of the savage smoked, now are to be seen populous towns and villages. The savage war dance is changed to the song of civilization and its blessings; and the music of the stream on whose banks the Indians sought repose, is now lost in the hum of machinery."[17]

After intensive wrangling, the state border was set at the St. Croix River instead of the Mississippi, creating a strange territorial issue. Several thousand Americans already lived between the St. Croix and the Mississippi but would have no territorial government. As Wisconsin moved toward statehood, congressional delegate Morgan L. Martin proposed the creation of Minnesota Territory to include the area that fell unorganized with the creation of the states of Iowa and Wisconsin, stretching from Iowa to Canada, from Wisconsin to the distant Missouri River. The proposal was rejected.

But the populated enclaves of the unorganized area—Fort Snelling,

1847: Exchange of Ceded Territory

In 1846, a treaty between the United States and the Ho Chunk nation began a series of removals, land cessions, and relocations among indigenous nations. In this treaty, the Ho Chunk ceded their land in Wisconsin, and "In consideration of the foregoing purchase from, or cession by, the said Indians, the United States hereby agree to purchase and give to the said Indians as their home, to be held as all Indians' lands are held, a tract of country north of St. Peter's and west of the Mississippi Rivers, of not less than eight hundred thousand acres, which shall be suitable to their habits, wants, and wishes: *Provided*, Such land can be obtained on just and reasonable terms."[1]

The treaty obligated the United States, then, to secure a land cession from the Ojibwe in the present-day state of Minnesota. The land targeted for this cession was identified by Henry Rice, a trader with the Ho Chunk and future US senator, who negotiated with the Ojibwe for its sale. Commissioner of Indian Affairs William Medill noted that

> Mr. Rice, . . . though without any authority from this Dept., entered into an informal treaty with the Chippewas, or a portion of them, for this section, for which it was agreed to pay the sum of $80,000, a trifle over nine cents per acre. This amount was regarded as excessive. The lands are now unoccupied and unused by the Chippewas and therefore comparatively valueless to them; and they are of no importance to the Govt. except for a home for the Winnebagoes. . . . In this view, five cents per acre at most would, it is believed, have been a large price to offer for these lands.

Sibley's trading post at the current site of the Twin Cities, the pinelands along the St. Croix, and the copper fields of the Arrowhead Region— already had a history as American territory. The people who lived there demanded a government, with its attendant militia. They conceived a bizarre idea to justify the formation of a government. They claimed, despite the lack of any precedent, that when Wisconsin became a state, Wisconsin Territory continued its existence, covering only the area of Minnesota east of the Mississippi. They further claimed that they were entitled to a territorial delegate to Congress and elected Henry Sibley to the position. He was actually seated in Congress in January 1849, after months of political maneuvering, creating an unprecedented situation: both Wisconsin Territory and Wisconsin the state had US representatives. Sibley's term lasted only until Minnesota Territory was created to cover that larger area that extended into the Dakotas. In July 1849, after a two-month vacation, Sibley returned to Washington

Henry Rice, however, was appointed commissioner (with Isaac Verplanck) for a treaty with the Ojibwe that in 1847 secured the land to which the Ho Chunk would relocate.[2]

In his instructions to the commissioners, Medill had also suggested a course for the future: "There is another portion of country immediately adjoining that selected for the Winnebagoes . . . which it is also desirable to procure from the Chippewas for a home for the Menominees in Wisconsin." So three weeks later, Rice and Verplanck held a second conference with another band of the Ojibwe, and secured another six hundred thousand acres.[3]

The following year, Medill himself traveled to Lake Poygan, near Green Bay, to negotiate a removal treaty with the Menominee. The sojourn of the Ho Chunk and Menominee in present-day Minnesota, however, was short-lived. In 1854, the Menominee, "upon manifestation of great unwillingness on the part of said Indians to remove to the country west of the Mississippi River, . . . and a desire to remain in the State of Wisconsin," ceded their land in Minnesota Territory back to the United States, and "the President consented to their locating temporarily upon the Wolf and Oconto Rivers."[4]

The Ho Chunk were moved to a reservation further south in present-day Minnesota, next to the Dakota. After the Dakota War in 1862, a group of white community leaders in Mankato and the surrounding county formed a group called the Knights of the Forest. They lay in ambush for any Ho Chunk person who attempted to leave the nearby reservation, in effect turning the reservation into a concentration camp. The group lobbied successfully to have all Ho Chunk people forcibly removed from the state to a reservation in present-day Nebraska.[5]

as a delegate from the new territory. The new governor, who showed up with his brother and his own private secretary, was a former US congressman from Pennsylvania named Alexander Ramsey.[18]

A long succession of territorial governors—from St. Clair through Dodge to Ramsey—appealed to and encouraged the popular appetite for indigenous land among American citizens. Territorial governments, along with the Office of Indian Affairs and the military, were part of an ever-expanding bureaucratic machine that kept the relentless business of treaties in operation.

SIGNERS: OFFICERS AND OFFICEHOLDERS

On a single day in 1789, Congress passed two pieces of legislation that would make bureaucratic infighting and personal political rivalry elements of US "Indian Policy" for generations. The first one established the Department of War. The cabinet-level "principle officer to be called the Secretary" would be in charge of "matters respecting military or naval affairs, . . . or relative to the granting of lands to persons entitled thereto, for military services rendered to the United States, or relative to Indian affairs."[19]

At the time, "Indian affairs" involved both negotiating treaties and prosecuting a war in the Northwest Territory, and the Department of War was saddled with competing goals: it had to both fight indigenous nations and rein in the settlers who, by encroaching on indigenous land, provoked further conflict. This charge would grow even more complicated over time. Indian agents in the War Department were appointed by the president to maintain a permanent presence among indigenous nations, in a system outside the regular army chain of command. The War Department built and maintained forts to protect settlers from indigenous nations (and often vice versa). From 1806 to 1822, it also ran the factory system, in which the major business of some forts became trade with indigenous nations. All of these complications had their genesis in that initial legislation, passed on August 7, 1789.

Later on that same day, Congress passed another bill that seemed innocuous enough at the time. The Northwest Territory had already been established under the Articles of Confederation in 1787; this act merely re-established it under the Constitution. But in that two-year interim, Governor Arthur St. Clair had been assigned "the duties of superintendent of Indian affairs" in the territory. This set a precedent: territorial governors would be in charge of local relations with indigenous nations. And the original ordinance also stated that "The governor . . . shall be commander in chief of the militia, appoint and commission all officers in the same below the rank of general officers."[20]

So practically from the start, two bureaucratic juggernauts— territorial government and the Department of War, each with its own armed forces—would engage in Indian affairs. Consequently, hundreds of officers and officeholders signed treaties. Their names at the end of the documents are entirely expected and even reassuring from a colonialist point of view. These were the professionals who, following orders or championing the cause of the pioneers, managed the relentless business of treaties on behalf of the American people.

Most military personnel signed treaties in one of two situations. First, they might be assigned to "frontier posts" by their superiors. The Department of War maintained a military presence along the line between indigenous nations and American settlers, wherever that moving line might be, overseeing trade and (ostensibly) discouraging conflict between indigenous nations and American settlers. It was not an accident that Arthur St. Clair and James Wilkinson were each the commanding general of the US Army while, simultaneously, the governor of a huge territory that expanded US presence far into "Indian country." William Hull was a lieutenant colonel in the Continental Army before his appointment as governor of Michigan Territory.

The career trajectories of many soldiers in the eighteenth and nineteenth centuries—especially those who rose to national prominence— passed through intersections with indigenous people. Zachary Taylor, as a typical example, was placed in command of a garrison in Tennessee as a twenty-four-year-old lieutenant. His subsequent career was a series of command postings at forts on the front line of US interaction with indigenous nations: Green Bay, Fort Jessup in Louisiana, Fort Snelling in present-day Minnesota, Fort Crawford at Prairie du Chien, Fort Smith in Arkansas. Though punctuated by service in the Seminole Wars and the war between the United States and Mexico, Taylor's career consisted overwhelmingly of fort life, generally too dull to distract him from collecting plantations, bank stock, and slaves.

A majority of US–Indian treaties were signed at military outposts, and fort commanders were often commissioned by the federal government to negotiate treaties, as Taylor was with the Dakota in 1836. The forts sometimes housed or hosted Indian agents and civilian treaty commissioners, and military personnel signed treaties as witnesses in those cases, as Taylor did with the Ojibwe and Ho Chunk in 1829.

The second situation in which military personnel might sign treaties occurred when military units were sent on expeditions to make war or, in war's aftermath, to make peace with indigenous nations. There, the military was the direct representative of the federal government. After the St. Louis fur trading consortium Ashley's Hundred provoked violence along the Missouri River in the 1820s, General Henry Atkinson led an expedition up the river, making treaties with a dozen indigenous nations. For most of the men of the First and Sixth Infantry under Atkinson's command, this expedition was their only experience in making treaties. But for others, it was a stepping-stone to notable careers. Three of the men on the expedition—brevet major Stephen Watts Kearny and captains R. B. Mason and Bennett Riley—went on to become generals. In US–occupied territory after the war with Mexico, they were successive military governors of California. Kearny was also military governor of Mexico City. Officer Jason Rogers, who signed eight of the Atkinson treaties, was later the military governor of the Mexican city of Monterrey.[21]

High-ranking military officers are usually politically astute, and US–Indian affairs were an avenue to political capital. Clearing indigenous title through treaties, combined with victories in times of war, propelled military men to national popularity. Four events proved to be especially productive résumé builders for generals with political ambitions: the Black Hawk War of the early 1830s, military involvement in Indian removal later in the decade, the Seminole War at the beginning of the 1840s, and the 1846–48 war between the United States and Mexico. The men who emerged from the war with Mexico with the greatest glory had been involved in the earlier three events.

Winfield Scott was a general for fifty years, from the Jefferson administration to the Lincoln administration. He fought in the War of 1812 before commanding US troops in the Black Hawk War, where he signed treaties with the Sauk and Meskwaki and the Ho Chunk; then he led the US military removal of the Cherokee before commanding US troops in Mexico. He became famous enough there to win the Whig nomination for president in 1852. General William Worth—second-in-command to Scott in the Black Hawk War and Cherokee removal, Zachary Taylor's successor in command of troops during the Seminole War, on assignment in Washington when he signed a treaty with the Dakota in 1837—was immensely popular after the war with Mexico;

he authorized a biography in preparation for a presidential run against Winfield Scott but died of cholera in 1849. And Zachary Taylor, after signing treaties at Fort Crawford, fought in the Black Hawk War and led US troops in Florida during the Seminole War. He rose to spectacular fame in Mexico and was elected president as a Whig nine months after the war ended, in 1848.

The other two generals who were elected president during the treaty-making era had more extensive résumés in Indian affairs than anyone else to occupy the office. William Henry Harrison was already a military notable from the Battle of Fallen Timbers when he was appointed governor of Indiana Territory, extinguished aboriginal title to millions of acres, and famously won the Battle of Tippecanoe against Tecumseh. And of course, Andrew Jackson, military governor of Florida during the first Seminole War in 1820, was elected in part due to his aggressive stance on US–Indian affairs.

Many other men used military service and Indian affairs as a springboard to political success, without reaching the presidency. John Bell was chairman of the US House Committee on Indian Affairs and wrote the Indian Removal Act; he parlayed this experience into the Constitution Party nomination for president in 1860. Andrew Jackson Donelson was raised by his uncle, Andrew Jackson, and served as aide-de-camp in Florida; in 1856, he was the vice presidential nominee of the American Party.

In fact, hundreds of men combined military experience and treaty making to run for public office, winning scores of races as state legislators, mayors, and US congressmen.

At the beginning of his adult life, William Carroll needed a helping hand from Andrew Jackson just to open a hardware store in Tennessee. But during the War of 1812, he was appointed by Jackson to be brigade inspector for the campaigns to Natchez in 1812 and against the Creek Indians in 1813; he was injured at the Battle of Horseshoe Bend. In 1817, he was named to the board of directors of the newly created Bank of Nashville but went bankrupt in the Panic of 1819. This experience allowed him to sell himself as a "common man," and he was elected governor of Tennessee for all but two years between 1821 and 1835. In 1838, he returned to Indian affairs when President Van Buren appointed him a special agent to the Creeks. (Critics charged that Carroll used this position to enrich himself through illicit land speculation.) John Blair Smith Todd, a first cousin of Mary Todd Lincoln, graduated from West Point in 1837, fought in Florida (signing a treaty there) and in Mexico, then became a trader and land speculator in the Dakotas; he engineered an 1858 treaty with the Yankton that cleared title to a large part of South Dakota and was elected a territorial delegate to Congress when Dakota Territory was incorporated in 1866.[22]

American settlers in the Pacific Northwest, arriving in large numbers in a relatively short period, were among the most aggressive in the history of US expansion. When Oregon Territory was created in 1849, General Joseph Lane, late of the war between the United States and Mexico, was named governor. He arrived in Oregon City to find tensions running high between settlers and local indigenous nations, particularly the Cayuse. Lane kept the situation from exploding by treating the killing of white people by Cayuse people as individual incidents rather than episodes in the narrative of a race war, working with indigenous leaders to try the offenders, and keeping the white settlers from forming lynch mobs. (He was the Democratic nominee for vice president in 1860.)

When Washington Territory was formed in 1853, however, the new governor took a different approach. The ambitious Isaac Stevens, first in his class at West Point, was a major in the army when appointed to the governorship. In preparing for the trip west to take up his new position, Stevens successfully bid on a government contract to survey a route for a transcontinental railroad, an ambitious moonlighting job that delayed his arrival in Olympia for months. Stevens was perhaps the most draconian of all governors in his duties as superintendent of Indian Affairs, forcing land cession treaties at gunpoint, inciting decades of conflict, and encouraging a territorial militia that devolved into a white supremacist gang.

Stevens appointed Benjamin Franklin Shaw, a timber and shipping magnate, to the position of lieutenant colonel in the militia; under Stevens's orders, Shaw enthusiastically attacked indigenous villages throughout the territory. When even settlers objected to his harsh treatment of indigenous people (including the summary execution of Leschi, a Nisqually leader), Stevens placed entire towns under arrest, charged with treason; the chief justice of the territorial supreme court issued a writ of habeas corpus for their release, and Stevens had the judge arrested, physically removed from the courtroom by Shaw and the militia.[23]

Throughout his tenure, Stevens was at odds with officers of the regular army. General John Wool, who had served in the army since the War of 1812, was particularly antagonistic to the overreaching Stevens. Wool, from his position as commander of the Pacific Department of the army, headquartered in San Francisco, ordered Lieutenant Colonel Silas Casey to use force, if necessary, in opposing Stevens.

> It is evident that Stevens . . . is dictated by a vindictive spirit, caused by his recent attempt to renew the war in the Walla Walla country. . . . If an attempt should be made by Governor Stevens or other persons to renew the war on Puget Sound you will resist it to the extent of your power. Should the whites attack the Indians, the power of the Indian agent ceases, and the whole power of peace and war will be vested in yourself. . . . [Militia] Volunteers will in no wise be recognized, and should any be sent into the field to make war on the Indians they will, if you have the power, be arrested, disarmed and sent home.[24]

This situation underscored a long-standing distinction among the soldiers in the United States. Until the Civil War, the federal government maintained a relatively small standing army, and in times of war, it called for additional volunteers. At times, states and territories were given quotas for filling the volunteer ranks with short-term enlistees (and sometimes used conscription to do so), but the volunteers were considered federal troops. The state and territorial militia, on the other hand, were a separate force in which membership was required by law, training and equipment were usually minimal, and the drumbeat of war followed the tempo of local rather than national concerns. In times of conflict, governors would "call out" the militia, and leading citizens would form regiments that they themselves would command, under the supervision of federally appointed generals.

The interests of settlers, who were the militia members, often undermined or challenged federal policy in relation to indigenous nations. During the Revolution, federal commissioners negotiated the neutrality of the Lenape Delaware, but members of the Eighth Pennsylvania regiment assassinated the pro–United States leader of the Lenape and drove that nation into an alliance with the British. Fort Harmar, in the Northwest Territory, was built to keep settlers from encroaching on indigenous land north of the Ohio River, but after the city of Marietta was established, its mission shifted to protecting settlers. As early settlers encroached illegally on land from Georgia to Ohio, the federal government was trying desperately to curtail the antagonism and growth of a multinational coalition that would oppose any US expansion; consequently, US military presence and treaty making on the early "frontier" presented opposition to the interests of settlers. The illegal, free-for-all rush of lead miners into Illinois and Wisconsin in the 1820s was opposed by the creation of federal mining districts, where order was maintained by the regular army. And decades later, when Peter Davy of Minnesota organized an 1867 gold mining expedition to the Black Hills in violation of treaties with the Lakota, his group was turned away from the gold fields by federal troops.[25]

Of course, federal policies toward indigenous nations were not always so protective. Those policies often favored business interests that demanded the extinguishment of aboriginal title to land and were executed by military leaders who were sometimes rabid in their antagonism toward indigenous people.

The governors and other officials in the organized territories were political appointees, so they supported the prevailing attitudes of the administration in power. But they also had to deal with the settlers who formed the territorial legislatures and militia and were usually avid supporters of the extinguishment of aboriginal land titles at any cost; the governors were in fact at times the leaders and instigators of settler aggression against indigenous people. And in order to maintain a functioning territorial government, the people in charge usually included the powerful business interests that underpinned the local economy: land speculators, fur traders, miners. These business interests, like the settlers, drove US expansion.

Lewis Cass, William Clark, Henry Dodge, Newton Edmunds of Dakota Territory, and other territorial governors came to their appointments through service in territorial militias and championed fur traders, miners, and US expansion. John Reynolds, governor of Illinois during the Black Hawk War, personally led militia forces against the Sauk and Meskwaki. John Evans, prior to his appointment as governor of Colorado Territory, was an investor in the Chicago & Evanston Railroad. (Evanston, Illinois, was named after him.) Unsurprisingly, he was a railroad booster as governor and encouraged mining. The only treaty he negotiated secured for the United States "the right to locate, construct, and maintain railroads" through Ute reservations. His policy against indigenous people was so aggressive that it created an atmosphere in which the Sand Creek Massacre—one of the most heinous acts in US history—was a local political plus for him; the disgraced John Chivington, who led federal troops in the massacre, later became Evans's business partner.

In this mare's nest of conflicting political interests—federal, settler, business—the only consistent theme was aggressive support for US expansion. Treaties were important events in this process, and about one out of every five men who signed a US–Indian treaty held elective office at some point in his career. In 1848, alternative paths to glory and political stature converged in the presidential election. Americans were given a choice between two treaty signers: Zachary Taylor, military hero, and Lewis Cass, territorial governor and consummate politician. Cass's running mate was William Orlando Butler, son of one of the Fighting Butler Brothers.

In 1824, another layer of Indian Affairs bureaucracy was added to those of the military and territorial government. The "Indian Office" began as a three-person operation housed in the Department of War: Thomas McKenney, formerly head of the Office of Indian Trade, and two clerks. McKenney was essentially a low-level assistant to the Secretary of War until 1829, when Congress created the position of commissioner to run the Office of Indian Affairs (renamed the Bureau of Indian Affairs in 1947). Each commissioner brought his own thoughts about federal policy to the job, but those thoughts fell into a rather narrow intellectual range: Should indigenous people be "civilized," or is that task too difficult? Should their ethnic identity be destroyed in a process of cultural assimilation, or should they be isolated from everyone else in the country? Created on the eve of the Indian Removal Act, the Office of Indian Affairs generated wild debate within strict policy parameters.

The Indian Office was in charge of the budget for Indian removal, and it took over the work of the Indian agents, including distributing the annuity payments that were promised to indigenous nations for their land cessions. Commissioners were first and foremost political appointees, often with no experience in Indian relations. The emphasis on money and the lack of any moral compass to guide the agency created a cesspool of corruption.

Carey A. Harris was a lawyer and newspaperman from Tennessee, a family friend of Andrew Jackson. Harris received a lucrative contract as public printer for the city of Washington when Jackson became president; before Jackson left office in 1836, he appointed Harris as the second commissioner of Indian Affairs. Harris signed seven treaties in the two years he occupied this office, including the 1837 treaty in which the Dakota ceded their land east of the Mississippi. Of all the men who have served as commissioner of Indian Affairs, Harris was among the most corrupt. When an assistant, Daniel Kurtz, cautioned Harris about "drawing too freely upon the large funds at his disposal," Harris prohibited anyone in his office from reading correspondence that had not been vetted by his wife, Martha. But in October 1838, Martha allowed a letter to reach Kurtz that revealed a scheme to secure Chickasaw lands through fraud; Harris was gone by the end of the year. His resignation must have been a painful outcome for Harris: he was about to funnel $300,000 in funds intended for Chickasaw orphans into a bank he had started in Arkansas.[26]

William Medill was a US representative from Ohio and, briefly, second assistant postmaster general before his appointment as US commissioner of Indian Affairs in 1845. (He later served as governor of Ohio and the first comptroller of the US Treasury.) In three years, Commissioner Medill signed only the Menominee treaty of 1848 that ostensibly moved the tribe to land ceded by the Ojibwe. In his report to Congress in 1848, Medill seemed baffled by distrust of the government exhibited by indigenous nations. Reporting on a census of indigenous nations, Medill wrote of "The difficulty in making the Indians comprehend the object of the inquiries, and their superstitious disinclination to furnish information respecting themselves or their affairs. . . . [S]ome of those more advanced in civilization and intelligence seem obstinately to have taken up the impression, that the information is desired for some sinister and improper object, having reference to a change in their present position, or an interference in their domestic concerns."[27]

One of the Indian agents who worked under Medill in Minnesota was David B. Herriman. As a young man, he escaped from a bar fight in New Jersey and fled to the West. In Indiana, he saved enough money from a two-dollar-a-day job to buy land that he sold for $400. He reinvested this in land that he sold for $10,000. In 1850, he was appointed an Indian agent in Minnesota, where he became complicit in schemes to defraud the Ojibwe of goods intended as treaty payments. At one point, he used reservation land to grow hay that he sold to recent immigrants. He laid out the town of Wadena on land that he owned and built a mansion there. Herriman's obituary stated that "His ruling passion was for making money and he succeeded."

Luke Lea, who was commissioner from 1850 to 1853, did not claim to know much about indigenous people, but he did claim to know what they needed: less land. Lea felt that smaller reservations would encourage indigenous people to give up their traditional practices more quickly. In his report to Congress for 1851, Lea made the case for hastening assimilation by reducing the size of reservations:

> On the general subject of the civilization of the Indians many and diversified opinions have been put forth; but ultimately, like the race to which they relate, they are too wild to be of much utility. The great question, How shall the Indians be civilized? yet remains without a satisfactory answer. The magnitude of the subject, and the manifold difficulties inseparably connected with it, seem to have bewildered the minds of those who have attempted to give it the most thorough investigation. . . . Therefore leave the subject for the present, remarking only, that any plan for the civilization of our Indians will in my judgment, be fatally defective, if it do not provide in the most efficient manner, first, for their concentration; secondly, for their domestication; and, thirdly, for their ultimate incorporation into the great body of our citizen population.

He also mentioned in his report that the Dakota had ceded "a large and valuable extent of country west of the Mississippi," tens of millions of acres that comprised most of the Dakota homeland. This treaty, true to Lea's policy, confined the Dakota people to a reservation ten miles wide for fifty miles along the Minnesota River.[28]

Lea's successor as commissioner, George Washington Manypenny, was a newspaper editor and "manager of public works" in Ohio. Manypenny shared Lea's views on reservations and civilization, but the indigenous people with whom he interacted did not, as he noted in 1853: "If they dispose of their lands, no reservations should, if it can be avoided, be granted or allowed. . . . To make reservations for an entire tribe on the tract which it now owns, would, it is believed, be injurious to the future peace, prosperity, and advancement of these people. . . . The commissioner, as far as he judged it prudent, endeavored to enlighten them on this point, and labored to convince them that it was not consistent with the true interest of themselves and their posterity that they should have tribal reservations."[29]

In the same 1853 report to Congress, Manypenny noted that "the large and populous tribe of Chippewas, the great body of whom are in Minnesota, still own an extensive tract of country east of the Mississippi, of which, on account of its great mineral wealth, it will become necessary to obtain possession at an early day." In fact, Reuben Carlton and his partners were already identifying locations for copper mines in the Arrowhead Region, and the area was ceded by the Ojibwe during Manypenny's tenure.

James Denver was a lawyer and newspaper owner from Ohio who served as a US representative from California when appointed commissioner of Indian Affairs. Denver held the post from 1857 to 1859, except for a short interim during which he was governor of Kansas Territory. (The city that bears his name was founded under his governorship.) In his report to Congress, Denver asserted the same point of view about reservations that his predecessors shared: "Their reservations should be restricted so as to contain only sufficient land to afford them a comfortable support by actual cultivation, and should be properly divided and assigned to them, with the obligation to remain upon and cultivate the same." He added that recent land cessions by the Ojibwe had "ceded nearly the whole of the lands owned by them to the government," and he insisted that in the land that the Ojibwe people had reserved, "it should be the policy to concentrate and confine them, and every exertion used to induce them to adopt the habits and pursuits of civilized life." In this same confident spirit of paternal benevolence, Commissioner Denver also related to Congress that "Energetic measures have been adopted by the government [of California] to suppress" the practice of kidnapping Indian children and selling them for servants. Denver oversaw the reduction of the Dakota reservation from ten miles wide to five miles wide.[30]

In 1872, the Senate investigated a deal struck long before, during the tenure of James Denver as commissioner; the complicated arrangement centered on an agreement between Samuel Folsom of the Choctaw Nation and John T. Cochrane, a lawyer, in what was called the "Net Proceeds Case." Cochrane and associates including John Luce had received a contract to collect $1.8 million from the government, on behalf of the Choctaw, in exchange for one-third of the amount. Folsom at the time was trying to secure as much of the money for himself as he could, in complicated deals that involved hiding bags of gold in fireplaces in New Hampshire. Just before Cochrane died, he sold his interest in the case to other attorneys, creating years of financial and legal wrangling. The Senate testimony revealed that two of the attorneys involved in the mess were Luke Lea and James W. Denver. Cochrane, Luce, Lea, and Denver were involved in US–Indian affairs in many capacities, including as signatories to treaties with the Wyandot, Creeks, Pawnee, and Dakota during the 1840s and 1850s.[31]

Alfred Greenwood was a US representative from Arkansas when

appointed commissioner in 1859. During his tenure, Texans murdered indigenous people in coordinated gang violence, forcing the removal of several tribes from the state. When the US Indian agent—Robert Neighbors, a longtime advocate of Comanche rights—returned from the relocation process, he also was murdered. The opposite situation, in some ways, also existed during Greenwood's term, in Nebraska City. When Indian agent William W. Dennison failed to deliver $40,000 in annuity payments in 1860, tribal leaders accosted him in a store, said their children were starving, and tied Dennison "head to foot" with a rope they took from the store shelf. Local citizens mounted an immediate investigation and found that Dennison had made false claims about expenses and still held the money in his own bank account; they arranged for the money to be transferred as soon as an escort could be arranged, and sent food along. "This was the last seen of Major Dennison" in Nebraska City. With the outbreak of the Civil War, Dennison became an employee of the Treasury Department of the Confederacy, and Alfred Greenwood resigned his post to become tax collector for the Confederate state of Arkansas.[32]

William Dole, a Republican Party hack from Indiana, was appointed commissioner of Indian Affairs by Lincoln in 1861. By then, the Indian Office was corrupt from top to bottom. In Kansas, James Burnett Abbott was appointed an Indian agent to the Shawnee, also in 1861. His qualifications included manufacturing shoes; selling pens, pencil cases, forks, spoons, and spectacles; electro-plating; and smuggling guns to abolitionists. While agent, Abbott and his confederates initiated a scheme to illegally secure Shawnee land. The ongoing conspiracy was described by Shawnee leaders in a letter sent to one of Dole's successors in 1867. It involved fabricating personal titles to reservation land for individual Shawnee people—land that was in fact held in common by all Shawnee people. "This is done with the design of speculating in lands," the leaders wrote,

for while held in common no title can be obtained by the speculator. Foremost in this dishonest and dishonorable business is the late agent, James B. Abbot. This man has already made a snug fortune out of the Shawnees . . . and now says that about one hundred of these persons have made severalty selections [received individual titles], but as very few of them seem to know anything about it, it is evident that a fraud has been practiced on them by Abbott, who was then agent, and his co-workers. According to the true intent and meaning of the treaty of 1854, these reserves cannot be gradually disintegrated as individuals may desire—much less can they be apportioned out by the agent and those he recognizes as the Shawnee council, to suit their speculative purposes.

These concerns were never addressed by the government.[33]

Much of the worst corruption under the Dole administration focused on Minnesota. Clark W. Thompson—a Minnesota banker and railroad speculator—was placed in charge of the Northern Superintendency, with responsibility for relations with dozens of indigenous nations; his appointment continued an ongoing feeding frenzy among private contractors, politicians, and bureaucrats who made their money from Indian affairs. The US senator from Minnesota, Morton Wilkinson, secured a $50,000 appropriation ostensibly intended to make improvements on a Ho Chunk reservation; Wilkinson admitted to Thompson that the real purpose of the funds was to provide "a chance to employ our friends this fall." One particularly egregious example of Thompson's corruption involved Dakota and Ho Chunk people who were exiled from Minnesota in 1863. Well aware that rations were running out within weeks of their relocation to Crow Creek in present-day Nebraska, Thompson waited for starvation to set in before ordering provisions for the winter. His cronies then procured last-minute contracts to move food and cattle from distant Mankato, Minnesota, to the reservation; the rotting pork and inedible beef that were delivered as winter arrived proved inadequate for even short-term relief. Dakota women and children starved to death.[34]

In 1861, Luther Webb became an Indian agent to the Ojibwe, headquartered at Bayfield, Wisconsin. The man he employed as an interpreter, Benjamin Armstrong, quit the job within a year, worried about his own reputation: "I found that Agent Webb and four or five others were bribing boys and children to come in and swear that they were entitled to an eighty acre piece of land that the Treaty of 1854 provided for half-caste and mixed blood people, and were paying them from ten to twenty dollars apiece for their scripts, as circumstance required. I made up my mind that I would be drawn into the rascally scheme by implication, if I remained in the employ of the government under General Webb, so I threw up my position and left Bayfield."[35]

The fraudulent acquisition of "mixed blood" scrip was the final flowering of a thirty-year process that included legislation sponsored by US senator Henry Rice of Minnesota. By the 1860s, unscrupulous employees of the Indian Office were issuing, buying, and selling scrip wholesale. (William Dole himself was engaged in the practice until the 1870s.) Webb remained in his position until 1867, when he was appointed as commissioner of Indian Affairs for New Mexico. He turned down the job to engage in an Arkansas railroad scheme.[36]

Dole's successor, Dennis Cooley, advocated raising the pay of Indian agents to attract a better class of candidates for the job. He noted that "The fact that innumerable applicants stand ready to take any places which are vacated is not, in my judgment, an argument against an increase of pay; it is simply a proof of the commonly received idea of the outside profit of the business."[37]

The position of Indian agent, though not necessarily high in social status, was always an attractive career move, in large part because it could be so lucrative. David Brydie Mitchell was the governor of Georgia in 1817 when he resigned to become Indian agent to the Muscogee (but was fired in 1821 over charges of slave smuggling). In 1818, when former senator and territorial governor Thomas Posey was defeated in his bid to become Indiana's first state governor, he took a job as an Indian agent in Illinois. John Crowell moved from a position as Alabama's first US representative to Indian agent for the Muscogee in 1821 and kept the job until 1836. (Georgia's governor accused him of ordering the assassination of Muscogee leader William McIntosh.) William Carroll, long-term governor of Tennessee until 1835, became a treaty commissioner to the Creeks in 1838. Montfort Stokes was elected governor of North Carolina in 1830 but resigned in 1832, when he was appointed a member of the Board of Indian Commissioners and moved to Fort Gibson, in Oklahoma, to negotiate treaties, eventually becoming an agent for the Cherokee, Seneca, Shawnee, and Quapaw nations. R. R. Thompson "crossed the plains to Oregon City in 1846" and started life there without money, herding sheep for neighbors with his children. In 1848, he went to California and struck gold, returning with "a long purse." He bought land and went into the shipping and freight business, yet took an appointment as Indian agent for six years. It was part of a career in which Thompson built an estate that, at the time of his death in 1918, was valued at $2.5 million. All these men were treaty signers.[38]

Of all the US Indian agents in history, perhaps the most corrupt was Perry Fuller of Kansas. His is not a well-known name today, but in the

1860s, the *New York Times* could put his name in a headline without explaining who he was. Orphaned at the age of six in Illinois, he was cared for by a guardian who was a minor land speculator who used Abraham Lincoln as a lawyer. In 1854, Fuller moved to Kansas, purchased land, and set up a store near three reservations. He cleared $40,000 in his first year, in large part by selling whiskey. He first came to the attention of law enforcement when the strychnine in his whiskey killed his customers; he escaped any consequences by terrorizing the local Indian agent.

In 1858, Fuller founded the town of Mineola, Kansas, which consisted of little more than his house, and bribed legislators to consider moving the territorial capital there. When they arrived for an inspection tour and found that the site was not a transportation hub with an imposing structure for a capitol building, the plan fell through.

The next year, Fuller became the US Indian agent and signed treaties with the Ojibwe and the Sauk and Meskwaki. He brazenly stole goods intended for annuity payments in present-day Kansas—wagon trains full of goods—and sold them in his own stores. He developed a ring of corrupt indigenous leaders who funneled virtually all cash annuity payments into his pocket; the exposure of this corruption led to a suspension of all annuity payments in Kansas. With the advent of the Civil War, he received contracts to supply consistently shoddy merchandise and rotten meat to the army; he stole cattle from indigenous people who were being moved from one reservation to another, selling it back to them in exchange for annuity payments. One of his fellow Indian agents was William Ross, the brother of a budding politician named Edmund Ross.

At the end of the Civil War, Fuller was no longer an Indian agent, though he was involved enough in US–Indian affairs to sign a treaty with the Seminole in 1866. In that year, Kansas senator James Lane committed suicide, an act attributed by many people to a *Chicago Tribune* exposé linking him to Perry Fuller—an indication of how toxic Fuller was. But by then, Fuller had amassed so much cash in trade and Indian affairs that he could spend money on bribery that had national implications. He distributed $40,000 to the Kansas legislature to have Edmund Ross appointed by the legislature to the position of US senator.

Ross was the deciding vote in the impeachment of Andrew Johnson, and days after the vote, he suggested to Johnson that Perry Fuller be named director of the US Internal Revenue Service. Instead, Fuller was appointed collector of customs for the Port of New Orleans, where he took kickbacks for overlooking import duties on coffee and sugar.[39]

✕✕✕✕✕ ◆ ✕✕✕✕✕

During and after the Civil War, the United States was embroiled in a series of conflicts with indigenous nations in the West that cost money and provoked outrage on many fronts: the Dakota War of 1862, the Bear River Massacre of Shoshone people in 1863, the Sand Creek Massacre of Cheyenne and Arapaho in 1864, "Red Cloud's War" from 1866 to 1868, and attacks by indigenous people along white "emigration" routes. Periodically, the United States would send out teams of military officers and political emissaries in attempts to resolve these conflicts. In 1865, a six-member "peace commission" traveled through the West to make treaties. General William Harney, who had participated in Atkinson's expedition forty years earlier, was one member of the group. Also included was Jesse Leavenworth, Indian agent and son of treaty signer Henry Leavenworth (who built Fort Snelling); no less a judge of character than John Chivington, perpetrator of the Sand Creek Massacre, had called Leavenworth "the meanest old whoremonger and drunkard in all the mountains." William Bent, the prosperous trader who had tried to warn the Cheyenne about the Sand Creek Massacre, and his assistant, Thomas Murphy, were also members, as was Kit Carson. John B. Sanborn, a Washington lawyer who investigated several incidents involving the army and indigenous nations, and Judge James Steele, representing the Indian Office, rounded out the group. They signed treaties with the Cheyenne, Arapaho, Apache, Comanche, and Kiowa at Fort Smith, in Arkansas, in October.

Also traveling the West in 1865 was another peace commission with more ambitious goals. Nine bands of the Lakota, spread over long distances, were invited to treaty negotiations at Fort Sully in present-day South Dakota, near the site where Pierre Chouteau had established a fur trading post decades earlier. This group included Newton Edmunds, the governor of Dakota Territory; General Samuel R. Curtis, a consultant to the Union Pacific Railroad; General Henry Sibley, who had led militia forces against the Dakota; Edward B. Taylor, a Nebraska newspaper owner, Indian agent, and head of the Northern Superintendency of Indian Affairs; missionary Henry W. Reed; and Orrin Guernsey, the brother-in-law of commissioner of Indian Affairs Dennis Cooley. This group made a lot of headway in resolving issues in the West by brokering agreements that Congress, while ratifying the treaty, failed to keep.

This necessitated another peace commission in 1868. Its members represented a wide range of opinions on US–Indian affairs. Nathaniel G. Taylor, a former congressman and acting commissioner of Indian Affairs, advocated "civilizing" Indians. Senator John B. Henderson, of the Committee on Indian Affairs, had sponsored the bill that created the peace commission. Samuel F. Tappan was a "Christian crusader," chaired the commission to investigate Sand Creek, and supported indigenous rights. John B. Sanborn, who had traveled west in one of the 1865 groups, and General William S. Harney, who traveled in the other group, were also members of this peace commission. Before departing, General William T. Sherman, commander of the Division of Missouri, said of the western nations that "it makes little difference whether they be coaxed out by Indian commissioners or killed." He was later replaced by General Christopher C. Augur. The final member was General Alfred H. Terry, US military commander of the Dakotas. On their way to Medicine Lodge in Kansas, where they hoped to conduct negotiations, they picked up nine newspaper reporters—a new development in US–Indian relations.[40]

The nine journalists invited to join the expedition represented "the leading newspapers of the country" and were evidently selected for their accommodating attitude toward the commissioners. One of the reporters was a friend of the commission chairman's son, Alfred A. Taylor. Though he was only a teenager, Alfred was named secretary to the treaty commission and extended this nepotistic arrangement to get his journalist friend included on the trip. He later reminisced that "by reason of the fact that my father was Commissioner of Indian Affairs, and being acquainted with the officials, I used to get items . . . for his paper."[41]

Embedding independent journalists on a treaty expedition was a relatively rare event, but the importance of the press was not lost on men who signed treaties. In fact, scores of treaty signers owned newspapers themselves at some point in their careers and used them in a final aspect of the relentless business: mythmaking.

6 ■ Mythmakers

T he size of the once vast Northwest and Louisiana Territories was reduced over time as states were carved out of their areas and admitted to the Union. By the end of the 1840s, Minnesota Territory became the heir to those larger political entities. The United States acquired control of tens of millions of acres of land from Dakota and Ojibwe people during the Minnesota Territorial period.

From its inception, and throughout its nine-year history, the Minnesota territorial legislature was a mechanism by which political and economic leaders could capture indigenous land and resources for themselves. Treaty signers featured prominently among the territory's leadership, occupying political offices and starting corporations through legislative acts that dominated profit making from townsite development, timber, mining, and transportation.

Today, the excesses of Minnesota legislators are often considered abuses of a benign American system rather than as a system of American abuse. But they were typical of the self-serving "pioneers" of colonialist settlement in states across the Midwest and the nation. That system captured natural resources through the business of making treaties and used those resources to form American businesses and fortunes. But they also went on to create romantic stories about that transformation. Treaty signers were among the founders of historical societies and other institutions that presented their own stories as the history of America. These stories, however, were so one-sided that they diverged from the course of history into myth. Though it often sounds like history, in its inclusion of voyages, battles, and settlers, the American myth is not a historical narrative; it is an identity narrative, intended to illustrate who true Americans are, or should be. The institutions that treaty signers helped to create pursued a mythical purpose, revealed in the 1853 act to incorporate the State Historical Society of Wisconsin: "To collect, embody, arrange and preserve in authentic form, a library of books, pamphlets, maps, charts, manuscripts,

---

Top right: Great Seal of the State of Illinois (1868 version), detail.

papers, paintings, statuary, and other materials . . . to rescue from oblivion the memory of its early pioneers, and to obtain and preserve narratives of their exploits, perils and hardy adventures."[1]

TERRITORY: 1849–1858

On March 3, 1849, Congress organized Minnesota Territory. It comprised the area—170,000 square miles—that was not included in Wisconsin and Iowa when they became states. The territory stretched from Lake Superior in the east into the Dakotas as far as the Missouri River. Yet only five thousand square miles—three percent of the territory— had been ceded to the United States by indigenous nations, in the 1837 treaties of the Ojibwe and Dakota. The American population lived in that small triangle of ceded land and in trading outposts scattered from Lake Superior to Fort Pierre Chouteau on the Missouri. (The Ojibwe had also ceded land in 1847, but for Ho Chunk and Menominee removal.)

About three hundred people lived in St. Paul at the time; the population had recently risen in response to rumors that the town would be a territorial capital. That information was confirmed on April 9, 1849, when news of Congress's action reached the little town by steamboat. Almost six weeks later, Alexander Ramsey arrived with his family on another steamboat to take up his position as territorial governor. He had not booked a room at either of the two hotels in town, so he traveled a few miles farther up the river, and his family stayed at Henry Sibley's house for a month.

Ramsey was a lawyer from Pennsylvania who had served as a US representative until two years earlier. He was joined in St. Paul by his brother Justus and by his personal secretary, Thomas Foster, a Pennsylvania newspaper editor. They were all Whigs like Zachary Taylor, the recently elected president who appointed Ramsey, and they were opposed to the radical democratic impulses that Andrew Jackson had introduced into American politics. Ramsey liked law.

He quickly moved to set the date for a territorial election. On August 1, Henry Sibley became the territory's delegate to Congress, running as a Democrat and unopposed. As Wisconsin Territory's congressional delegate, he had pushed through the bill to create Minnesota Territory. Seats for two houses of a territorial legislature were also filled. Nine men were elected to the territorial council, and eighteen were elected to the territorial house of representatives. In other territories, the establishment of a legislature took years; under Ramsey, the election was over less than four months after citizens found out they lived in a territory.[2]

Much of the business of the first legislative session focused on establishing the apparatus of government: setting the rules for legislative action, defining county and judicial district borders, selecting a printer to produce written versions of the laws that were passed. One act did incorporate the St. Paul and St. Anthony Plank Road Company, to build a road between two of the three towns in the territory. (The town of St. Anthony, built on the east side of the Mississippi at the Falls of St. Anthony, was the precursor to Minneapolis; the west side was still closed to settlement.) Among the proprietors of the company were Henry Sibley; his associate in the American Fur Company William Forbes; and William Randall, who was about to become very wealthy as one of the owners of the land on which St. Paul would be built. The next legislative session met in January 1851. Among its accomplishments was the incorporation of the Mississippi Boom Company, which would move logs from the pine region to mills in St. Anthony. One of the proprietors of that company was trader Joseph R. Brown.

Several of the men elected to the first two legislatures had been present at land cession treaties. William H. Forbes had signed the 1837 Ojibwe land cession treaty. Trader Alexis Bailly had signed an 1837 treaty with the Ho Chunk. Trader Allan Morrison had signed the 1826 Ojibwe treaty that was a follow-up to Prairie du Chien as well as the 1847 Ojibwe land cession treaties. Legislators D. T. Sloan and William Whipple Warren had also signed one of the 1847 Ojibwe treaties.

For other members of early legislative sessions—Joseph R. Brown, Henry Sibley, Reverend Gideon Pond, traders Alexander Faribault and David Olmsted, adventurer Martin McLeod, merchant Henry Jackson, painter James McBoal, and Alexander Ramsey's brother Justus—a fifteen-year series of opportunities to sign treaties was about to begin.

One of Ramsey's first acts as governor—even before he sent out a call to elect a legislature—was the creation of a land office in St. Paul. In 1849, there was very little land to buy in Minnesota Territory, and there were very few Americans to buy it. But the fur traders of Minnesota, led by Henry Sibley, were witnessing the end of the fur trade era and were engineering an enormous land cession. Working in Washington, delegate Sibley took a heavy hand in the selection of commissioners for the treaty, while his associates in Minnesota Territory worked among the Dakota, paving the way for the diversion of government funds to the pockets of traders. The land cession was to cover twenty million acres. It was much the same area that the Dakota had agreed to cede in 1841, at the unratified treaty negotiated by James Duane Doty, and the Dakota were hurt by the decline in the fur trade, but they were still reluctant to cede nearly their entire homeland. Commissioner of Indian Affairs Luke Lea joined Ramsey in a bad cop/bad cop negotiating team. Lea threatened during the negotiations to bring one hundred thousand troops to the territory to take the land for no compensation if the Dakota did not sign; Ramsey withheld the food until negotiations improved. In July and August 1851, the Dakota made the cession in exchange for about $3 million in compensation; $305,000 would be in cash, to help them relocate to a reservation ten miles wide along the Minnesota River. But traders had negotiated a side deal for the immediate payment of debts, and they walked away with $240,000 of that cash. More than half of that amount went to Henry Sibley, either directly from the treaty money or from traders who owed him money.[3]

In the next legislative session, traders, politicians, and treaty signers began immediately to reap the largesse of the land cession. The first act of the 1852 legislature permitted Pierre Bottineau—an interpreter for Sibley, scout for various expeditions to the West, and long-term resident of St. Anthony—to build a ferry across the Mississippi. Americans were crossing the river. D. T. Sloan and Paul H. Beaulieu were given the right to build ferries across the Mississippi and Minnesota Rivers later in the session.

Two of Minnesota's most powerful politicians, Henry Sibley and Henry Rice, had more ambitious plans. Though they had fallen out over fur trade deals, they joined a group that incorporated the Mississippi Bridge Company through a legislative act. Rice had signed the 1847 Ojibwe treaties and played an instrumental role in negotiating the Dakota land cessions.

During the next two legislative sessions, however, the treaty signers' exploitation of the land cession mushroomed in the passage of a series of legislative acts. Scores of towns were established throughout the ceded area (including St. Paul) on land that the treaty signers themselves had acquired at the land office.

Dakota Treaties of 1851

In July 1851 at Traverse des Sioux, and the next month at Mendota in Minnesota Territory, the four bands of the Dakota ceded their homeland, more than twenty million acres.

It was a wrenching process for the Dakota, necessitated by ecological collapse that ruined their hunting. As treaty commissioners Luke Lea and Alexander Ramsey observed, "It was soon perceived that although there was a vague and indefinable idea on the part of these people, that it was necessary for them to sell at least a portion of their country in order to secure them against the misery and almost starvation which . . . for the last few years had been inflicted upon them, yet when they were brought to meet the proposition in a distinct and intelligible form, they appeared to shrink with undisguised reluctance from taking a step so important in its results."[1]

Article 3 of the treaty set aside a small tract of land for a reservation ten miles wide and fifty miles long straddling the Minnesota River from Traverse des Sioux to the northwest. "It was with much trouble" wrote Ramsey and Lea, "that they could be induced to agree to go to the upper part of the Minnesota Valley where the reservation has been made for the four bands together. This region is sufficiently removed to guarantee the Indians against any pressure on the part of the white population for many years to come."[2]

The commissioners had a lot riding on the establishment of this reservation. The quick adoption of agriculture was their vision of the Dakota people's future; hunting would be impossible, and the reservation would be stocked with blacksmith shops and farming implements. "In this new home, which is of comparatively small extent," the commissioners noted, "they will be so consentrated [sic] as to be readily controlled and influenced for their real welfare."

The Dakota treaties of 1851 are infamous for the behind-the-scenes wheeling and dealing of fur traders, who siphoned hundreds of thousands of dollars from the government payment for the land cession and left the Dakota people more impoverished and dependent on the United States than they had been before the treaty. And the clause that established the reservation was stricken out by the Senate, where the idea of removing the Dakota far to the west was preferable. A subsequent action by Congress restored the reservation, but several years were required for the Dakota people to move there.

Six months after the treaties were signed, however, Henry Jackson (who signed them) had formed the Mankato Claim Company with Alexander Ramsey's brother Justus. The initial sales of land to settlers would be in their new town, fifteen miles from the reservation's edge at Traverse des Sioux.[3]

In 1853 and 1854, the territorial legislature passed eleven acts to create corporations that involved treaty signers: six railroads, two bridge construction companies, and three plank road construction companies whose incorporators included a revolving cast of treaty signers. These were the men at the intersection of politics, trade, timber, mining, land speculation—and Indian affairs: Alexander Ramsey, Justus Ramsey, Henry Rice, Charles Borup, Charles Oakes, William LeDuc, Henry Sibley, Marcus Grinnell, James Duane Doty, Joseph R. Brown, Nathan Myrick, A. L. Larpenteur, Martin McLeod, Benjamin Thompson, Philander Prescott, Joel Bassett, Alexander Faribault, William H. Forbes. Many of them were involved in more than one of the eleven companies created in those first legislative sessions; all had signed, or would sign, land cession treaties. Henry Sibley's brother-in-law and Henry Rice's brother were also the founders of other companies.

The state's routes for many of these railroads would traverse the Dakota land cession. In the early 1850s, though, construction was actually not the primary focus of creating a railroad company in Minnesota. Railroad companies were simply a spectacular way to attract capital from eastern investors, and in fact the incorporators could make more money for themselves if no construction took place. The railroad companies were authorized to raise millions of dollars in capital, which would be placed in territorial banks and would jump-start the local economy.

With the Dakota homeland taken and its exploitation begun, Minnesota politicians undertook the policy of Commissioner of Indian Affairs James Denver to "concentrate and confine" the Ojibwe. In 1854 and 1855, the Ojibwe ceded the Arrowhead Region along Lake Superior's western shore and another large area in the interior of the territory. Six years after forming the Minnesota Territory, the United States had extinguished aboriginal title to 85 percent of the present state.

In the interim, Ramsey had been replaced as governor. Zachary Taylor died in office, and his successor, Millard Fillmore, was replaced by Franklin Pierce, a Democrat. In 1855, Ramsey became mayor of St. Paul. But he participated in the continued corporate grab at the territorial legislature in 1855 and 1856, joining the owners of the St. Paul and St. Anthony Railroad Company, the St. Paul Gas Light Company (with Charles Oakes), the Fort Snelling Bridge Company (with his brother Justus, Charles Oakes, Joseph R. Brown, and Nathan Myrick), the Lake Superior and Northern Pacific Railroad Company (with Richard

1854 and 1855: Treaties with the Ojibwe

In 1854 and 1855, Ojibwe people ceded two large tracts of land that today are within the borders of the state of Minnesota. An 1854 treaty ceded the three-million-acre Arrowhead Region; a treaty in 1855 ceded an irregularly shaped tract of about nine million acres stretching at points to the western and northern borders of the state. Although the land cessions border one another, and the treaties were signed within five months of one another, important distinctions mark their histories.

Lake Superior was the geographic focus of the first treaty. Several years earlier, the United States had tried to get Ojibwe people who lived around the lake—in Minnesota, Wisconsin, and Michigan—to move west in a heavy-handed maneuver that had tragic consequences. The time and location of an important annuity payment had been changed to late in the year and far to the west, in Sandy Lake (now Minnesota). The idea was that, after traveling so far, all the Ojibwe people at the payment site would stay there at least for the winter and perhaps permanently. But Ojibwe people, knowing that their villages in the east were at stake, made the long round trip to Sandy Lake and home. Hundreds died of cold and sickness along the way.

In exchange for the 1854 land cession, Ojibwe bands successfully negotiated for permanent reservations throughout the lake region, coming to be known as the "immovable" Ojibwe. They also retained the right to making a living in the ceded territory. Those rights are still in force today.[1]

Ojibwe bands to the west, where the Mississippi River runs inland from the lake, negotiated the 1855 treaty. The main negotiators were giants in treaty making: Bagone-giizhig (Hole in the Day), who was consolidating his leadership position among local Ojibwe bands, had already begun farming, and astutely balanced representation of his people with personal gain, and Henry Rice, fur trader and politician, who was angling for payments on old debts. In this treaty, too, Ojibwe people retained sovereignty over reservations that are maintained today in Minnesota.[2]

The interests of copper mining companies featured prominently in the background of the 1854 treaty. An 1847 treaty had created the position of blacksmith for the Ojibwe; one of the signers of that treaty was a soldier named Reuben Carlton, who took the job. Once in the area, Carlton began scouting locations for copper mines in the Arrowhead Region. On September 25, 1854—five days before the region was ceded—the R. B. Carlton Company was created "for the purpose of obtaining mineral locations and lands." Partners in the company came to include J. W. Lynde, who signed the 1854 treaty, and treaty signers Nathan Myrick and E. A. Hatch. Signers of the 1854 treaty also included Daniel Cash, partner in the Ontanagon Mining Company, and Hugh McCullough, a large investor in the Pittsburgh and Isle Royal Copper Mining Company.[3]

Chute, the former front man for the Ewing Brothers, and Indian agent David B. Herriman), and the Northern Pacific Railroad.

As white settlement grew along the Mississippi toward the new town of St. Cloud, homegrown treaty signers welcomed into their fold at the legislature a rabidly proslavery newspaper owner named S. B. Lowry, who had signed the treaty that removed Ho Chunk people to Ojibwe land in 1846. He was given the right to establish a ferry near St. Cloud and co-incorporated the St. Cloud Bridge Company, the Watab Bridge Company (with Nathan Myrick), and the Lake Superior and Central Minnesota Railroad Company (with Ramsey).

Other railroads incorporated in 1855–56 included the Root River Valley and Southern Minnesota, the Transit, and the Minneapolis and Cedar Valley. Treaty signers among their incorporators included Sibley, Faribault, Olmsted, Borup, Benjamin Thompson, and Ramsey's private secretary from Pennsylvania, Thomas Foster. Additional legislation incorporated businesses—boom companies, bridge companies, manufacturing companies, ferries—that involved Joseph R. Brown and his son Angus, Joel Bassett, George Culver, Richard Chute, Martin McLeod, David Olmsted, Andrew Myrick, William Randall, and John F. A. Sanford. Sanford's Supreme Court case with Dred Scott was approaching an infamous conclusion that would exceed the proslavery dreams of editor S. B. Lowry.

Though the territorial legislatures from 1849 to 1856 produced the long litany of railroads, ferries, road companies, and other businesses listed above, it was the final session of the territorial legislature in 1857 that became famous as the Wildcat Legislature. More than forty treaty signers were among the owners of businesses that were incorporated during the 1857 legislative session. Four more railroads were among them and, notably, so was the North Shore Mining Company of Reuben Carlton, which had helped engineer the 1854 Ojibwe land cession treaties to acquire the rights to copper deposits.

Handing out corporate titles in 1857 required an extra "special session." The first act of that special session was meant to take advantage of a land grant from the federal government. Some of the land so recently acquired from the Dakota and Ojibwe would be turned over to the state to assist in actually constructing railroads. It was a huge boon to all of the men who had formed railroad companies, who now controlled more land as well as eastern capital.[4]

✕✕✕✕✕ ◆ ✕✕✕✕✕

As the prospect for Minnesota statehood materialized in 1857, several issues required resolution. One was the shape of the state. Most territorial residents, including Henry Rice, who was by then the delegate to Congress, preferred a north-south orientation, stretching from the Iowa border to Canada. But some residents lobbied for a state that ran east and west from the Mississippi to the Missouri, into the land of the Yankton and Lakota peoples, and extended north from Iowa for only a hundred miles or so.

Henry Rice was powerful enough to carry that decision, but another factor also had an impact on the shape of Minnesota. John Blair Smith Todd, a fur trader whose cousin was married to Abraham Lincoln, was interested in turning his trading posts into townsites: Yankton, Vermillion, Sioux Falls. He was competing in this enterprise with Minnesota territorial land speculators such as Joseph Renshaw Brown, who had his own designs on Sioux Falls through his Dakota Land Company. Brown would have political and economic clout in the new state and an upper hand in incorporating towns within the state's borders. Todd himself was also politically ambitious, but he had no political capital to run against Ramsey, Sibley, and Rice for elective office. So he supported Rice's north-south plan, which would leave his posts outside the state's boundaries.

A month before Congress approved Minnesota statehood, Todd organized a delegation of Yankton representatives for a trip to Washington, where they ceded millions of acres surrounding Todd's trading posts. When Dakota Territory was organized in 1861, he was elected the first territorial delegate to Congress.

Another issue to be tackled before statehood was the creation of a constitution. Territorial residents were elected to a convention for that purpose, but slavery had become a lethally divisive issue with the Dred Scott decision. Republicans and Democrats who were charged with writing a constitution refused to meet in the same room or even sign a single copy of the final document. The constitution was put before the public for approval in a referendum that also elected the first state legislators. While Congress was debating the state constitution, the legislators met—prematurely, without authorization—and passed an amendment to the Constitution. The amendment would authorize the legislature to direct $5 million in public money to state railroads.[5]

During the ensuing rancorous public scandal, a political cartoon appeared in St. Paul that depicted supporters of the amendment as gophers, undermining the stability of the state. This last act in the long history of Minnesota Territory gave the new state its nickname.[6]

1858: Treaty with the Yankton

As Minnesota moved toward statehood in 1858, two townsite development companies competed to effect the formation of Dakota Territory. One of these was the Dakota Land Company, formed by political powerhouses including Joseph Renshaw Brown, his brother Nathan, and J. W. Lynde. The company had already started several towns in Minnesota Territory; Joseph Brown and Lynde were also co-owners of the Nebraska and Pacific Mail Transportation Company and of the Mississippi River and Lake Superior Ship Canal Company. Lynde had signed land cession treaties with the Ojibwe in 1847 and 1854.

The Dakota Land Company staked a claim to the area that is now Sioux Falls, South Dakota. The site was barely outside the planned boundary for the state of Minnesota and barely within the region ceded by the Dakota people in 1851. When a new western territory was formed, the land company reasoned, Sioux Falls would be the logical choice for a capital.

The local Yankton people resisted the idea of white settlers flooding into the region, and their stance made land sales impossible. The Dakota Land Company resorted to subterfuge to convince settlers and politicians that their townsite was a viable operation. Joseph Brown, who also owned newspapers, brought a printing press into the area to give glowing accounts of the land and present an impression of political stability; the company convinced politicians that ten thousand settlers lived west of the Minnesota border, when the actual number was about forty. The Dakota Land Company needed a territory to be organized quickly and without scrutiny to carry off their plans.

Unfortunately for them, a fur trade company that operated among the Yankton people had its own territorial ambitions. John Blair Smith Todd wanted to be a territorial delegate himself and wanted the sites of his trading posts to become the leading towns of the new territory. Todd pulled off a coup on the eve of Minnesota statehood. Using the trust he had built as a trader—a trust that the Dakota Land Company lacked—Todd engineered a land cession treaty with the Yankton. The ceded land lay along the Missouri River, where Todd's trading posts were located. The next month, Minnesota became a state, and Todd was successful in delaying the formation of Dakota Territory until he could get his townsites up and running.

In 1860, Todd's cousin Mary Todd Lincoln became the First Lady when her husband, Abraham Lincoln, was elected president. When the territory was formed in 1861, it included all of present-day North and South Dakota, most of Montana and Wyoming, and part of Nebraska; J. B. S. Todd was elected to represent it in Congress.[1]

SIGNERS: MAKING HISTORY

The 2,300 men who signed treaties on behalf of the United States participated in events that made history. Many of them also participated in making the history of those events, injecting their colonialist points of view into the collective memory of the United States. The treaty signers themselves helped to create and propagate the American myth; their work informed public perception of US history and of indigenous people.

Caleb Atwater moved to Circleville, Ohio, in 1815, after being ruined by disastrous business investments in New York. He was elected to the Ohio legislature and rose to prominence as "The Father of Ohio Public Education." In 1829, he signed treaties between the United States and the Ojibwe and Ho Chunk peoples. Atwater was a rather prolific author and a member of the American Antiquarian Society, the Rhode Island Historical Society, and other learned bodies. He wrote *A History of the State of Ohio*, the first book-length treatment of the subject. The content ranges from geological information to poetry left untranslated from the Latin, and effusive passages about the success of Ohioans in extinguishing aboriginal title to land.

> We envy not those who possess the silvery heights of Potosi, the mines of Golconda and Peru, while we possess the soil of Ohio, the mines of Ohio, the free institutions of Ohio, the people of Ohio, and Ohio's temperate and healthful climate. . . . We have had flowing towards us, a flood of immigrants who love liberty. . . . During this very period, we have had two wars to pass through, prosecuted by England, with all her means of annoyance; and she was assisted, too, by hordes of the wildest, most cruel, most brave, and warlike savages on the globe.[7]

Atwater also wrote a piece called "Western Antiquities," in which he posited that earthen mounds constructed throughout North America "owe their origin to a people far more civilized than our Indians, but far less so than Europeans." He suggested that this race practiced traditions originated by the builders of the Tower of Babel, using as his historical guide "the Bible, the most authentic, the most ancient history of man."[8]

Two other government treaty signers wrote more significant works about indigenous people. William Whipple Warren, son of aggressive white trader Lyman Warren and Mary Cadotte, an Ojibwe woman, signed one of the 1847 land cession treaties of the Ojibwe as an interpreter; he authored *History of the Ojibways*. The book is grounded in his mother's oral traditions and is still widely considered to be an important source of information about the Ojibwe people.

Henry Schoolcraft, the mineralogist and powerful Indian agent for Michigan Territory, wrote extensively about indigenous people. His first wife, Obabaamwewe-giizhigokwe (or Jane Johnston), was an Ojibwe poet and translator; through Henry Schoolcraft her cultural knowledge passed, in garbled form, to Henry Wadsworth Longfellow, who based "Song of Hiawatha" on reimagined versions of her stories. After she died in an asylum, Schoolcraft married Mary Howard, the author of *The Black Gauntlet*. Her book, written at Schoolcraft's urging and dedicated to him, was a direct response to *Uncle Tom's Cabin*, from a proslavery point of view: "Were I an absolute Queen of these United States, my first missionary enterprise would be to send to Africa, to bring its heathen as slaves to this Christian land, and keep them in bondage until compulsory labor had tamed their beastliness, and civilization and Christianity had prepared them to return as missionaries of progress to their benighted black brethren."[9]

Schoolcraft had found his soul mate. In 1847, he received a government commission to compile *Historical and Statistical Information Respecting the History, Condition and Prospects of the Indian Tribes of the United States*. With Mary's help, he spent ten years compiling and publishing the cumbersome, six-volume, 3,500-page compendium. The government lost interest in the project before it was completed; an index to the work was not published for more than one hundred years.

Other treaty signers in the vein of Caleb Atwater created more straightforward, colonialist histories of colonized places. In a preface written for *The Illustrated History of Nebraska*, in 1897, J. Sterling Morton noted that "the narrative of the first struggles between barbarism and civilization on these plains is unwritten. . . . The time and the opportunity for a history of Nebraska has arrived. It is our duty to gather together in good and enduring form all the stories and heroisms of the frontier territory and to truthfully portray the moral and mental strength of the courageous men and women who made it so strong and vigorous."[10]

Morton had moved to Nebraska at the age of twenty-two, just as the Omaha people were ceding their homeland; he staked a land claim that became the site of Nebraska City, started a proslavery newspaper, became rich in land speculation, and eventually built a fifty-two-room mansion that replicated the White House. Morton signed a treaty with the Pawnee in 1857, just before his appointment as secretary of Nebraska Territory. As the US secretary of agriculture from 1893 to 1897, Morton started Arbor Day. He then resumed his writing career, starting the *Conservative* newspaper in which, thirty years after the Civil War, he presented his unrepentantly racist views. In 1899, writing in praise of "The White Man's Burden" by Rudyard Kipling, for instance, he suggested that, "The earth and its fulness are, from present indications, the predestined heritage of the people called Anglo-Saxon."[11]

Though Morton died in 1902, before the completion of *Illustrated History*, he did secure contributions from other prominent Nebraskans who finished the job: former governor Robert Furnas, who had signed treaties with the Omaha and Ho Chunk in 1865, wrote a chapter on forestry; the Reverend James Kerr, who signed three treaties in 1854, including the Omaha land cession, wrote the history of Nebraska's Presbyterian church; and Hiram P. Bennett, like Morton an immigrant to Nebraska in 1854 and later a US delegate to Congress from Colorado Territory, wrote a chapter entitled "The Story of Falki, War Chief of the Pawnees." The work was a fairly unvarnished look at the political organization of Nebraska, but betrayed a colonialist bias in its apologetic description of "claims clubs." In 1854, before it was legal for settlers to acquire land, these clubs were "organized for the protection of the property rights of the early settlers in the absence or inadequacy of the laws." In other words, illegal vigilante groups assaulted nonmember settlers who also tried to occupy indigenous land illegally.

The excesses of these clubs, however, are revealed only in passing (for example, in the biographical sketch of a victim of the club in Bellevue, which "did not hesitate to resort to intimidation, threats, and even acts of violence"). The fuller treatment of these clubs excused them as instances in which "necessity had become the mother of invention" and called the claims clubs "a practicable and efficient substitute for statutory rule or measure," noting, "The primary government of the territory was a pure democracy. The first formal laws were those passed by the claim clubs." The US Supreme Court ruled these "formal laws" unconstitutional in 1870.[12]

Lawyer Hezekiah Hosmer moved to the Maumee Valley of Ohio in 1836 and later edited the *Toledo Blade* newspaper. In 1858, he wrote the book *Early History of the Maumee Valley*. "This beautiful valley was to the Indian enchanted ground," he wrote. "Here, the Indian maidens were more beautiful, and the gallants of the sterner sex more manly and daring." He seemed under the impression that all indigenous people on the continent were a single group that loved the Maumee Valley more than anywhere else. And he notes the decline of the local indigenous communities into "a miserable remnant . . . nothing but vagrants and drunkards," an important story but a narrative still so prevalent even today that it might pass, in the American public consciousness, for the entire modern history of indigenous people. Two years later, Hosmer published a novel, *Adela, The Octoroon.* In 1864, he was appointed, improbably, to be chief justice of the Montana Territory supreme court, and he witnessed several treaties of the 1865 peace commission.[13]

Moses K. Armstrong—surveyor, newspaper publisher, and partner in the Northern Pacific Railroad—wrote *History and Resources of Dakota, Montana and Idaho* in 1866, the same year he signed the treaty of Fort Berthold. He also wrote *Early History of Mower County, Minnesota* (1876), *The Early Empire Builders of the Great West* (1901), and other books. Cortland B. Stebbins and Benjamin Ferris both signed a treaty with the Seneca in 1842. Stebbins went on to write *History of the Plymouth Congregational Church, Lansing, Michigan, 1864–1893.* Ferris had just written *A History of the Original Settlements on the Delaware: From its Discovery by Hudson to the Colonization under William Penn* (1846). Frederick Follet, who wrote *History of the Press of Western New-York* in 1847, signed a treaty with the Seneca in 1857.

In creating history, many of these treaty signers were telling their own stories. And because they occupied prominent positions in society at large, and in the vanguard of aggressive US expansion, their stories shaped the American myth and affected the way that American history has been told.

"An Act to incorporate the Historical Society of Michigan" was passed by the territorial legislature in 1828, nine years before Michigan became a state. Listed by name in the act are eighteen men "desirous of contributing their collective aid towards the discovery and preservation of such facts, records, and traditions, as may tend to elucidate the history of this portion of the Union."[14]

Among those eighteen founders of the Michigan Historical Society were seven prominent citizens who represented the United States at treaties with indigenous people. Lewis Cass had already signed nineteen treaties when the society was formed and would sign three more. John Biddle, mayor of Detroit and former Indian agent, had signed a treaty with the Wyandot in 1815. Army surgeon Zina Pitcher had signed one treaty with the Ojibwe in 1826; he would sign another in 1837 along with Major Henry Whiting, army quartermaster and author of poems about the Wyandot. Henry Schoolcraft had just signed the last of nine treaties, all of which involved the Ojibwe people and two of which had also involved Charles C. Trowbridge, then president of the Bank of Michigan, another founder. Thomas Rowland, a militia officer who had once been paid "the sum of thirty-three dollars and eighty-eight cents . . . for erecting a gallows for the execution of a certain Indian," had signed one of the Cass treaties.[15]

The vision that these men shared, "to elucidate the history of this portion of the Union," rose from a specifically American relationship to the past. They wanted to tell the history of a particular place, but only over the course of a limited time: the area had been "a portion of the Union" for just forty years. That attitude omitted a lot of the past, and it omitted the past of a lot of the people. On the society's first anniversary, president Lewis Cass made it clear that his history would have a definite starting point, distinguishing the territory timeline from the rest of the past: "Our country is yet fresh and green. . . . Our only monuments are the primitive people around us.—Broken and fallen as they are, they yet survive in ruins, connecting the present with the past, and exciting emotions like those which are felt in the contemplation of other testimonials of human instability." In 1828, the "monuments" still controlled 80 percent of Michigan Territory.[16]

Among the founders of the Indiana Historical Society, created in 1830, were at least seventeen men who had already signed treaties forty times and would sign another thirty times in the years to come. Their subjects of interest included "the history of the Indian tribes within the state" and "the civil and political history of the state from its earliest settlement." Both of those stories—of Indian tribes and of civil history—would be told through "lectures . . . or the communication of disquisitions." Of course, tribal members would not deliver any of those presentations. They had been removed from Indiana in treaties engineered by historical society members such as Abel C. Pepper of the Potawatomi "Whiskey Treaties," who was in charge of the state's

Indian removal; William Conner, who stayed when his Delaware family left; and Allen Hamilton and John Tipton, who conspired to capture annuity payments as indigenous nations departed.[17]

After signing several early treaties with the Iroquois, Egbert Benson became the first president of the New-York Historical Society in 1802. Christopher Higgins arrived in the Pacific Northwest on Governor Isaac Stevens's railroad survey and signed a treaty in 1855; he cofounded the Montana Historical Society in 1865. Later that year, his cofounder, Hezekiah Hosmer (the author of *Adela, The Octaroon*), signed five treaties. Six treaty signers, including James Duane Doty, his cousin M. L. Martin, and newspaper publisher A. G. Ellis, signed the original constitution of the Wisconsin Historical Society. Robert Furnas and J. Sterling Morton, "impressed with the importance of collecting and preserving, in particular, such historical material as shall serve to illustrate the settlement and growth of the state of Nebraska," cofounded the Nebraska Historical Society in 1878.[18]

On October 30, 1849, the Minnesota territorial legislature passed "An Act to incorporate the Historical Society of Minnesota": "The object of said Society shall be the collection and preservation of a Library, Mineralogical and Geological specimens, Indian curiosities and other matters and things connected with, and calculated to illustrate and perpetuate the history and settlement of said Territory." The history of the territory did not amount to much at that point, having started less than eight months earlier. But the incorporation of this society is one of the clearest statements of how Americans would come to delineate the past: indigenous identity and traditions as "curiosities"; settlement told as "history."[19]

Nine of the nineteen founders mentioned by name in the act were treaty signers, either before or after the incorporation of the society: Henry Sibley, Henry Rice, Henry Jackson, David Olmsted, A. M. Mitchell, Charles W. Borup, William H. Forbes, Martin McLeod, and Justus Ramsey. Early presidents of the society included Alexander Ramsey, Henry Rice, and Henry Sibley; John B. Sanborn, who signed two treaties in 1848, was president of the society fifty-five years later.

The historical societies of the Midwest helped reinforced a mythological "boat or wagon beginning" to US history. Indigenous people were here (past tense) for millennia, the myth states, yet nothing of note happened in all of that time. Then someone—Columbus, the Pilgrims, the settlers of Marietta, Zebulon Pike, or families on the Oregon Trail—arrived in a boat or a wagon at a place that was new to them, and history started. The early historical societies told stories that began, in most cases, just *after* treaties between the United States and indigenous nations opened indigenous land to white settlement.

As institutions, historical societies change over time—in their missions, their constituencies, their choice of stories, and their methods for relating the past to a contemporary public. The Minnesota territorial legislature, near the end of its final session in 1857, however, incorporated a different kind of organization, with a more focused and inflexible purpose. More than one hundred men were named in the act; with "their associates," they formed an Old Settlers Association. The object of the organization was "to collect and disseminate all useful information in relation to the early history and settlement of Minnesota, and it shall be the duty of said Association to record and preserve the names of its members and the date of their arrival in the Territory, the State or County from which they emigrated, together with such other information relating to the early history of the Territory of Minnesota and its early settlers as may be of interest to the people of the Territory."[20]

These "old settlers" included Alexander Ramsey, who at age forty-two had been in the territory for eight years. A quarter of the members were men who had signed, or would sign, treaties with indigenous nations: only 20 percent of the territory was open to settlement in 1857. The group was required by law to host a meeting once per year until all of its members were dead, and it was still meeting forty years later. At the 1873 meeting, missionary Gideon H. Pond—signer of the Dakota land cession of 1851—reminisced about visiting a Dakota village of five hundred people years before: "Men, women and children were all engaged in hunting, chopping, fishing, swimming, playing, singing, yelling, whooping, and wailing. . . . The clamor and clatter on all sides made me feel that I was in the midst of barbarism."[21]

After describing an incidence of violence by an Ojibwe group, and the retaliation by the Dakota, Pond draws a contrast with life in St. Paul, ten years after the ethnic cleansing of Dakota people from Minnesota was completed by the army and militia: "Glorious contrast! Cities now stand thick along your rivers. Civilized man is everywhere. Schools, academies, colleges, and churches fill the land. Grace, mercy and peace!"

The Old Settlers Association was one of many such organizations created throughout the Midwest in the last half of the nineteenth century. Most of these were local in nature, and as the "old settlers" died, the organizations in their turn provided the genesis for local historical societies. In 1897, though, one hundred "old settlers" still survived in St. Paul to create a new statewide organization called the Minnesota Territorial Pioneers. It was formed "that the memories and friendships of those early days may be perpetuated, and to assist in the preservation of our history covering that period." At its second annual meeting, A. L. Larpenteur—signer of the same Dakota treaty as Pond—beautifully summarized the tenor of the organization and, more broadly, the point of settler-focused history. "Minnesota, thou art dear to me," he said. "I saw thee first when thou hadst to be fed and hadst not a dollar of taxable property. I leave thee in wealth and feeding the world. Thou hast today a property valuation of over one thousand million of dollars."[22]

Men who signed treaties between the United States and indigenous nations generated tens of millions of pages in journals, reports, ethnography, legal documents, and legislation that are now primary historical documents. Collectively, their work affected public policy and, more broadly, public perception of indigenous people and of the history of US–Indian relations in subtle and not-so-subtle ways.

From the virtually limitless expressions of a colonialist mind-set found in the writing of treaty signers, Henry Dodge provides a relatively subtle example. In 1837, he negotiated with the Ojibwe the White Pine Treaty, the transfer of millions of resource-rich acres in present-day Minnesota and Wisconsin. In explaining his selection of borders for the land cession to the secretary of war, he wrote, "The country which I proposed to purchase from the Chippewa was I considered of the first importance to the people of the State of Illinois, Missouri, and the Territory of Wisconsin for its Pine Timber; and I was satisfied in my own mind that if a purchase was not made of this pine region of country by the United States, there was great danger of our citizens being brought into a state of collision with the Chippewa Indians, that would have resulted in bloodshed, and perhaps war."[23]

As a younger man, Dodge had moved to Wisconsin to mine lead. He squatted on Ho Chunk land in defiance of Ho Chunk protests, treaty stipulations, and orders from the US military; he helped provoke the Black Hawk War and then raised an armed militia to fight it enthusiastically. Dodge's careful phrasing ("There was great danger of [Wisconsin's citizens] being brought into a state of collision") implied passivity unknown to Dodge or the settler mentality. Such language—from the Captain of an Aggressive Civilization, of all people—helped cultivate the enduring shibboleth that, somehow, the United States was not an aggressor nation in its westward expansion, that continued wars were defensive reactions to attacks by hostile "Indians."

Much of the writing by treaty signers—certainly the writing that was most accessible to the general public at the time—appeared in the newspapers that they owned, published, and/or edited. Elihu Stout started the *Western Sun*, the first newspaper in the Northwest Territory, in 1808, and he sold it to John Rice Jones in 1845. Joseph Charless was the owner of the first newspaper west of the Mississippi, the *Missouri Gazette*, when he signed one of the William Clark treaties after the War of 1812. In the 1840s, Robert Newell published the first newspaper west of the Rockies, the *Oregon Spectator*. Patrick Edward Connor started the first non-Mormon newspaper in Utah, the *Daily Union Vendette*, at Fort Douglas, shortly before perpetrating the Bear River Massacre. Several early papers in Minnesota were owned by treaty signers: the *Dakota Weekly Journal* in Hastings (fur trader Alexis Bailly); the *Minnesota Democrat* (fur trader and lead miner David Olmsted); the *Henderson Democrat* (fur trader and land speculator Joseph R. Brown). In fact, treaty signers owned scores of newspapers, from Florida and New York to the Pacific Northwest.[24]

In addition to presenting a colonialist point of view—even when they violently disagreed about policy particulars—newspaper owners among the treaty signers supported the expansion of the property system in one important way: newspapers were often the organs of land speculation. John Suydam and Albert Gallatin Ellis, who signed treaties with the Menominee, started the first paper in Wisconsin, the *Green Bay Intelligencer*. One of their journalist peers later recalled that, though they ran articles on politics, "They were mainly devoted, however, to the work of introducing the new Territory of Wisconsin to the favorable attention of immigrants and the eastern world generally."[25]

The champions of the US property system understood the power of the press. Treaty signer and newspaper owner Addison Phileo made Henry Dodge famous. William Worth hired a biographer. And the 1867–68 peace commission invited nine national journalists to accompany them and their contingent of soldiers and scouts to treaty signings. Curiously enough, among those journalists (who signed the treaties alongside the soldiers and politicians) was Henry Morton Stanley, representing the *New York Tribune*. The next year, Stanley would travel to Africa in search of Dr. David Livingstone, the first of several expeditions that would ultimately lead to a cruel, Stanley-led conquest of the Congo on behalf of the King of Belgium. But in 1867, history hit the mythmaker perfecta when journalist Henry Stanley and scout William "Buffalo Bill" Cody traveled across the plains together to sign treaties with indigenous nations of North America.[26]

In 1848, Commissioner of Indian Affairs William Medill expounded on US–Indian relations in his annual message to Congress:

> While, to all, the fate of the red man has, thus far, been alike un-satisfactory and painful, it has, with many, been a source of much misrepresentation and unjust national reproach. Apathy, barbarism, and heathenism must give way to energy, civilization, and Christianity; and so the Indian of this continent has been displaced by the European; but this has been attended with much less of oppression and injustice than has generally been represented and believed. If, in the rapid spread of our population and sway, with all their advantages and blessings to ourselves and to others, injury has been inflicted upon the barbarous and heathen people we have displaced, are we as a nation alone to be held up to reproach for such a result? Where, in the contest of civilization with barbarism, since the commencement of time, has it been less the case than with us; and where have there been more general and persevering efforts, according to our means and opportunities, than those made by us, to extend to the conquered all the superior resources and advantages enjoyed by the conquerors?[27]

Savagery and civilization. Upon this distinction the US property system rests. Colonialists brought with them from Europe an assumption of superiority. They found ample evidence to refute that assumption. For one telling, practical instance, many Europeans who lived for extended periods among indigenous people seemed to prefer that life. And in fact, the premise behind Indian removal, the factor that allowed Andrew Jackson to call ethnic cleansing a "benevolent policy," was that US society was so toxic to indigenous people.

The enduring debate of the treaty-making era, from a US point of view, was the question of whether indigenous people should be *assimilated into* US society or *removed from* it. Common to both options was an unrelenting assault on indigenous social structures and relationships to the natural world. At every opportunity, the United States included clauses in treaties that "alloted" reservation land to individuals, in a conscious effort to destroy traditional indigenous relationships to land. "In the details of these treaties," Alexander Ramsey and Luke Lea reported, after securing the cession of Dakota homeland, ". . . it was our constant aim to do what we could to break up the community system among the Indians, and cause them to recognize the individuality of property."[28]

This policy was eventually encapsulated by Senator Henry Dawes, who sponsored an act to allot all reservation land to individuals in small lots (and to sell the "excess" land to non-Natives, an enormous land grab). Dawes said, "The defect of the system is apparent. They have got as far as they can go, because they own their land in common. . . . There is no enterprise to make your home any better than that of your neighbors. There is no selfishness, which is at the heart of civilization."[29]

However, US "civilization" efforts did not encourage selfishness among indigenous people. Many of these attempts were sponsored and conducted by Christian churches and by groups such as the American Bible Association. (Missionaries signed more than one hundred treaties.) Many indigenous people, as a result, became Christians. The biblical injunction, found in Genesis, that man should subdue the earth was antithetical to many indigenous world views, but Christianity is a large religion, and some indigenous people found in it a spiritual sustenance in their transition to a new world. Allotment and religion were only parts of a larger, consistent policy of destroying traditional indigenous identity. Languages, too—in which traditional relationships to the natural world are embodied—were also assaulted in reservation schools and boarding schools (including the Choctaw Academy, a cash cow started with government funds by treaty signer Richard Mentor Johnson).

The choice to destroy indigenous culture was seldom questioned anywhere in US society. Even the missionaries who organized opposition to the Indian Removal Act intended indigenous identity to disappear. In fact, John Marshall—in *Johnson v. M'Intosh*—made the issue unquestionable from a legal standpoint.

Although we do not mean to engage in the defense of those principles which Europeans have applied to Indian title, they may, we think, find some excuse, if not justification, in the character and habits of the people whose rights have been wrested from them.

. . . The tribes of Indians inhabiting this country were fierce savages whose occupation was war and whose subsistence was drawn chiefly from the forest. To leave them in possession of their country was to leave the country a wilderness.

. . . However extravagant the pretension of converting the discovery of an inhabited country into conquest may appear . . . if a country has been acquired and held under it; if the property of the great mass of the community originates in it, it becomes the law of the land and cannot be questioned.

The irony of a Supreme Court justice stating that laws cannot be questioned was evidently lost on Marshall.[30]

Visual artists attended treaties, giving us notable presentations of these events and of indigenous people. George Catlin, who thought of himself as the "Indian's historian," produced famous portraits of indigenous leaders and signed Sauk and Meskwaki and Shawnee treaties in the 1830s. Railroad surveyor and artist Gustavus Sohon signed—and recorded in paintings and sketches—treaties in Washington Territory in 1855. James Otto Lewis signed the treaty at Prairie du Chien in 1825; his painting of that event emphasized US military might among the attendees from many indigenous nations.[31]

Men who signed US–Indian treaties designed many of the territorial and early state governmental seals that marked official documents. The consciously chosen imagery on these seals expressed, endorsed, and celebrated a colonialist point of view. The seals were usually quite small, yet they were often packed with visual images. The seal of Indiana Territory, designed by William Henry Harrison, is an example: a picture in which buffalo are disappearing and trees are falling portrays the story Harrison wanted to tell. Wisconsin's first territorial seal, designed in consultation with Henry Dodge, reflected how important lead mining was to the region and to Dodge himself: it featured only a pile of rocks and an arm holding a pickaxe. But treaty signer Ebenezer Childs introduced legislation to include more information on the seal. Its replacement—only two and a half inches in diameter—depicted a farmer behind a plow and two horses, an indigenous person look-ing toward the west, a sheaf of wheat, a pile of metal ingots, a pile of lumber, a lighthouse, a steamboat, a yacht, a flour mill, the territory's original capitol building, and the motto *Civilitas Successit Barbarum* (Civilization has taken the place of barbarism).[32]

In Minnesota Territory, the legislature recommended an official seal that showed "an Indian family, with lodge and canoe, encamped, a single white man visiting them, and receiving from them the calumet of peace." Instead, as historian Edward D. Neill remembered, territorial governor Alexander Ramsey and territorial delegate Henry Sibley "de-vised at Washington the territorial seal. The design was: Falls of St. An-thony in the distance, an emigrant ploughing the land on the borders of the Indian country, full of hope, and looking forward to the posses-sion of the hunting-grounds beyond. An Indian amazed at the sight of the plough, and fleeing on horseback towards the setting sun." When Minnesota became a state, Sibley was governor, and he continued to use the seal (substituting "state" for "territory" on its outer rim). With minor changes, it remains the state seal today.[33]

The iconography of a settler narrative appeared on official docu-ments throughout territorial and state governments. A surviving letter from the designer of one seal leaves no room for ambiguity in interpreting the imagery of emigrant and Indian. The Minnesota His-torical Society's seal, used from 1857 until it was retired in 2012, was delivered with a letter from Daniel A. Robertson, who designed it and witnessed its production in New York. Robertson was not a treaty signer, but he worked with treaty signers. He owned the *Minnesota Democrat* newspaper until he sold it to treaty signer David Olmsted, and he cofounded the town of Mankato with Justus Ramsey. He was a member of the territorial legislature and the Minnesota Historical Society, and he wrote to Neill, then the head of the society, to describe exactly what the images in the seal represented.

> The female figure representing American intelligence and progress . . . in her right [hand] holds the hour glass, typical of time, the sands of which denote that the time has come for the Indian to depart. The light in the East is sending forth its rays above an ancient Mound. *Lux* over the light, *tenebris* [Latin for "darkness"] over the darkness—on the Indian side. On the East side our Railroad cars, the sign of prog-ress and civilization, the sheaf and sickle, of agriculture; the globe, books, scrolls, pen, and inkstand & compass, of history, literature, &

science. On the left are the pine lands, which are wanted for civilization and therefore the Indian must leave them. Submitting to his inevitable fate, he is looking upon the new world of civilization and science, and at the same time advancing to his bark canoe to take his departure, carrying with him the *gun,* the only useful article he has appropriated from all the achievements of civilization. . . . The seal viewed as a work of the kind, you will not often find surpassed.

Nor could it easily be surpassed as an expression of a colonialist version of history.[34]

Today, such iconography predictably, appropriately, yet only occasionally stirs public controversy. More remarkable, perhaps, is that when these devices were created, their racist messages provoked no controversy whatsoever.

A number of treaty signers were also mapmakers who imposed and reinforced a particular cultural perspective on the landscape by emphasizing imagined political boundaries. J. N. Nicollet signed treaties with the Dakota and the Ojibwe while creating a map of the hydrographic basin of the Upper Mississippi in 1835–37. Daniel D. Smith, who signed a treaty with the Kickapoo in 1819, later created and sold a four-by-six-foot map of Illinois, certified as "very good" by governors Shadrach Bond and Ninian Edwards. Maps that resulted from the Lewis and Clark expedition struck a loud chord in the American imagination: their maps demonstrated the vast space available west of the Mississippi into which indigenous people from east of the river could be moved.[35]

On these and many other maps, the colonialist point of view is most consistently reinforced in place names. "In the beginning was the Word": this opening to the Gospel of John, echoing the first creation story in Genesis, often has been used as a meditation on the power of language, and in particular the power to name things. The United States is saturated with the names of treaty signers, which are so ubiquitous that they go unnoticed. Thousands, perhaps tens of thousands, of streets in the United States are named after treaty signers. Rice Street, named after Henry Rice, passes the capitol building in St. Paul, Minnesota. Doty Street, named after James Duane Doty, runs past the capitol in Madison, Wisconsin. The capitol building in Springfield, Illinois, can be approached on (Newton) Edwards Street from the west and (Andrew) Jackson Street from the east. One of the major thoroughfares in

Omaha is Blondo Street, named after Maurice Blondeau, the Meskwaki "half breed" who signed sixteen treaties with William Clark.

Hundreds of towns are named after treaty signers. Some of these names are meant to honor their namesakes: more than twenty-five townships are named Cass. More than twenty-five states have a town named Jackson. Gadsen, in Alabama and Arizona; Du Quoin, Illinois; Denver, Colorado; Fort Dodge, Fort Worth, and Fort Leavenworth are named after treaty signers. Other cities—Pierre, Evansville, Shreveport, and many others—are named after a treaty signer who at some point owned the site where the town was built.

And hundreds of counties are named after treaty signers. William Henry Harrison is the namesake of counties in four states; Richard M. Johnson in five states; Lewis Cass and Isaac Shelby in five states each; Andrew Jackson in twenty-two states. In the three-state area of Minnesota, Wisconsin, and Iowa, counties are named after William Aitkin, Joseph Renshaw Brown, Reuben Carlton, Lewis Cass (in two states), William Clark, Henry Dodge (in two states), Alexander Faribault, Andrew Jackson (in all three states), John Rice Jones, Morgan Martin, Martin McLeod, Allan Morrison, J. N. Nicollet, David Olmsted, John Pope, Alexander Ramsey, Henry Rice, Henry Sibley, and J. B. S. Todd, all of whom played local roles in transforming indigenous land into private property. Counties in these states are also named for national figures who signed treaties: Reuben Walworth, Richard Mentor Johnson, Winfield Scott, Isaac Shelby, Isaac Stevens, Zachary Taylor, James Calhoun, William Henry Harrison, Anthony Wayne, and William Worth.

These names are written on a landscape in which relationships with the natural world that organize human society were violently and fundamentally changed in a remarkably short time. Each name is part of the story of that transformation. But what could be more natural, in a system of private property, than for the owners to name the place?

Epilogue

When Minnesota became a state in 1858, Dakota people were left with a ten-mile-wide strip of land along the Minnesota River; Ho Chunk people lived at a nearby reservation. Ojibwe people still controlled much of the northern area of the state. The next ten years would see momentous changes.

In 1862, following a short war between Dakota people and the United States, 304 Dakota men were sentenced to be hanged and thirty-eight were executed in the largest mass execution in US history. The United States abrogated all past treaties with the Dakota. The next year, Dakota and Ho Chunk people were exiled from the state, on boats owned by Pierre Chouteau Jr., to a reservation in Nebraska. A St. Paul paper, referring to escaped Dakota leader Little Crow, wrote, "He belongs to an age and an order which no longer exists, and which has no place in the grand economy of the modern world."[1]

Little Crow was captured and killed three months later; the state would pay a bounty for his scalp. Later in the summer, while cavalry still roamed the borders of the state in a hunt for other escaped Dakota people, Alexander Ramsey began heavy-handed negotiations for Ojibwe land. By 1867, indigenous people within the borders of the state lived on several reservations in northern Minnesota.

In the next four years, the US military engaged indigenous nations further to the west, and US peace commissions traveled by train to sign treaties. In 1871, during a squabble between the Senate and the House of Representatives over control of Indian affairs, funding for future treaty making was cut off. The legislation stated that "No Indian nation or tribe within the territory of the United States shall be acknowledged or recognized as an independent nation, tribe, or power with whom the United States may contract by treaty; but no obligation of any treaty lawfully made and ratified with any such Indian nation or tribe prior to March 3, 1871, shall be hereby invalidated or impaired."[2]

In 1886 a Supreme Court case, *United States v. Kagama*, supported the shaky idea that Congress has plenary (absolute) power over indigenous tribes—the opening to nearly one hundred years of wildly inconsistent public policy. The next year, Congress passed the General Allotment Act, which gave individuals on reservations title to small amounts of land; the government then sold any "excess" reservation land to non-Natives. As a result of this and follow-up acts, the 150 million acres of land still held by indigenous people in 1887 diminished by 90 million acres. In 1879, the establishment of Carlisle Indian Industrial School began an era in which children were taken from their families and stripped of their native culture and language in the belief that the indigenous population would die out unless it assimilated into white culture. In an 1892 speech, Carlisle founder Richard Pratt gave his educational philosophy: "All the Indian there is in the race should be dead. Kill the Indian in him, and save the man." In 1924, all indigenous people within the boundaries of the United States were made US citizens.

Another era in US–Indian relations started in 1934, with the Indian Reorganization Act. Some tribal lands were restored to indigenous nations, and tribal governments were formed to oversee reservation life. Most, but not all, of these governments survived a policy of "Indian termination" pursued by Congress beginning in the 1940s, in which legislative acts refused to recognize indigenous sovereignty. In the 1950s, Indian Relocation Acts sought to remove indigenous people from reservations to urban areas through economic incentives. Beginning in the 1960s, activism by indigenous people led to a new era of self-determination. In 1978, for instance, Congress passed the Indian Religious Freedom Act, which stopped government-sponsored restrictions on the practice of traditional indigenous religions.[3]

Through all of these changes in policies, indigenous nations maintained their commitment to retaining their sovereignty and, in carefully selected moments when the United States might live up to its promise to act "in utmost good faith," laid the legal groundwork to maintain and assert the rights they had retained in treaties.

Overlaying this history is the American myth. In its boat-or-wagon beginning to local history, the myth renders treaties invisible and emphasizes the settler as a quintessential American. In its insistence on American history as a long March of Progress, the myth consigns the whole sorry mess of US–Indian affairs, including ethnic cleansing, to a distant past. The American myth that guides so much public discourse in the United States disconnects US–Indian relations from its central place in the history of the country. But the system that expanded across the continent through treaties with indigenous people does not belong exclusively to the bygone past. In its vulnerability to corporate interests, in its assertion of a peculiar formation of race, in its assumptions based on property as the proper relationship between people and the natural world, the US–Indian treaty-making machine was the genesis of the system we all live in today.

Acknowledgments

This book is dedicated to my wife, Mona M. Smith. Her inspiration, support, emotional and intellectual companionship, and introductions to people and concepts have made this book possible.

The first germ of the book was planted fifteen years ago in research I provided for one of Mona's video projects. I noted then that in 1837 Ojibwe bands in what is now Minnesota signed the White Pine treaty, and Dakota people signed a treaty with US negotiator Joel Poinsett, for whom the flower is named. That unexpected juxtaposition of pines and poinsettias was my first indication that strange connections might be found in examining the treaties.

Years later, as a birthday gift for Mona, I collected a glossary of Dakota words and their translations, taken from names of Dakota people who signed treaties with the United States. In the course of that small, personal project I found a website, then recently created at the University of Oklahoma, that provided a searchable digital version of every official US–Indian treaty, taken from the work of Charles Kappler. With this resource, all treaty signatures could be efficiently collected in a single database. I will always be grateful to the creators of that website (now significantly changed and no longer as usable), which shaped my research for the next ten years.

When I sorted the names of US treaty signers, connections among them immediately arose to challenge my sense of the history of US–Indian relations. After some initial research, I was introduced through Mona to Cris Stainbrook of the Indian Land Tenure Foundation. This meeting changed the direction of my life. A contract with ILTF to conduct research on the treaty signers, and to capture emerging narratives about their connections, transformed my personal pursuit into a more public, organized inquiry. Cris and other people then associated with ILTF—Terry Janis, Jamie Podratz, and their impressive board of directors—provided funding, logistical support, and tough questions that improved my project. In the ILTF–supported phase of my research, I met David Woodard of Concordia University, the University of Minnesota's Pat Nunnally and Karen Till (who is now at the

University of Maynooth in Ireland), and, through Karen, graduate student Demetri Deib. I've enjoyed and benefitted from many productive conversations with them.

As the scope of my research expanded to include more than a thousand treaty signers, support from ILTF enabled me to get help with data collection and management. Wičáŋȟpi Iyótaŋ Wiŋ, Adrienne Pabst, Jess Annabelle, Riley Nesheim-Case, and Nathaniel Nesheim-Case provided not only practical help and a burst of enthusiasm but also confirmation that details from the lives of the treaty signers seem as weird to other people as they do to me. Nathaniel and Riley have been mainstays of the project for more than ten years.

Eventually, I began presenting my research in public. One presentation in particular had a large impact on my life. Matthew Brandt, then a vice president at the Minnesota Humanities Center (MHC), invited me to share my research there. Annamarie Gutsch, then head of the Minnesota Indian Affairs Council (MIAC), was in attendance, and my involvement in several projects resulted. One was facilitating a MIAC–administered strategic plan for Ojibwe and Dakota language revitalization. It was a humbling experience, to be working with that august group of indigenous educators, policy makers, cultural leaders, and language activists. I don't want to single out any names because each person was truly impressive. Their insights underscored the complexity of indigenous cultures, the endurance of indigenous communities, and the legacy of treaties.

I also was invited by Annamarie and Matt to join the design team for an exhibit entitled *Why Treaties Matter*. A collaboration among MIAC, MHC, and the Smithsonian's National Museum of the American Indian (NMAI), this exhibit focuses on treaty making by Dakota and Ojibwe communities in what came to be called Minnesota. It was my privilege to work with, and learn from, irrepressible Jim Jones of Leech Lake and forcefully thoughtful Tom Ross of the Pezihutazizi Oyate. Jim took me to meet with tribal leaders; Tom and I created the content for the website that accompanied the exhibit. This experience had a profound impact on my understanding of treaties, an impact deepened by the expertise of Marc Hirsh, Ed Shupman, and other knowledgeable, generous personnel from the NMAI.

Since then, I have been a consultant to other projects sponsored by MHC, including an educational reform effort in Omaha. I began looking for connections between my research and new subjects there, through interaction with other MHC personnel and with stellar educators and community leaders. Conversations in Omaha with Rose Mcgee of MHC, educator/activist Elmer Crumley, Alexs Pate of Innocent Technologies, and Wynema Morris of the Nebraska Indian Community College continue to resonate in my work today.

After a presentation about treaties in 2015 (again at MHC), editor in chief Ann Regan of the Minnesota Historical Society Press asked about my publishing plans. With her help I crafted a proposal to accommodate both the geographic focus of the press and the national networks that connect US treaty signers. In the months after I started work on the book in 2016, both of my parents died. During that protracted vigil I tried to write at times. Parts of this book were drafted in the well-appointed basement of my brother (and fellow writer) Todd and sister-in-law Alesa. Their generosity, and the sharing of a profound experience with all my spectacular siblings—Monica, Tam, Clark, and Jess and their spouses and partners and children—will always color my memory of writing this book.

Even as I pushed every publishing deadline to its limit and beyond, Ann Regan maintained a preternaturally calm and supportive presence, and this book would be nowhere without her genuine kindness and bottomless bag of author management strategies. Mattie Harper of the Minnesota Historical Society's Native American Initiatives unit generously provided information on the Bonga family. Nathaniel Nesheim-Case and Jessica Rice helped in the last-minute push to finalize the end notes. Eventually, copyeditor Betty Christiansen made that phase of the project painless, and managing editor Shannon Pennefeather, in shepherding the book through production, went so far as to make that process pleasant. Special thanks to David Wilkins, who holds the McKnight Presidential Professorship in American Indian Studies at the University of Minnesota Twin Cities, and Joseph Bauerkemper, assistant professor in American Indian Studies at the University of Minnesota Duluth, for their assistance with the "For Further Reading" list.

I am fortunate to have a circle of generous, intelligent, and captivating friends, family, and acquaintances who have allowed me to talk about treaty signers in just about any social situation over the years. Consequently, many people have had a hand in shaping my research, writing, and presentations. Some are deeply conversant with the subject of US–Indian treaties; others are experts in education and education reform, social justice, many artistic disciplines, jurisprudence, history, biology, psychology, public policy. Their gentle interrogation from many points of view has made my work better. Some of the conversations I consider most important to my work—in addition to those with people listed above—have involved Michael Agnew, Jewell Arcoren, Andy Arsham, Christine Baeumler, Jim and Carol Bauer, John Burke, Stephen Carpenter, Art Cullen, Tim Frederick, Steve Higgins, Gerry Kearns, Sonja Kuftinec, Shanai Matteson, Ken Meter, Marty Miller, William Millikan, Don Olson, Joel Rowland, Bruce White, and Carolyn Wolski.

Many of my most thought-provoking conversations arise from membership in three groups. Healing Place Collaborative, started by Mona, is an indigenous-led, artist-led association of people from diverse backgrounds and professions who share an interest in the Mississippi as a place of healing and a place in need of healing; every conversation I have with HPC partners is stimulating. I also work with a team of scholars each year in the MHC Summer Educators Institute: Yvonne RB Banks, Tlahtoki Xochimeh, Heid Erdrich, Sun Yung Shin, Rose McGee, Ethan Neerdaels, Ramona Stately, and Mona, and staff members Eden Bart and Sung Ja Shin. I learn a lot from them, and from the Minnesota educators with whom we spend our time. My work is also informed by Kris Sorensen and fellow board members of In Progress, a media production nonprofit. The history of US–Indian relations can be harrowing at times; the young participants in In Progress, as they express their diverse cultural and personal identities through art—like the members of that language revitalization task force and the Healing Place Collaborative, and like the educators of Omaha and Minnesota—give me hope.

Finally, I want to acknowledge three friendships. When I have encountered the most distressing subjects in the historical record, the ever-generous Louis Alemayehu has opened his heart and home to help me to decompress. Novelist Sheila O'Connor is an accomplished teacher of writing; her insights into the writing process are among the many treasures that her friendship has given me. And I find that I can trace many of my life's best and most important features to my friendship with Juanita Espinosa. She has challenged and supported me in many ways over decades, not least by first introducing me both to Mona and to the subject of US–Indian treaties.

Notes

Notes to Introduction

1. In this book, the word *Indian* reflects a colonialist usage in official US documents (e.g. *Indian treaties, Indian Affairs, Indian agent*). Indigenous nations are referred to with more widely and currently accepted names, regardless of how they are labeled in treaties (e.g., Ho Chunk rather than Winnebago), although the official names of the treaties are retained.

2. Notably by Francis Paul Prucha in *American Indian Treaties: The History of a Political Anomaly* (Berkeley: University of California Press, 1994). John O'Sullivan, "Annexation," *United States Magazine and Democratic Review* 17 (July–August 1845): 5–10.

3. Johnson v. M'Intosh, 21 US 543 (1823).

4. Adam Smith, *Wealth of Nations, Book IV,* chapter 7, part 3.

5. In the annotation to this book, I provide sources for information about specific treaty signers. For some references covering the actions of groups of signers ("Among the founders of the Indiana Historical Society, created in 1830, were at least seventeen men who had already signed treaties forty times and would sign another thirty times in the years to come."), this is not practical. Their signatures, noted in the Treaty Signers Project, are found among the scores of official treaties signed by the United States and indigenous nations.

6. See later references in this text for J. Sterling Morton, Arbor Day; Henry Stanley in the Congo; Douglass Houghton and copper mining; Stephen Watts Kearny, cavalry; Winfield Scott, troops in Mexico City ("Halls of Montezuma"). For other signers, see Barney Warf, ed., *Encyclopedia of Geography* (Thousand Oaks, CA: Sage Publications, 2010), 1946 (Jedidiah Morse); Jesse S. Myer, *Life and Letters of Dr. William Beaumont* (St. Louis, MO: C. V. Mosby Company, 1912), 102–54 (Beaumont); David M. King, "United States Joint Operations in the Tripolitan Campaign of 1805" (thesis, US Army Command and General Staff College, 1994) (William Eaton, "Shores of Tripoli"); Elizabeth Robins Pennell and Joseph Pennell, *The Life of James McNeill Whistler* (Philadelphia: J. B. Lippincott, 1908), 1:6 (William Whistler, uncle of James McNeill Whistler); http://www.earlychicago.com, which is based on Ulrich Danckers et al., *A Compendium of the Early History of Chicago to the Year 1835, When the Indians Left* (River Forest, IL: Early Chicago, Inc., 2000) (Juliette Gordon Low, founder of US Girl Scouts, granddaughter of J. H. Kinzie); Douglas C. Harrison, *The Clarks of Kentucky* (Bloomington, IL: iUniverse, 2011), xi (Meriwether Lewis Clark Jr., founder of Kentucky Derby); *Symmes's Theory of Concentric Spheres* (Cincinnati, OH: Morgan, Lodge and Fisher, 1826) (John Cleves Symmes Jr., brother-in-law of William Henry Harrison); Zella Armstrong and Janie P. C. French,

Notable Southern Families (Chattanooga, TN: Lookout Publishing, 1922), 2:181 (Matthew Wallace, brother-in-law of Texas founder Sam Houston).

7. The canons were established by Menominee Tribe of Indians v. United States, 391 US 404 (1968); Arizona v. California, 373 US 546 (1863); Squire v. Capoeman, 351 US 1 (1856), and other cases, cited in Jill de la Hunt, "The Canons of Indian Treaty and Statutory Construction: A Proposal for Codification," *University of Michigan Journal of Law Reform* 17 (Spring 1984): 681n2.

Notes to Section 1: Speculators

1. "The Royal Proclamation, October 7, 1763," Avalon Project, Yale Law School, available at http://avalon.law.yale.edu/; George Washington to William Crawford, 17 September 1767, Founders Online, National Archives, https://founders.archives.gov/documents/Washington/02-08-02-0020.

2. US Congress, Ordinance of 1794, Founders Online, National Archives, https://founders.archives.gov/documents/Jefferson/01-06-02-0420-0006.

3. Charles Hall, *Life and Letters of Samuel Holden Parsons* (Binghamton, NY: Otsenengo Publishing, 1905), 479; US Congress, *Indian Land Cessions in the United States, 1784–1894*, 56th Cong., 1st Sess., House Doc. 736, serial 4015, 650–51.

4. On the Ohio Company, see Alfred P. James, *The Ohio Company: Its Inner History* (Pittsburgh, PA: University of Pittsburgh Press, 1959). Other accounts of the Ohio Company and the settlement of Marietta include L. A. Alderman, "Marietta, Ohio, Historically Considered," in *The National Magazine: A Monthly Journal of American History* 7 (1887–88): 541–44; Charles Moore, *The Northwest Under Three Flags* (New York: Harper & Brothers, 1900), 332–34.

5. Northwest Ordinance, 1787, available at http://avalon.law.yale.edu/18th_century/nworder.asp.

6. Rhoda Gilman, *Henry Hastings Sibley: Divided Heart* (St. Paul: Minnesota Historical Society Press, 2004), 6, 9–10; Thomas J. Summers, *History of Marietta* (Marietta, OH: The Leader Publishing Co., 1903), 294.

7. Ebenezer Denny, *Military Journal of Ebenezer Denny* (Philadelphia: Historical Society of Pennsylvania, 1859), 140.

8. Arthur St. Clair to Alexander Hamilton, 9 August 1793, Founders Online, National Archives, https://founders.archives.gov/documents/Hamilton/01-15-02-0158.

9. R. Douglas Hurt, *The Ohio Frontier: Crucible of the Old Northwest, 1720–1830* (Bloomington: Indiana University Press, 1996), 120–42; A. R. Bauman, *General "Mad" Anthony Wayne and the Battle of Fallen Timbers* (Bloomington, IN: Author House, 2010), 19.

10. B. F. Bowen, *History of Clinton County Ohio* (Indianapolis: B.F. Bowen & Co., 1915), 38.

11. "Outline Review of the Life, etc. of William Henry Harrison," *Quarterly Review of Methodist Episcopal Church* 1 (1847): 359. See also Robert M. Owens, *Mr. Jefferson's Hammer: William Henry Harrison and the Origins of American Indian Policy* (Norman: University of Oklahoma Press, 2011).

12. Epigraph: A. M. Sakolski, *The Great American Land Bubble* (New York: Harper & Brothers, 1932), 31–32. This is the first comprehensive study of land speculation in the United States and the source of much of the information used here.

13. An event that Frederick Jackson Turner noted in "The Significance of the Frontier in American History," presented as a paper in 1893 and published in *The Frontier in American History* (New York: Henry Holt and Company, 1921), 261: "The Western wilds . . . constituted the richest free gift that was ever spread out before civilized man."

14. *Resolutions, Laws, and Ordinances, Relating to the Pay, Half Pay, Commutation of Half Pay, Bounty Lands, and Other Promises Made by Congress to the Officers and Soldiers of the Revolution* (Washington, DC: Thomas Allen, 1838), 20; US Congress, *Virginia Military Land Warrants,* House of Representatives, Report No. 633, 30th Cong., 1st Sess., 1848, 8.

15. Michael Hattem, "Newburgh Conspiracy," in George Washington Digital Encyclopedia, edited by Joseph F. Stoltz III, Mount Vernon Estate, 2012– , http://www.mountvernon.org/digital-encyclopedia/article/newburgh-conspiracy/; text of Newburgh Petition in Gaillard Hunt, ed., *Journals of the Continental Congress,* vol. 24, 1783 (Washington, DC: Government Printing Office, 1922), 291.

16. Louise Burnham Dunbar, *A Study of "Monarchical" Tendencies in the United States, from 1776 to 1801* (Urbana: University of Illinois, 1923), 60; Patrick Allen Pospicek, "Society of the Cincinnati," in George Washington Digital Encyclopedia, http://www.mountvernon.org/digital-encyclopedia/article/society-of-the-cincinnati/.

17. Sakolski, *Great American Land Bubble,* 114.

18. Recounted in David W. Miller, *The Taking of American Indian Lands in the Southeast: A History of Territorial Cessions and Forced Relocation, 1607–1840* (Jefferson, NC: McFarland & Company, 2011), 71.

19. David B. Dill Jr., "Portrait of an Opportunist: The Life of Alexander Macomb," *Watertown Daily Times,* September 9, 1990, annotated and revised by Marshall Davies Lloyd, at http://mlloyd.org/gen/macomb/text/amsr/wt.htm.

20. Dill, "Portrait."

21. Ellis Paxson Oberholtzer, *Robert Morris: Patriot and Financier* (New York: Macmillan, 1903), 313.

22. Norman Wilkinson, "The 'Philadelphia Fever' in Northern Pennsylvania," *Pennsylvania History* 20 (January 1953): 44; "Summary Information," Pennsylvania Population Company Papers (Collection 489), Historical Society of Pennsylvania.

23. For a description of the Glasgow fraud, see Russell Koonts, "'An Angel Has Fallen!': The Glasgow Land Frauds and the Establishment of the North Carolina Supreme Court" (MA thesis, North Carolina State University, 1995).

24. Thomas Perkins Abernathy, *The South in the New Nation* (Baton Rouge: Louisiana State University Press, 1961), 136–69; Thomas Marshall Green, *Historic Families of Kentucky* (Cincinnati, OH: R. Clarke & Company, 1889), 261.

25. These imprisonments are all noted in Sakolski, *Great American Land Bubble,* 66, 135, 165–66.

26. Sakolski, *Great American Land Bubble,* 233.

27. Charles Mulford Robinson, "The Life of Judge Augustus Porter, A Pioneer in Western New York," *Publications of the Buffalo Historical Society* 7 (1904): 245–46.
28. James L. Roark et al., *The American Promise, Volume I: To 1877: A History of the United States* (New York: Macmillan, 2012), 338.
29. Hammond, quoted in Richard Sylla, "The U.S. Banking System: Origin, Development, and Regulation," in *History Now* (online journal of the Gilder Lehrman Institute of American History) 24 (Summer 2010).
30. *The History of Fond du Lac County, Wisconsin* (Chicago: Western Historical Company, 1880), 186, 333–36, 467. For the inquiry into issuance of bank notes, see US House, 25th Cong., 3d Sess., Report of the Secretary of the Treasury Respecting Banks of Wisconsin Territory (Washington, DC: Government Printing Office, 1839) (House Doc. 232), 5. For biographical information on Arndt, see John Stover Arndt, *The Story of the Arndts* (Philadelphia: Christopher Stower Company, 1922), 182–88.
31. "Agreement between John Lewis and James Wilkinson for locating land," American Memory, Library of Congress, http://memory.loc.gov/cgi-bin/query/h?ammem/fawbib:@field(NUMBER+@band(icufaw+amc0004)).
32. Sakolski, *Great American Land Bubble*, 235.
33. United States, Office of Indian Affairs, *Annual Report of the Commissioner of Indian Affairs* (Washington, DC: Government Printing Office, 1851), 284.
34. *Sydney Morning Herald,* October 8, 1857, 8.
35. Wells, Minnesota, "City History," http://www.cityofwells.net/index.php/city-history.

Notes to Section 2: Traders

1. Thomas Jefferson to William Henry Harrison, February 27, 1803, in Francis Paul Prucha, *Documents of United States Indian Policy* (Lincoln: University of Nebraska Press, 2000), 22.
2. Samuel P. Snell, Ryan L. Jackson, Angie R. Krieger, "Lost and Forgotten Historic Roads: The Buffalo Trace, a Case Study" (n.d.), posted on Hoosier National Forest website, https://www.fs.usda.gov/Internet/FSE_DOCUMENTS/stelprdb5444947.pdf; William Henry Harrison to James Madison, 8 September 1801, Founders Online, National Archives, https://founders.archives.gov/documents/Madison/02-02-02-0140.
3. Robert Miller, "The Federal Factory System" (March 7, 2009), in *Encyclopedia of United States Indian Policy,* Congressional Quarterly Press, Sage Publications, available: https://ssrn.com/abstract=1355236; Jefferson to Harrison, February 27, 1803. A map of factory locations and dates of establishment is in Francis Paul Prucha, *Atlas of American Indian Affairs* (Lincoln: University of Nebraska Press, 1990), 55.
4. "Treaty with the Kaskaskia, 1803," in Charles J. Kappler, *Indian Affairs: Laws and Treaties*, 2:66–68, available at http://dc.library.okstate.edu/digital/collection/kapplers.
5. To Thomas Jefferson from Albert Gallatin, 20 August 1804, Founders On-

line, National Archives, https://founders.archives.gov/documents/Jefferson/99-01-02-0262.

6. *Historic Rock Island County* (Rock Island, IL: Kramer & Company, 1908), 8–9.
7. Text of Louisiana Purchase is at https://www.archives.gov/exhibits/american_originals/original.html.
8. James Madison to William Hull, 10 December 1805, summarized at Founders Online, National Archives, https://founders.archives.gov/documents/Madison/02-10-02-0624.
9. Clarence Edwin Carter, ed., *The Territorial Papers of the United States* (Washington: Government Printing Office, 1934), 12:196–200, as quoted in Richard E. Jensen and James S. Hutchins, eds., *Wheel Boats on the Missouri: The Journals and Documents of the Atkinson-O'Fallon Expedition, 1824–1826* (Lincoln: Nebraska State Historical Society, 2001), 2.
10. Mary Ellen Rowe, *Bulwark of the Republic: The American Militia in Antebellum West* (Westport, CT: Praeger, 2003), 28–30. On Smith T, see Dick Steward, *Frontier Swashbuckler: The Life and Legend of John Smith T* (Columbia: University of Missouri Press, 2000).
11. Kira Gale, *Meriwether Lewis: Assassination of an American Hero* (Omaha, NE: River Junction Press, 2015), 352; J. F. Darby, *Personal Recollections of John F. Darby* (St. Louis, MO: G. I. Jones and Company, 1880), 59–60.
12. Bates to Henry Dearborn, June 22, 1807, in Thomas Maitland Marshall, ed., *The Life and Papers of Frederick Bates* (St. Louis: Missouri Historical Society, 1926), 148–49.
13. Ray Vaughn Denslow, *Territorial Masonry: The Story of Freemasonry and the Louisiana Purchase, 1804–1821*, chapter 9; Robert J. Wheeler, "St. Louis Missouri Lodge No. 1 History," http://stlmasons.org/history.
14. To Thomas Jefferson from Meriwether Lewis, 15 December 1808, Founders Online, National Archives, https://founders.archives.gov/documents/Jefferson/99-01-02-9323.
15. "St. Louis Missouri Fur Company Articles of Incorporation," as quoted in General Thomas James, *Three Years among the Indians and Mexicans*, ed. Walter B. Douglas (St. Louis: Missouri Historical Society, 1916), available at https://user.xmission.com/~drudy/mtman/html/mfc/artassoc.html.
16. Jefferson to Harrison, February 27, 1803.
17. Louis Pelzer, "Private Land Claims of the Old Northwest," *Iowa Journal of History* 12 (1914): 383.
18. See, for example, Adam Jortner, *The Gods of Prophetstown: The Battle of Tippecanoe and the Holy War for the American Frontier* (New York: Oxford University Press, 2011). In *War and Peace*, Tolstoy wrote of "the comet which was said to portend all kinds of woes and the end of the world."
19. Epigraph: H. B. Cushman, *History of the Choctaw, Chickasaw and Natchez Indians* (Greenville, TX: Headlight Printing, 1899), 386.
20. For the Iroquois Confederacy's success in manipulating trade relations with colonialist powers, see Dorothy V. Jones, *License for Empire: Colonialism by Treaty in Early America* (Chicago: University of Chicago Press, 1982); for analogous relationships involving the Choctaw Nation, see Richard White, *The Roots*

*of Dependency: Subsistence, Environment, and Social Change Among the Choc-
taws, Pawnees, and Navajos* (Lincoln: University of Nebraska Press, 1988).

21. For more on this confusion of terms, see Walker Connor, "A Nation Is a Nation, Is a State, Is an Ethnic Group, Is a . . . ," *Ethnic and Racial Studies* 1 (1978):
379–88.

22. Cherokee Nation v. Georgia, 30 US (5 Pet.) 1 (1831).

23. 25 U.S. Code 71, Future treaties with Indian tribes.

24. Royal B. Way, "The United States Factory System for Trading with the Indians,
1796–1822," *Mississippi Valley Historical Review* 6 (September 1919): 226, 234.

25. Zebulon Montgomery Pike, *The Expeditions of Zebulon Montgomery Pike, to
Headwaters of the Mississippi River, through Louisiana Territory, and in New
Spain, During the Years 1805-6-7,* ed. Elliot Coues (New York: Francis P. Harper,
1895), 1:1.

26. Pike, *Expeditions,* 1:227.

27. Pike, *Expeditions,* 1:237.

28. Pike, *Expeditions,* 1:44.

29. Pike, *Expeditions,* 1:145.

30. Pike, *Expeditions,* 1:12–13.

31. Louis A. Tohill, "Robert Dickson, the Fur Trade, and the Minnesota Boundary," *Collections of the Minnesota Historical Society* 6 (December 1925): 332–35;
profile of Dickson in David Lavender, *The Fist in the Wilderness* (Lincoln: University of Nebraska Press, 1998), 46–48.

32. Mary Ellen Rowe, "Bernard Pratte," in Lawrence O. Christensen et al., *Dictionary of Missouri Biography* (Columbia: University of Missouri Press, 1999), 623.

33. Stella M. Drumm, "More about Astorians," *The Quarterly of the Oregon Historical Society* 24 (December 1923): 338–44.

34. Drumm, "More about Astorians," 341.

35. For a description of the Chouteaus' involvement in this transition, see Stan
Hoig, *The Chouteaus: First Family of the Fur Trade* (Albuquerque: University of
New Mexico Press, 2008), 164–66.

36. "Treaty with the Chippewa, 1842," Kappler, *Indian Affairs,* 2:542–45.

37. Lucille Kane, "The Sioux Treaties and the Traders," *Minnesota History* 32 (June
1951): 65–80.

38. Lucius F. Hubbard et al., *Minnesota in Three Centuries: 1655–1908* ([New York]:
Publishing Society of Minnesota, 1908), 2:280.

39. R. David Edmunds, "'Designing Men, Seeking a Fortune': Indian Traders and
the Potawatomi Claims Payment of 1836," *Indiana Magazine of History* 77 (June
1981): 109–22.

40. William H. C. Folsom, *Fifty Years in the Northwest* (St. Paul, MN: Pioneer
Press Company, 1888), 572 (Oakes); Francis Paul Prucha, "Army Sutlers and
the American Fur Company," *Minnesota History* 40 (Spring 1966): 26–31
(Stambaugh).

41. For background on early Chicago meat packing and Hubbard's role in it, see
Margaret Walsh, *The Rise of the Midwestern Meat Packing Industry* (Lexington:
University Press of Kentucky, 1982), 62; for the origins of Grand Haven, see
George Newman Fuller, *Economic and Social Beginnings of Michigan* (Lansing,
MI: Wynkoop Hallenbeck Crawford Company, 1916), 427–38.

Notes to Section 3: Men of Industry

1. "Ratified treaty no. 153, documents relating to the negotiation of the treaty of August 25, 1828, with the Winnebago, and United Potawatomi, Chippewa, and Ottawa Indians," frame 7 (White Crow), frame 11 (Snake Skin), frame 20 (Little Priest). For digital access to this treaty record and others cited below, see "For Further Reading."

2. For a concise treatment of Cass's career up to the War of 1812, see Willard Carl Klunder, *Lewis Cass and the Politics of Moderation* (Kent, OH: Kent State University Press, 1996), 1–15.

3. "Treaty of Ghent, 1814," Avalon Project, Yale Law School, available at http://avalon.law.yale.edu/.

4. Cited in R. Douglas Hurt, *Nathan Boone and the American Frontier* (Columbia: University of Missouri Press, 2000), 104.

5. Reuben Thwaites, "Notes on Early Lead Mining in the Fever (or Galena) River Region," *Collections of the State Historical Society of Wisconsin* 29 (1895): 286.

6. Calhoun to Cass, January 14, April 5, 1820, in American State Papers, *Indian Affairs*, 2:319, 320, cited by Ralph H. Brown, ed., "With Cass in the Northwest: Journal of C. C. Trowbridge," part 1, *Minnesota History* 23 (June 1942): 128; Henry Schoolcraft, *Narrative Journal of Travels from Detroit Northwest to the Sources of the Mississippi River in the Year 1820* (Albany: E. & E. Hosford, 1821), 343.

7. "Treaty with the Ottawa and Chippewa, 1820," Kappler, *Indian Affairs*, 2:187–88; Ralph H. Brown, ed., "With Cass in the Northwest: Journal of C. C. Trowbridge," part 3, *Minnesota History* 23 (1942): 340.

8. Barbara Saunders and Lea Zuyderhoudt, *The Challenges of Native American Studies: Essays in Celebration of the Twenty-fifth American Indian Workshop* (Leuven, Belgium: Leuven University Press, 2004), 223; Gaye Wilson, "The Return of Lewis and Clark," Thomas Jefferson Encyclopedia, Monticello, https://www.monticello.org/site/jefferson/return-lewis-and-clark.

9. "Ratified treaty no. 139, documents relating to the negotiation of the treaty of August 19, 1825, with the Sioux, Chippewa, Sauk and Fox, Menominee, Iowa and Winnebago Indians and part of the Ottawa, Chippewa, and Potawatomi of the Illinois Indians," frame 15, available at http://digital.library.wisc.edu/1711.dl/History.IT1825no139; a transcript of the treaty negotiations was printed in "Mission to the Indians," *Niles' Weekly Register* 29 (1825–26): 187–92.

10. "Treaty with the Sioux and Chippewa . . . 1825," Kappler, *Indian Affairs*, 2:253; "Treaty with the Chippewa, 1826," Article 3, Kappler, *Indian Affairs*, 2:269.

11. William Salter, *Life of Henry Dodge, from 1782 to 1833* (Burlington, IA: n.p., 1890), 12.

12. Epigraph: Schoolcraft, *A View of the Lead Mines of Missouri* (New York: Charles Wiley, 1819), 245. Thwaites, "Notes on Early Lead Mining," 279.

13. For Austin/Smith T rivalry, see Steward, *Frontier Swashbuckler*, 26–51, 68–69, 209; Schoolcraft, *View of the Lead Mines*, 19, 116; David B. Gracy II, "Austin, Moses," Handbook of Texas Online, http://www.tshaonline.org/handbook/online/articles/fau12.

14. Pike, *Expeditions*, 32.

15. United States, *Laws of the United States, Resolutions of Congress under the Con-federation, Treaties, Proclamations, and Other Documents, Having Operation and Respect to the Public Lands* (City of Washington: Printed and sold by Jonathan Elliot, 1817), 34–38.

16. Schoolcraft, *View of the Lead Mines,* 21–22, 135 (list).

17. Schoolcraft, *View of the Lead Mines,* 106; Ronald Rayman, "Confrontation at the Fever River Lead Mining District," *The Annals of Iowa* 44 (Spring 1978): 279.

18. Consul Willshire Butterfield, *History of Lafayette County, Wisconsin* (Evansville, IN: Whipporwill Publications, 1881), 423 (Hemstead); Rayman, "Confrontation at the Fever River Lead Mining District," 278–95; Louis Pelzer, *Henry Dodge* (Iowa City: State Historical Society of Iowa, 1911), 31–33, and "Lead Mining in Southwestern Wisconsin," Turning Points in Wisconsin History, Wisconsin Historical Society, https://www.wisconsinhistory.org/turningpoints/tp-026/ (Dodge).

19. As quoted in Ronald N. Satz and Laura Apfelbeck, *Chippewa Treaty Rights: The Reserved Rights of Wisconsin's Chippewa Indians in Historical Perspective* (Madison: University of Wisconsin Press, 1996), 56.

20. See David J. Krause, *The Making of a Mining District: Keweenaw Native Copper, 1500–1870* (Detroit, MI: Wayne State University Press, 1992), 97, 140.

21. *Acts of the Legislature of the State of Michigan, Passed at the Annual Session of 1848* (Lansing, MI: Bagg & Harmon, 1848), 138, 153, 155, 331, 341.

22. Matthew W. Hall, *Dividing the Union: Jesse Burgess Thomas and the Making of the Missouri Compromise* (Carbondale: Southern Illinois University Press, 2015), 63. The quotation is from Shadrach Bond to Ninian Edwards, February 7, 1813, in E. B. Washburne, ed., *The Edwards Papers: Being a Portion of the Collection of the Letters, Papers, and Manuscripts of Ninian Edwards* (Chicago: Fergus Printing Company, 1884), 3:94.

23. As recounted in Salter, *Life of Henry Dodge,* 10.

24. Summarized in Stan Hoig, *Beyond the Frontier: Exploring the Indian Country* (Norman: University of Oklahoma Press, 1998), 83–84.

25. Jacob Barker et al., *Trial of Jacob Barker, Thomas Vermilya, and Matthew L. Davis, for alleged conspiracy: testimony as reported by Hugh Maxwell, Esq., district attorney, and certified for the use of the Supreme Court* (New York: Coke Law-Press, 1827), 8; *Rathbun-Rathbone-Rathburn Family Historian* 10 (January 1990): 4–5; Philip Sturm, "The Rathbone Well," e-WV: The West Virginia Encyclopedia, March 11, 2014.

26. Levi Colbert to Andrew Jackson, November 22, 1832, National Archives Microfilm Publication M-234, Roll 136, Letters Received by the Office of Indian Affairs, 1824–1881, available at http://archive.li/22yzx; A. P. Whitaker, "Tennessee Public Schools, 1834–1860," *Tennessee Historical Magazine* 2 (1916): 16.

27. Franklin T. Oldt, ed., *History of Dubuque County, Iowa* (Chicago: Goodspeed Historical Association, 1911), 55, 59, 60–62, 85.

28. W. S. Bell, "Perry W. McAdow and Montana in 1861–1862," *Montana: The Magazine of Western History* 2 (January 1852): 46, including n18 (Adams); Mary Ellen Snodgrass, *Settlers of the American West: The Lives of 231 Notable Pioneers* (Jefferson, NC: McFarland, 2015), 33 (Campbell); Jon Lane and Susan Layman,

South Pass City and the Sweetwater Mines (Charleston, SC: Arcadia Publishing, 2012), 10 (Carter).

29. Joseph Alexander Leonard, *History of Olmsted County, Minnesota* (Chicago: Goodspeed Historical Association, 1910), 41.

30. David A. Walker, "Lake Vermilion Gold Rush," *Minnesota History* 44 (Summer 1974): 47–49.

31. "Dousman, Hercules Louis (1800–1868), Land Speculator and Businessman," Dictionary of Wisconsin History, Wisconsin Historical Society, https://www .wisconsinhistory.org/Records/Article/CS1655; James Taylor Dunn, *The St. Croix: Midwest Border River* (New York: Holt, Rinehart and Winston, 1965; repr., St. Paul: Minnesota Historical Society Press, 1979), 78–81.

32. William Lee Jenks, *St. Clair County, Michigan: Its History and Its People* (Chicago: Lewis Publishing Company, 1912), 1:371 (Whiting and Rice); James Cook Mills, *History of Saginaw County, Michigan: Historical, Commercial, Biographical* (Saginaw County, MI: Seemann & Peters, 1918), 394 (Williams brothers); Reuben G. Thwaites, "Some Wisconsin Indian Conveyances, 1793–1836," *Collections of the State Historical Society of Wisconsin* 15 (1900): 16–17, and *History of Fond du Lac County, Wisconsin,* 186 (Arndt); William E. Lass, "The First Attempt to Organize Dakota Territory," in William L. Lang, ed., *Centennial West: Essays on the Northern Tier States* (Seattle: University of Washington Press, 1991), 7, 21 (Brown).

33. Deborah Beaumont Martin, *History of Brown County, Wisconsin: Past, Present* (Chicago: S. J. Clarke, 1913) 1:187 (Arndt); John Fletcher Williams, *A History of the City of St. Paul and of the County of Ramsey, Minnesota* (St. Paul: Minnesota Historical Society, 1876), 41 (Brown); Charles C. Trowbridge, "History of Allegan County," *Pioneer Collections: Report of the Pioneer Society of Michigan* (Lansing, MI: W. S. George & Company, 1883), 4:173–75 (Trowbridge); Pine River Logging Co. v. United States, 186 U.S. 279 (1902) (Bassett Supreme Court Case); "Joel Bean Bassett," *The Book of Minnesotans: A Biographical Dictionary of Leading Living Men of the State of Minnesota* (Chicago: A. N. Marquis & Company, 1907), 33–34 (Bassett biographical information).

34. "Sudden Death of Pioneer Warrior," *Oregonian,* February 4, 1908, 7 (Shaw); Robert E. Ficken, *The Forested Land: A History of Lumbering in Western Washington* (Seattle: University of Washington Press, 2012), 27–30 (Keller and the Northwest lumber industry).

35. "Treaty with the Cherokee, 1791," Kappler, *Indian Affairs,* 2:30.

36. Edythe Johns Rucker Whitley, *Overton County, Tennessee: Genealogical Records* (Baltimore, MD: Genealogical Publishing Co., 1979), 46; *Acts of Tennessee,* Chapter 73, November 14, 1801, as cited in Alvin B. Wirt, *The Upper Cumberland of Pioneer Times* (n.p.: A.B. Wirt, 1954), 21.

37. Charles J. Ritchey, "Martin McLeod and the Minnesota Valley," *Minnesota History* 10 (December 1929): 387–402; Norene Roberts with Clark Dobbs, "Lower Minnesota River Valley Cultural Resource Study," prepared for the Minnesota Department of Natural Resources, June 1993, 55–56, 175; "Snelling-Mendota Ferry Still Transports Tourists After 120 Year Service," *Minneapolis Journal,* July 8, 1923.

38. R. G. Robertson, *Rotting Face: Smallpox and the American Indian* (Caldwell, ID: Caxton Press, 2001), 84–85, 140–41, 144–45.
39. Arthur C. Wakeley, *Omaha: The Gate City* (Chicago: S. J. Clarke Publishing Co., 1917), 99, 199–260; W. T. Block, "Olive, Hardin County, Texas, an Extinct Saw Mill Town and the Olive-Sternenberg Partnership That Built It," *Texas Gulf Historical and Biographical Record* 21 (1990): 6.
40. Richard A. Schermerhorn, *Schermerhorn Genealogy and Family Chronicles* (New York: Tobias A. Wright, 1914), 93–97.
41. Thomas Ricaud Martin, *The Great Parliamentary Battle and Farewell Addresses of the Southern Senators on the Eve of the Civil War* (New York: Neale Publishing Company, 1905), 212.
42. Annie H. Abel, "History of Indian Consolidation West of the Mississippi," *Annual Report of the American Historical Association* 1 (1908): 384; George Gibson to J. B. Gardiner, June 5, 1832, *Correspondence on the Subject of the Emigration of Indians Between the 30th November, 1831, and 27th December, 1833*, S. Doc. No. 512, 23rd Cong., 1st Sess. (1833), 109.
43. Willis Brew, *Alabama, Her History, Resources, War Record and Public Men* (Montgomery, AL: Barrett and Brown, 1872), 256. The Articles of Incorporation of the Mississippi Texas Land Company are available in the Digital Collections of the Briscoe Center for American History, University of Texas at Austin, http://www.cah.utexas.edu/db/dmr/image_lg.php?variable=BC_0194a.
44. John Livingston, *Portraits of Eminent Americans Now Living* (New York: Lamport & Company, 1854), 3:337–51.
45. Mary Lethert Wingerd, *North Country: The Making of Minnesota* (Minneapolis: University of Minnesota Press, 2010), 220–23.
46. Patrick Leopold Gray, *Gray's Doniphan County History: A Record of the Happenings of Half a Hundred Years* (Bendena, KS: Roycroft Press, 1905), 41–43.

Notes to Section 4: Political and Personal Boundaries

1. President's Message to Congress, December 7, 1830, *Register of Debates*, 21st Cong., 2nd Sess. (Washington: Gales & Seaton, 1830), appendix p. ix.
2. United States Statutes at Large, 21st Cong., 1st Sess., 1830, 411–12.
3. Link available at Indian Removal Act, Primary Documents in American History, Library of Congress Web Guides, https://www.loc.gov/rr/program/bib/ourdocs/Indian.html.
4. One of the first recorded uses of this new meaning appears in Thomas Hobbes, *Leviathan,* chapter 24: "A People comming into possession of a Land by warre, do not alwaies exterminate the antient Inhabitants."
5. Sakolski, *Great American Land Bubble*, 224; Willis Frederick Dunbar and George S. May, *Michigan: A History of the Wolverine State,* 3d rev. ed. (Grand Rapids: W. B. Eerdmans Publishing Co., 1995), 187; Robert B. Ross and George Catlin, *Landmarks of Detroit: A History of the City* (Detroit, MI: Evening News Association, 1898), 296–97.
6. Clarence Monroe Burton et al., *The City of Detroit, Michigan, 1701–1922* (Detroit, MI: S. J. Clarke Pub. Co., 1922), 2:1204.

7. Reynolds to Cass, July 7, 1831, in *The Black Hawk War, 1831–1832*, comp. Ellen M. Whitney (Springfield: Illinois State Historical Library, 1973), 36:101.

8. B. P. Settle to John Reynolds, July 25, 1831, *Black Hawk War*, 113.

9. James Stewart to Stevens T. Mason, June 7, 1832, *Black Hawk War*, 546.

10. William Clark to Lewis Cass, June 8, 1832, *Black Hawk War*, 550.

11. For conflicting casualty estimates, see James L. Isemann, "Black Hawk War," in J. E. Brown, ed., *Historical Dictionary of the U.S. Army* (Westport, CT: Greenwood Press, 2001), 61; "The Black Hawk War," Turning Points in Wisconsin History, Wisconsin Historical Society, https://www.wisconsinhistory.org/turningpoints/tp-012/?action=more_essay.

12. *Journal of the Proceedings of the Sixth Legislative Council of the Territory of Michigan* (Detroit, MI: S. M'Knight, 1834), 159.

13. For more details on these confusing developments, see Dunbar and May, *Michigan*, 204–20; Alice Smith, *The History of Wisconsin, Volume 1: From Exploration to Statehood* (Madison: State Historical Society of Wisconsin, 1973), 235–72.

14. Bonnie Steppenhoff, *From French Community to Missouri Town: Ste. Genevieve in the Nineteenth Century* (Columbia: University of Missouri Press, 2006), 84–85.

15. John Carroll Power, *History of Early Settlers of Sagamon County* (Springfield, IL: Edwin A. Wilson & Co., 1876), 61; Mark Wyman, *The Wisconsin Frontier* (Bloomington: Indiana University Press, 1998), 151; Salter, *Life of Henry Dodge*, 26.

16. Sidney Rigdon, *Oration delivered by Mr. S. Rigdon, on the 4th of July, 1838, at Far West, Caldwell County, Missouri* (n.p. [Missouri]: Journal Office, 1838), 12; Missouri Executive Order 44, text available at World Heritage Encyclopedia, http://central.gutenberg.org/articles/missouri_executive_order_44.

17. W. B. Stevens, *St. Louis, the Fourth City, 1764–1909* (St. Louis, MO: S. J. Clarke, 1909), 3:1015.

18. Relationships mentioned here for the Chouteau clan can be tracked through Hoig, *The Chouteaus*.

19. Relationships mentioned here among the Kinzie/Forsyth clan can be tracked through the website http://www.earlychicago.com, based on Danckers et al., *Compendium of the Early History of Chicago to the Year 1835*, which includes source notes on its research; Eunice Trippler and Louis A. Arthur, *Eunice Trippler: Some Notes of Her Personal Recollections* (New York: Grafton Press, 1910); John Tomas Scharf, *History of Saint Louis City and County: From the Earliest Periods to the Present Day, Including Biographical Sketches of Representative Men* (St. Louis, MO: L. H. Everts, 1883), vol. 1.

20. Trippler and Arthur, *Eunice Trippler*, 16, 63.

21. Katharine T. Corbett, *In Her Place: A Guide to St. Louis Women's History* (St. Louis: Missouri Historical Society Press, 1999), 13.

22. Frederick John Kingsbury and Mary Kingsbury Talcott, *The Genealogy of the Descendants of Henry Kingsbury, of Ipswich and Haverhill, Mass.* (Hartford, CT: Hartford Press, 1905), 314–15.

23. S. L. Kotar and J. E. Gessler, *The Steamboat Era: A History of Fulton's Folly on*

American Rivers, 1807–1860 (Jefferson, NC: McFarland & Co, 2009), 48; "Manuel Lisa," Historic Missourians, State Historical Society of Missouri, https://shsmo.org/historicmissourians/name/l/lisa/. Mary was the third of Lisa's three wives.

24. For more on Lisa and his family, see Richard E. Oglesby, *Manuel Lisa and the Opening of the Missouri Fur Trade* (Norman: University of Oklahoma Press, 1963).

25. Denslow, *Territorial Masonry*, 32.

26. *The Constitution of the Aztec Club and the List of Members, 1893* (Washington, DC: Judd & Detweiler, 1893).

27. John W. Campbell, *History of the Friendly Sons of St. Patrick and of the Hibernian Society* (Philadelphia: Hibernian Society, 1892).

28. Thomas Helm, *History of Cass County, Indiana: From the Earliest Time to the Present* (Chicago: Brant and Fuller, 1886), 440.

29. Dudley Wright, ed., *Gould's History of Freemasonry Throughout the World* (New York: Charles Scribner's Sons, 1936), 5:30, 127, 131, 181, 198, 223, 352, 374, 412; 6:136, 381.

30. See, for example, Carl Watner, "Libertarians and Indians: Proprietary Justice and Aboriginal Land Rights," *Journal of Libertarian Studies* 7, no. 1 (1983): 147–56.

31. On the Bongas and racial identity, here and below, see Mattie Marie Harper, "French Africans in Ojibwe Country: Negotiating Marriage, Identity and Race, 1780–1890" (PhD diss., University of California–Berkeley, 2012), especially iii–iv, 34.

32. See, for instance, George M. Fredrickson, *Racism: A Short History* (Princeton, NJ: Princeton University Press, 2002).

33. John Locke, *The Second Treatise on Government,* Chapter V, Sections 26 and 27.

34. Locke, *Second Treatise,* Section 41.

35. Barbara J. Fields, Presentation for the Producers of "Race: The Power of an Illusion," 2001, archived at http://www.pbs.org/race/000_About/002_04-background-02-02.htm.

36. Francois Bernier, "A New Division of the Earth," as quoted in Ania Loomba and John Burton, *Race in Early Modern England: A Documentary Companion* (New York: Palgrave Macmillan, 2007), 272.

37. John Mitchell's article is in Royal Society of London, *Philosophical Transactions of the Royal Society* (1744) 43:102–50.

38. *Johnson v. M'Intosh,* 20–21.

39. Quoted as part of a reasoned exploration of this issue in Alex Alvarez, *Native America and the Question of Genocide* (Lanham, MD: Rowman & Littlefield, 2014), 132–36.

40. Message of Governor Alexander Ramsey, September 9, 1862, as quoted in James H. Baker, *Lives of the Governors of Minnesota,* in *Collections of the Minnesota Historical Society* 13 (1908): 42; Colette Routel, "Minnesota Bounties on Dakota Men during the U.S.–Dakota War," *William Mitchell Law Review* 40 (2013): 21–40 (bounties); Francis Paul Prucha, *The Great Father: The United States Government and the American Indians* (Lincoln: University of Nebraska Press, 1984), 145 (Pope quotation).

41. For a nuanced, book-length examination of the question of genocidal policies, see Alvarez, *Native America and the Question of Genocide*.

42. "Treaty with the Sauk and Foxes, 1824," Kappler, *Indian Affairs*, 2:207.

43. "Treaty with the Sauk and Foxes etc., 1830," Kappler, *Indian Affairs*, 2:307.

44. "Treaty with the Chippewa, 1826," Kappler, *Indian Affairs*, 2:269.

45. Frederick L. Johnson, "'Half Breed' Tract and Scrip," MNopedia, Minnesota Historical Society (2013), http://www.mnopedia.org/event/half-breed -tract-and-scrip.

Notes to Section 5: Bureaucrats

1. O'Sullivan, "Annexation."

2. K. Jack Bauer, *Zachary Taylor: Soldier, Planter, Statesman of the Old Southwest* (Baton Rouge: Louisiana State University Press, 1993), 87.

3. "Treaty with the Kaskaskia, etc, 1832," Article 1, Kappler, *Indian Affairs*, 2:376.

4. Major General Winfield Scott's Order No. 25 Regarding the Removal of Cherokee Indians to the West, May 17, 1838, Letters Received and Other Papers of Major General Winfield Scott Relating to the Cherokees, 1838–1838, Record Group 393: Records of U.S. Army Continental Commands, 1817–1947, National Archives, available at https://catalog.archives.gov/id/6172200.

5. *Vermont Telegraph*, August 22, 1838, as quoted and depicted in Toye E. Heape, "Trail of Tears National Historic Trail in Tennessee: Indian Removal in the Cherokee Nation," Native History Association website, http://www .nativehistoryassociation.org/totnht_background.php. The literature on Cherokee removal is vast. See, for example, Theda Perdue and Michael D. Green, *The Cherokee Removal: A Brief History with Documents* (Boston: Bedford/St. Martin's Books, 2005).

6. Henry Dodge, "Address to the Wisconsin Territorial Legislature, 4 August 1840," *Journal of the House of Representatives of the . . . Second Legislative Assembly of Wisconsin* (Madison, Wisconsin Territory: Charles C. Sholes, 1841), 12.

7. "The Voice of an Injured Territory," September 7, 1840, quoted in Smith, *From Exploration to Statehood*, 336.

8. E. W. Keyes, "The Winnebago Removal of 1840," *Milwaukee Sentinel*, October 7, 1895, available at Canku Ota website, http://www.turtletrack.org/ IssueHistory/Issues13/CO01_2013/CO_0113_Winnebago_Removal.htm.

9. Wingerd, *North Country*, 141–44.

10. Thomas Hughes, "The Treaty of Traverse des Sioux in 1851," *Collections of the Minnesota Historical Society* 10, no. 1 (1905): 102.

11. Pelzer, *Henry Dodge*, 165.

12. "Mexican War," Ohio History Central, http://www.ohiohistorycentral.org/w/ Mexican_War.

13. O'Sullivan, "Annexation."

14. Louis Picone, *The President Is Dead!: The Extraordinary Stories of the Presidential Deaths, Final Days, Burials, and Beyond* (New York: Skyhorse Publishing, 2016).

15. Thomas W. Cutrer, "Gaines, Edmund Pendleton," Handbook of Texas Online, http://www.tshaonline.org/handbook/online/articles/fga03.

16. "Treaty with the Winnebago, 1846," Kappler, *Indian Affairs*, 2:566. This is the removal engineered by Henry Rice, mentioned above. The subsequent move occurred when the heavily forested land proved unacceptable to the Ho Chunk—and, more importantly, highly desirable for its timber.

17. Henry Dodge, "Message to the Legislature, February 8, 1848," *Journal of the Council of the Fifth Legislative Assembly of the Territory of Wisconsin* (Madison, WI: H. A. Tenny, 1848), 10.

18. William E. Lass, "The Birth of Minnesota," *Minnesota History* 55 (Summer 1997): 267–79.

19. United States Statutes at Large, Volume 1, 1st Cong., 1st Sess., chapter 7.

20. United States Statutes at Large, Volume 1, 1st Cong., 1st Sess., chapter 13, sec. 1 (duties); Northwest Ordinance, 1787.

21. Jensen and Hutchins, eds., *Wheel Boats on the Missouri*, 45, 49n3, 68n50; H. D. Barrows, "Governors of California," *Annual Publication of the Historical Society of Southern California and of the Pioneers of Los Angeles County* 6 (1903): 33–34; Craig Choisser, "Kearny, Stephen Watts (1794–1848)," in Spencer Tucker, ed., *US Leadership in Wartime: Clashes, Controversy, and Compromise* (Santa Barbara, CA: ABC-CLIO, 2009), 1:229–31.

22. Jonathan M. Atkins, "William Carroll," Tennessee Encyclopedia of History and Culture, http://tennesseeencyclopedia.net/entry.php?rec=205; Lass, "The First Attempt to Organize Dakota Territory."

23. William L. Lang, *Confederacy of Ambition: William Winlock Miller and the Making of Washington Territory* (Seattle: University of Washington Press, 2014), 87–95. Lawyers present at the arrest protested in "Proceedings of a Meeting of the Bar, Washington Territory, May 7, 1856," available at https://www.sos.wa.gov/legacy/images/publications/SL_proceedingsbar/SL_proceedingsbar.pdf.

24. As quoted in Ezra Meeker, *Pioneer Reminiscences of Puget Sound: The Tragedy of Leschi* (Seattle, WA: Lowman & Hanford, 1905), 371.

25. Donald Jackson, *Custer's Gold: The United States Cavalry Expedition of 1874* (Lincoln: University of Nebraska Press, 1866), 6–7.

26. Ronald N. Satz, *American Indian Policy in the Jacksonian Era* (Lincoln: University of Nebraska Press, 1974), 157–59; Cody Lynn Barry, "Carey Allen Harris, 1805–1842," Encyclopedia of Arkansas History and Culture, http://www.encyclopediaofarkansas.net/encyclopedia/entry-detail.aspx?entryID=9370.

27. United States, Office of Indian Affairs, *Annual Report of the Commissioner of Indian Affairs for the year 1848*, 12. This report and those in the following notes are available at http://digicoll.library.wisc.edu/cgi-bin/History/History-idx?type=browse&scope=HISTORY.COMMREP.

28. United States, Office of Indian Affairs, *Annual Report of the Commissioner of Indian Affairs to the Secretary of the Interior for the year 1851*, 12–13.

29. United States, Office of Indian Affairs, *Annual Report of the Commissioner of Indian Affairs to the Secretary of the Interior for the year 1853*, 10.

30. United States, Office of Indian Affairs, *Annual Report of the Commissioner of Indian Affairs to the Secretary of the Interior for the year 1857*, 10.

31. Testimony of Albert Pike, John Luce, and James Denver in "Claims Against the Choctaw Nation," S. Doc. No. 1977, 49th Cong., 2nd Sess., Report 1977, Serial 2458 (1887), 33–66.

32. United States, Office of Indian Affairs, *Annual Report of the Commissioner of Indian Affairs to the Secretary of the Interior for the year 1859*, 5–6; Rupert N. Richardson, "Neighbors, Robert Simpson," Handbook of Texas Online, http://www.tshaonline.org/handbook/online/articles/fne08; J. Sterling Morton, *Illustrated History of Nebraska: A History of Nebraska from the Earliest Explorations of the Trans-Mississippi Region* (Lincoln, NE: Western Pub. and Engraving Co., 1907), 1:203–4n (Dennison); John Spurgeon, "Alfred Burton Greenwood," Encyclopedia of Arkansas History & Culture, http://www.encyclopediaofarkansas.net/encyclopedia/entry-detail.aspx?entryID=4626.

33. *History of the State of Kansas* (Chicago: A. T. Andreas, 1883), 243 (Farnsworth); *The United States Biographical Dictionary: Kansas Volume* (n.p. [Kansas]: S. Lewis & Company, 1879), 11 (Abbott); "Sale of Shawnee Lands in Kansas," in S. Doc. No. 40, 41st Cong., 2nd Sess. (1870), 33–34 (Shawnee letter).

34. Wilkinson to Thompson, July 21, 1862, cited in an extensive treatment of corruption in Indian Affairs during this period: David A. Nichols, *Lincoln and the Indians: Civil War Policy and Politics* (2000; repr., St. Paul: Minnesota Historical Society Press, 2012), 70. The contract for Crow Creek provisions is described in detail in William E. Lass, "The 'Moscow Expedition,'" *Minnesota History* 38 (Summer 1965): 227–40.

35. Benjamin G. Armstrong, *Early Life Among the Indians* (Ashland, WI: Press of A. W. Bowron, 1891), 35–78.

36. William Watts Folwell, *A History of Minnesota* (St. Paul: Minnesota Historical Society, 1921), 1:470–78 (Dole involvement, 472n9).

37. United States, Office of Indian Affairs, *Report of the Commissioner of Indian Affairs, 1865*, 2.

38. Royce Gordon Shingleton, "David Brydie Mitchell and the African Importation Case of 1820," *Journal of Negro History* 58 (July 1973): 327 (Mitchell); Charles Joseph Oval, *Governors of Indiana: Illustrated* (Indianapolis, IN: Oval and Koster, 1916), 16 (Posey); George R. Lamplugh, *Rancorous Enmities and Blind Partialities: Factions and Parties in Georgia, 1807–1845* (Lanham, MD: University Press of America, 2015), 116 (Crowell); Atkins, "William Carroll"; William Omer Foster, "The Career of Montfort Stokes in North Carolina," *North Carolina Historical Review* 16 (July 1939): 268; Grant Foreman, "The Life of Montfort Stokes in the Indian Territory," *North Carolina Historical Review* 16 (October 1939): 373–403; T. C. Elliot, "The Dalles-Celilo Portage: Its History and Influence," *Quarterly of the Oregon Historical Society* 16 (March-December 1915): 160–62 (Thompson).

39. Deborah Barker, "Perry Fuller: Indian Agent, Self-Made Man and White-Collar Criminal," paper presented at the Franklin County Historical Society 75th Anniversary Symposium, April 28, 2012, available at http://www.franklincokshistory.org/wp-content/uploads/2012/07/Perry-Fuller-talk.pdf; Richard A. Ruddy, *Edmund G. Ross: Soldier, Senator, Abolitionist* (Albuquerque: University of New Mexico Press, 2013), 103–9.

40. Kerry R. Oman, "The Beginning of the End: The Indian Peace Commission of 1867–1868," *Great Plains Quarterly* 2343 (Winter 2002): 35–51.

41. Alfred A. Taylor, "Medicine Lodge Peace Council," *Chronicles of Oklahoma* 2 (June 1924): 98.

Notes to Section 6: Mythmakers

1. "An Act to Incorporate the State Historical Society of Wisconsin, March 4, 1853," *The Charter and Revised Statutes relating to the State Historical Society of Wisconsin* (Madison, WI: Democrat Printing Company, 1884), 3.

2. Edward D. Neill and J. Fletcher Williams, *History of Ramsey County and the City of St. Paul* (Minneapolis, MN: North Star Publishing Co., 1881), 117–19.

3. Kane, "The Sioux Treaties and the Traders"; Wingerd, *North Country*, 193.

4. For text of legislative acts, see Minnesota Session Laws, 1st through 8th Territorial Legislature, Office of the Revisor of Statutes, https://www.revisor .mn.gov/laws.

5. Fred L. Morrison, "An Introduction to the Minnesota Constitution," *William Mitchell Law Review* 20 (1994): 295–96.

6. Hubbard et al., *Minnesota in Three Centuries*, 75.

7. Caleb Atwater, *A History of the State of Ohio: Natural and Civil* (Cincinnati, OH: Stereotyped by Glezen and Shepard, 1838), 351.

8. Caleb Atwater, *Writings of Caleb Atwater* (Columbus, OH: The Author, 1833), 18, 106.

9. Mary Schoolcraft, *The Black Gauntlet* (Philadelphia: J. B. Lippincott & Co., 1860), vii.

10. Morton, *Illustrated History of Nebraska*, xi.

11. *The Conservative* (Nebraska City), February 23, 1899, 1.

12. Hubert Howe Bancroft, *History of Nevada, Colorado, and Wyoming, 1540–1888* (San Francisco: History Co., 1890), 415–16 (on Bennett); Morton, *Illustrated History of Nebraska*, 296n3 (clubs organized), 645 (Bellevue victim), 230–31 (fuller treatment); Baker v. Morton, 79 US 12 Wall. 150 (1870).

13. H. L. Hosmer, *Early History of the Maumee Valley* (Toledo, OH: Hosmer & Harris, 1858), 9, 17; Mark C. Dillon, *The Montana Vigilantes: Gold, Guns, and Gallows* (Boulder: University Press of Colorado, 2013), 22.

14. *Laws of the Territory of Michigan* (Lansing, MI: W. S. George & Co., 1874), 2:674–75.

15. *Illustrated Historical Atlas of the County of Wayne, Michigan* (Chicago: H. Belden & Co., 1876), 64.

16. Michigan Pioneer and Historical Society, *Historical and Scientific Sketches of Michigan* (Detroit, MI: Stephen Wells and George L. Whitney, 1834), 8–9.

17. Indiana Historical Society, *Proceedings of the Indiana Historical Society 1830–1886* (Indianapolis, IN: Bobbs-Merrill Co., 1897), 1:12–17.

18. David Hosack, "1820 Inaugural Address," *Collections of the New-York Historical Society* (New York: E. Bliss and E. White, 1821), 3:271; "An Act to Incorporate the Historical Society of Montana," *Contributions to the Historical Society of Montana* (Helena, MT: State Publishers, 1896), 2:19; State Historical Society of Wisconsin, *The Wisconsin State Historical Library Building and the Several Libraries Contained Therein* (Madison: State Historical Society of Wisconsin, 1901), 9–12; "Origin of the Nebraska State Historical Society," *Transactions and Reports of the Nebraska State Historical Society* (Lincoln, NE: State Journal Co., 1885), 1:14–15.

19. State Revisor's Office, Laws of Minnesota, 1849 Chapter 44, p. 106.

20. State Revisor's Office, Laws of Minnesota, 1857 Chapter 98.

21. John H. Stevens, *Personal Recollections of Minnesota and Its People* (Minneapolis, MN: n.p., 1890), 398–99.

22. *Proceedings and Report of the Annual Meetings of the Minnesota Territorial Pioneers* 1–2 (1899): 3, 24.

23. "Ratified treaty no. 223, documents related to the negotiation of the treaty of July 29, 1837 with the Chippewa Indians," 8–9, http://digital.library.wisc.edu/1711.dl/History.IT1837no223.

24. George E. Greene, *History of Old Vincennes and Knox County, Indiana* (Chicago: S. J. Clarke Publishing Co., 1911), 472–73; Walter B. Stevens, *100 Years of the St. Louis Republic* (St. Louis, MO: The St. Louis Republic, 1908), 6; Warren J. Brier, "Political Censorship in the Oregon Spectator," *Pacific Historical Review* (August 1962): 235n2; J. H. Beadle, *Life in Utah; or the Mysteries and Crimes of Mormonism* (Philadelphia: National Publishing Company, 1872), 534; Daniel S. B. Johnston, "Minnesota Journalism in the Territorial Period," *Collections of the Minnesota Historical Society* 10 (1905): 256, 292, 294.

25. *Proceedings of the Wisconsin Editorial Association* (c. 1853): 21.

26. Taylor, "Medicine Lodge Peace Council," 100–102.

27. United States, Office of Indian Affairs, *Annual Report of the Commissioner of Indian Affairs for the Years 1846–1850*, 385.

28. "Report of Luke Lea and Alexander Ramsey to the Secretary of the Interior, August 6, 1851," 32nd Cong., 2nd Sess., House Documents, Otherwise Published as Executive Documents, vol. 2, part 3, p. 283.

29. *Seventeenth Annual Report of the Board of Indian Commissioners*, Appendix E: Third Annual Meeting of the Lake Mohonk Conference (Washington, DC: Government Printing Office, 1886), 90.

30. *Johnson v. M'Intosh*, 21 US 543, 591–92.

31. Swannee Bennett and William B. Worthen, *Arkansas Made: Photography, Art* (Fayetteville: University of Arkansas Press, 1990), 131; Paul D. McDermott and Ronald E. Grim, "Gustavus Sohon's Cartographic and Artistic Works: An Annotated Bibliography," *Philip Lee Phillips Society Occasional Papers Series* 4 (Washington, DC: Library of Congress Geography and Map Division, 2002); "Benjamin Hyde Edgerton: Wisconsin Pioneer," *Wisconsin Magazine of History* 4 (1920–21): 357.

32. Reuben Gold Thwaites, "Wisconsin's Emblems and Sobriquet," *Proceedings of the State Historical Society of Wisconsin at its Fifty-fifth Annual Meeting* (Madison, WI: The Society, 1908), 298–99.

33. Edward D. Neill, *The History of Minnesota, from the Earliest French Explorations to the Present Time*, 2nd ed. (Philadelphia: J. B. Lippincott, 1873), 516; Robert M. Brown, "The Great Seal of the State of Minnesota," *Minnesota History* 39 (Autumn 1952): 126–29. Neill was a friend of the Ramseys; the first edition of his book, published in 1856, was inscribed "To Anna Ramsey, my wife's friend, the name of whose husband, as the first governor, must always be identified with the history of Minnesota." The controversy over the state seal is ongoing: see https://newmnflag.org/about/history.

34. Charles E. Flandrau, *Encyclopedia of Biography of Minnesota: History of Minnesota* (Chicago: Century, 1900), 431; D. A. Robertson to E. D. Neill, August 13,

1856, in General Correspondence Files, 1849–April 1878, Minnesota Historical Society Institutional Archives. In 1978, Mary Jean Jecklin, a researcher in the society's Information Office, compiled the story behind the society's seal when the symbolism in the Minnesota state seal was being questioned; see Administration, Mary Jean Jecklin, Notes on MHS Seal, 1978, MNHS Institutional Archives. On Robertson, see Flandrau, *Encyclopedia of Biography of Minnesota*, 431.

35. Joseph N. Nicollet, "Hydrographical Basin of the Upper Mississippi River," 1843, is available at https://www.loc.gov/item/78692260/; for a description of Smith's mapmaking enterprise, see William T. Norton, *Centennial History of Madison County, Illinois* (Chicago: Unigraphic, 1912), 149–50.

Notes to Epilogue

1. William E. Lass, "Removal from Minnesota of the Sioux and Winnebago Indians," *Minnesota History* 38 (December 1963): 353–64, including quote from *St. Paul Weekly Press*, April 23, 1863.
2. 25 U.S.C. Section 71: Future Treaties with Indian Tribes.
3. For overviews of US policy, see Vine Deloria and Raymond J. DeMallie, *Documents of American Indian Diplomacy: Treaties, Agreements, and Convention, 1775–1979* (Norman: University of Oklahoma Press, 1999) and Donald L. Fixico, *Termination and Relocation: Federal Indian Policy, 1945–1960* (Albuquerque: University of New Mexico Press, 1986); Supreme Court Case: United States v. Kagama, 118 US 375 (1886); Dawes Act: Bruce G. Trigger et. al., *Cambridge History of the Native Peoples of the Americas* (New York: Cambridge University Press, 1996), 201; Pratt Speech: *Official Report of the Nineteenth Annual Conference of Charities and Correction* (1892), 46–59, reprinted in Richard H. Pratt, "The Advantages of Mingling Indians with Whites," *Americanizing the American Indians: Writings by the "Friends of the Indian," 1880–1900* (Cambridge, MA: Harvard University Press, 1973), 260–71; Indian Religious Freedom Act: Public Law 95-341, August 11, 1978.

Notes to Sidebars

Notes to "1780s: Failed Treaties of the Northwest Territory"

1. J. A. Murray, "The Butlers of the Cumberland Valley," in William Henry Egle, *Historical Register: Notes and Queries, Historical and Genealogical, Relating to Interior Pennsylvania* 1 (1883): 11–12.
2. Gary Clayton Anderson, *Ethnic Cleansing and the Indian* (Norman: University of Oklahoma Press, 2014), 100.
3. Simon Gratz, "Biography of General Richard Butler," *Pennsylvania Magazine of History and Biography* (1883): 7–10.

Note to "1795: Treaty of Greenville"

1. "William Wells," Ohio History Central, http://www.ohiohistorycentral.org/w/William_Wells.

Note to "1804: Treaty with the Sauk and Fox"

1. "Treaty with the Sauk and Foxes, 1804," Kappler, *Indian Affairs*, 2:74–77.

Notes to "1808: Treaty with the Osage"

1. Described as such by Clark years later: see Ann Rogers, *Lewis and Clark in Missouri* (Columbia: University of Missouri Press, 2002), 113.
2. "Treaty with the Osage, 1808," Kappler, *Indian Affairs*, 2:95–98.
3. To Thomas Jefferson from Meriwether Lewis, 15 December 1808, Founders Online, National Archives, https://founders.archives.gov/documents/Jefferson/99-01-02-9323.

Note to "1815: War of 1812 Peace Treaties"

1. See A. J. Dallas to Treaty Commissioners, June 11, 1815 (Miller); James Monroe to William Clark, March 11, 1815 (McNair); and James Monroe to Treaty Commissioners, March 11, 1815 (Wash)—all in American State Papers, Senate, 14th Cong., 1st Sess., *Indian Affairs*, 2:6, 8.

Notes to "1825: Treaty of Prairie du Chien"

1. "Indian Missions," *Niles' Weekly Register* 29 (1825–26): 188, 189 ("Ratified treaty no. 139," frames 16, 20–21).
2. "Treaty with the Sioux and Chippewa . . . 1825," Kappler, *Indian Affairs*, 2:253.
3. William Clark and Lewis Cass to James Barbour, Secretary of War, September 1, 1825, in "Ratified treaty no. 139," frame 41.

Note to "1828: Treaty with the Winnebago, etc."

1. "Ratified treaty no. 153, documents relating to the negotiation of the treaty of August 25, 1828, with the Winnebago, and United Potawatomi, Chippewa, and Ottawa Indians," frame 20.

Notes to "1830: Treaty with the Sauk and Fox, etc."

1. "Ratified treaty no. 159, documents relating to the negotiation of the treaty of July 15, 1830, with the Sauk and Fox, Mdewakanton, Wahpeton, Sisseton, Yankton, and Santee, Sioux, Omaha, Iowa, and Oto and Missouri Indians," frame 5.
2. Clark to Eaton, July 25, 1830, "Ratified treaty no. 159," frame 26; Clark and Morgan to Eaton, July 16, 1830, "Ratified treaty no. 159," frames 27 and 28.

Notes to "1837: Treaties with the Ojibwe and Dakota"

1. Henry Dodge to C. A. Harris, August 7, 1937, in "Ratified treaty no. 223, documents relating to the negotiation of the treaty of July 29, 1837, with the Chippewa Indians," frame 9.
2. "Ratified treaty no. 224, documents relating to the negotiation of the treaty of September 29, 1837, with the Sioux of the Mississippi Indians," frame 7 (Poinsett), frames 8, 11 (Big Thunder), frame 27 (He Who Comes Last), frame 31 (Morning Shadow), frame 30 (Good Road).

Notes to "1847: Exchange of Ceded Territory"

1. "Treaty with the Winnebago, 1846," Kappler, *Indian Affairs*, 2:566.
2. "Ratified treaty no. 250, documents relating to the negotiation of the treaty of August 2, 1847, with the Chippewa of the Mississippi and Lake Superior Indians," frames 2–3.
3. "Ratified treaty no. 250," frames 2–3.
4. "Treaty with the Menominee, 1854," Kappler, *Indian Affairs*, 2:626.
5. Lass, "Removal from Minnesota of the Sioux and Winnebago Indians."

Notes to "Dakota Treaties of 1851"

1. United States, Office of Indian Affairs, *Annual Report of the Commissioner of Indian Affairs for the Year 1851*, 18.
2. "Ratified treaty no. 258, documents relating to the negotiation of the treaty of July 23, 1851, with the Sisseton and Wahpeton Sioux Indians," frame 109.
3. *History of the Minnesota Valley, Including the Explorers and Pioneers of Minnesota, by Rev. Edward D. Neill, and History of the Sioux Massacre, by Charles S. Bryant* (Minneapolis, MN: North Star Publishing Co., 1882), 537.

Notes to "1854 and 1855: Treaties with the Ojibwe"

1. Edmund J. Danziger Jr., "They Would Not Be Moved: The Chippewa Treaty of 1854," *Minnesota History* 43 (1973): 175–85.
2. Anton Treuer, *The Assassination of Hole in the Day* (St. Paul, MN: Borealis Books, 2011), 114.
3. Warren Upham, "Minnesota Geographic Names: Their Origin and Historic Significance," *Collections of the Minnesota Historical Society* 17 (1920): 73 (Carlton); Henry Rice, "Mineral Regions of Lake Superior," *Collections of the Minnesota Historical Society* 2 (1860–67), 179–80 (Lynde, Myrick, Hatch); Ellis Courter, *Michigan's Copper Country* (Lansing: Michigan Department of Natural Resources, Geological Survey Division), 40–41 (Cash); John E. Parke, *Recollections of Seventy Years and Historical Gleanings of Allegheny, Pennsylvania* (Boston: Rand, Avery & Co., 1886), 338–39 (McCullough).

Note to "1858: Treaty with the Yankton"

1. Dana R. Baily, *History of Minnehaha County, South Dakota* (Sioux Falls, SD: Brown & Saenger, 1899), 9–20.

For Further Reading

R eaders who are interested in reading more about treaties and treaty making have many options beyond the titles listed in this book's end notes. The volumes listed below discuss federal laws relating to treaties and indigenous nations; include the stories of individual treaties; examine how US legal processes were constructed to enable treaty making; outline indigenous conceptions of diplomacy and justice; and demonstrate the power of treaties as vital documents that determine indigenous rights today.

In addition, primary documents provide immediate and powerful opportunities for exploring treaty making. In 1960, the National Archives microfilmed Bureau of Indian Affairs materials (held in National Archives Record Group 75) that define the treaty process—correspondence, treaty journals (which include transcripts of speeches by indigenous leaders), instructions to treaty commissioners, reports, letters, and in some cases copies of the treaties. The resulting ten rolls of "Documents Relating to the Negotiation of Ratified and Unratified Treaties with Various Tribes of Indians, 1801–1869" are now available online at the "Documents Relating to Indian Affairs" section of the Digital Collection at the University of Wisconsin–Madison Libraries (https://uwdc.library.wisc.edu/collections/history/indiantreatiesmicro/). This website also makes available the annual reports of the commissioner of Indian Affairs, which sometimes include transcriptions of treaty journals and reports.

In addition, the texts of treaties are published in volume 2 of Charles J. Kappler's *Indian Affairs: Laws and Treaties* (Washington, DC: Government Printing Office, 1903–41), familiarly known as Kapplers. This volume and the six others in the set are available online through the digital collections at Oklahoma State University: http://dc.library .okstate.edu/digital/collection/kapplers. Hundreds of treaties and agreements made by Indian nations that are unavailable in Kappler's work are included in two volumes edited by Vine Deloria Jr. and Raymond J. DeMallie: *Documents of American Indian Diplomacy: Treaties,*

Agreements, and Conventions, 1775–1979 (Norman: University of Oklahoma Press, 1999).

For an interactive map showing links to treaties, legislation, and executive orders, see http://www.ehistory.org/projects/invasion-of-america .html. Booklets relating to Ojibwe treaties are available at http://www .glifwc.org/publications/#Booklets and http://www.1854treatyauthority .org/images/The-Right-to-Hunt-and-Fish-Therein.final.pdf.

Banner, Stuart. *How the Indians Lost Their Land: Law and Power on the Frontier.* Cambridge, MA: Belknap Press, 2005.

Calloway, Colin. *Pen and Ink Witchcraft: Treaties and Treaty-Making in American Indian History.* New York: Oxford University Press, 2013.

Cohen, Felix S. *Handbook of Federal Indian Law.* Washington, DC: Government Printing Office, 1942.

DeJong, David H. *American Indian Treaties: A Guide to Ratified and Unratified Colonial, United States, State, Foreign, and Intertribal Treaties and Agreements, 1607–1911.* Salt Lake City: University of Utah Press, 2015.

Fixico, Donald L., ed. *Treaties with American Indians: An Encyclopedia of Rights, Conflicts, and Sovereignty.* Santa Barbara, CA: ABC-CLIO, 2008.

Harjo, Suzan Shown. *Nation to Nation: Treaties Between the United States and American Indian Nations.* Washington, DC: Smithsonian Books, 2014.

Jones, Dorothy V. *License for Empire: Colonialism by Treaty in Early America.* Chicago: University of Chicago Press, 1982.

Pevar, Stephen L. *The Rights of Indians and Tribes.* 4th ed. New York: Oxford University Press, 2012.

St. Germain, Jill. *Indian Treaty-Making Policy in the U.S. and Canada, 1867–1877.* Lincoln: University of Nebraska Press, 2005.

Wilkins, David E. *Hollow Justice: A History of Indigenous Claims in the United States.* New Haven, CT: Yale University Press, 2013.

Wilkins, David E., and Tsianina Lomawaima. *Uneven Ground: American Indian Sovereignty and Federal Law.* Norman: University of Oklahoma Press, 2002.

Williams, Robert Jr. *Linking Arms: American Indian Treaty Visions of Law and Peace, 1600–1800.* New York: Oxford University Press, 1997.

Index

and St. Louis Missouri Fur Trading
Company, 47; and Stoddard, 41; as
treaty signer, 43, 47, 68, 107
Chouteau, Pierre, 48, 104, 145
Chouteau, Pierre Jr.: and American
Fur Company, 59; and Bernard
Pratte and Company, 57; and
Ewing family, 60; and fur trade, 57;
involvement in townsite develop-
ment, 64; Masonic Lodge founder,
46; Pierre, SD, named for, 64; *St.
Peters* steamship carrying smallpox,
88; steamship on Missouri River,
87; and Valle, 88; and Western
Department, 59
Chouteau family: and American Fur
Company, 58; and fur trade, 57;
kinship group, 108–9; mining in
St. Genevieve, 76; steamships, 87;
traders for, 58; treaties, 48, 94
Chute, Richard, 152, 154
Cincinnati, OH, 22, 27, 157
Clark, George Rogers, 21, 40, 41, 104
Clark, Thomas N., 86, 87
Clark, William: acquiring indigenous
resources, 69; attempts to negotiate
treaty with Osage, 46; and Battle of
Fallen Timbers, 22; and Black Hawk
band, 98; and Cass, 71; and Chouteaus, 109; founding member of
Masonic Lodge, 46; as governor of
Missouri Territory, 66; and Indian
Affairs, 71; and Indian removal, 122;
and Kennerly, 104; land boundaries, 73; land cession treaties, 47,
67–69, 71–72, 78, 87, 94–96, 100,
103; places named after, 171; and
political purge of Burr supporters,
46; St. Louis Missouri Fur Trading
Company, 47; as superintendent of
Indian Affairs, 100; as territorial
governor, 136; as treaty commissioner, 67
colonialist: ambitions, 14; bias, 159;
economy, 60; fur trade, 59; governments, 44; histories, 158; mindset,
164; nations, 50; point of view,

4, 157, 165, 168, 170; power, 7–9,
50–51; regime, 3; societies, 52;
squatting on indigenous land, 44;
traders, 52, 56–67
Colorado Territory, 136, 159
Comanche, 116, 141, 145
Congress: firing of Harmar, 20; incorporating Northwest Territory,
18; and "Indian Policy," 130; Indian
Removal Act, 94; and "Indian termination," 174; Land Ordinance of
1784, 15; Northwest Ordinance, 17;
passing General Allotment Act, 174;
passing Indian Religious Freedom
Act, 174; and paying national debt,
16; setting up factories, 40
Connor, Henry, 63, 118
Connor family, 57, 63, 69, 106
Constable, William, 30, 32, 33
Continental Army, 16, 26, 110, 131
Cooley, Dennis, 143, 145
copper: in Arrowhead Region, 153;
around Great Lakes, 70, 76, 80;
mining, 70, 153; Ojibwe land
cession treaties, 154; role in land
acquisition, 66; and treaty-making
interests, 80–81
Corbeau, Petit, 56, 96
Council of Three Fires, 14, 23, 44, 75,
98
Crawford, William, 15, 102
Creeks, 90, 122, 133, 140, 143
Currin, Robert P., 82, 91

Dakota: and American Fur Company,
59; execution, 173; fur trade effect
on, 150; and "half-breed tracts,"
117; and Henry, 102; land cession,
37, 60, 63, 96, 100–2, 122–23, 125,
137, 139, 148, 150–51, 152, 154, 156,
167; Ojibwe, 56; and Pike, 54; and
Ramsey, 116; removal, 87, 117, 142,
163; societies, 6; and Taliaferro,
119; treaties with, 13, 37, 44, 55, 67,
71–72, 82, 96, 100, 125, 127, 131–32,
140, 164, 170; vs. Black Hawk's
band, 97

French: administration, 44; and British traders, 56; and Indian War, 14; land claims, 43; and Louisiana Purchase, 8; merchants in St. Louis, 43; traders, 40, 44, 55
Fuller, Perry, 143, 144
fur trade: British, 45, 54; collapse of, 60, 62, 64; and diplomacy, 47; effect on Dakota, 150; as foundation of private fortunes, 64; and indigenous people, 52, 60, 63; and land speculators, 37; Minnesota, 57; posts, 105, 145; Spanish and French, 44; and sutlers, 62; and treaties, 59, 86; and wealth, 60–61, 63–64; among Yankton, 156
Furnas, Robert, 111, 159

galena, 76, 79
Galena, IL, 81, 95, 99, 108
Galena River, 77, 79
Gardiner, James, 91, 92
Genesis, 7, 113, 167, 170
Georgia, 30, 32, 135, 143
Gibson, John, 22, 53, 110
Glasgow, James, 31, 32
Godfroy family, 57, 58, 63, 69, 106
gold: mines, 83, 136; rushes, 83
Gorham, Nathaniel, 29–30, 33
Graham, Duncan, 55, 56
Graham, Richard, 68, 103
Gratiot, Henry, 75, 79, 106, 108
Great Britain: and French and Indian War, 14; Indian policy, 14; and Michigan Territory, 50; and treaties, 3, 13, 15; and treaty obligations, 4; war with United States, 14, 50
Great Lakes, 20, 80–81
Green Bay, WI, 34, 85, 124, 129, 131
Greenwood, Alfred, 140, 141

Harmar, Josiah, 19–20
Harney, William S., 68, 103, 145–46
Harris, Carey A., 137, 138
Harrison, William Henry, 66, 133; Battle of Fallen Timbers, 22; Battle of Tippecanoe, 49; domain of, 44; and

Illinois Territory, 47; and land cessions, 44; places named after, 171; as president, 124; treaties, 41–43, 94; and Treaty of Greenville, 53
Hastings, MN, 37, 64, 165
Hempstead family, 79, 81, 108
Herriman, David B., 138, 154
Ho Chunk (Winnebago): description of white people, 65; land cession, 74, 79, 128; miners on unceded land, 74, 79, 164; and Pike, 54; removal, 38, 91, 122–24, 127, 142, 148, 154; on reservations, 173; resettlement of, 122, 129; treaties, 71, 75, 79, 132, 149, 157, 159
Homestead Act, 5, 25
Hosmer, Hezekiah, 159, 160, 162
Howard, Benjamin, 47, 50
Hubbard, Gurdon, 63, 88
Hull, William, 32, 44, 50, 66, 94

Illinois: ceded land in, 22, 41–42, 98; land speculation manias, 38; mines in, 65, 77, 99, 136; salt in, 81–82; statehood, 69; trading posts, 63; treaties, 41, 67
Illinois Territory, 47, 49, 67
Indian Affairs: and Bogy, 108; and Clark, 71, 98, 100; and Denver, 140; and Dole, 141; and Harris, 137; and Henderson, 146; and Medill, 138; and Stevens, 134; and treaties, 145, 152; and Webb, 143
Indian Office, 137, 141, 143, 145
Indian removal: beginning of, 69; Clark's role in, 95; Dodge's role in, 99; indigenous resistance to, 122; Jackson's dismissal of, 93; in Michigan, 80; and Pepper, 162; premise behind, 166; "transportation" as euphemism for, 90
Indian Removal Act: and Bell, 124, 133; missionaries against, 167; and Office of Indian Affairs, 137; passed by Congress, 94; and treaties, 12, 122
Indiana: ceded land in, 22, 69; and Connor family, 57; Council of Three Fires ceding land in, 98; Freemason

family, 63; Bois Fort band of, 83; claims to land in Illinois, 78; Council of Three Fires, 14, 23; Dakota intentions toward, 56; defrauded by Herriman, 138; Ho Chunk removed to Ojibwe land, 154; knowledge of copper deposits, 80; and land boundaries, 73; land cessions, 37, 60, 63, 80–81, 83, 87–88, 91, 100–2, 110–11, 118, 128, 138, 140, 147–49, 152, 154; miners invading land, 79; and Pike, 54; removal of, 80, 122, 127; treaties with, 20, 37, 61, 63, 70–72, 74, 79–82, 84–85, 87–88, 102, 106, 108, 111, 129, 132, 144, 150, 156–57, 161, 164, 170; US relations with, 80; Webb as Indian agent to, 142
Oklahoma, 71, 82, 143
Oklahoma Land Rush, 5–6, 25
Olmsted, David: as founder of Minnesota Historical Society, 162; as newspaper owner, 165, 169; places named after, 171; as treaty signer, 149, 154
Omaha (nation), 109, 158–59
Omaha, NE, 88, 89, 171
Oregon City, OR, 134, 143
Oregon Trail, 88, 162
Osage: ceded territory, 48; land cession, 71; land title in Missouri, 71; meeting with Clark, 48; meeting with Jefferson, 41, 48; and Pierre and Chouteau, 47; and Sibley, 71; trade with the Chouteaus, 40, 42; treaties with, 46, 48, 69, 82
Ottawa: claims to land in Illinois, 78; Council of Three Fires, 23; removal from Ohio, 91; resettlement of, 122; treaties with, 20, 70–71, 102, 106
Oto, 96, 122
Ouisconsin River (Wisconsin River), 70, 74

Pacific Northwest, 85, 88, 134, 162, 165
Parsons, Samuel Holden, 16, 17, 26
Paul, Gabriel, 103, 108
Pawnee, 108, 122, 140, 159

Pennsylvania, 30–31, 33, 53
Phelps, Oliver, 28, 29, 30, 32, 33
Phileo, Addison, 99, 165
Piankeshaw, 20, 40, 108, 122
Pike, Zebulon: and the American myth, 162; and Blondeau (the younger), 78; negotiating treaties, 45; Santa Fe expedition, 45; Upper Mississippi expedition, 45, 54, 55, 56; visiting Mines of Spain, 77
pioneers, 6, 11, 13, 19, 50
Polk, William, 31, 33
Pond, Gideon H., 149, 163, 164
Pope, John, 117, 171
Porter, George Bryan, 97, 98, 100
Posey, Thomas, 50, 143
Potawatomi: attack on traders, 61; claims to land in Illinois, 78; and Council of Three Fires, 14, 23; land cession treaties, 60; leaders, 61; resettlement of, 122; treaties, 20, 63, 71, 102, 106, 161
Prairie du Chien, WI: borders drawn at, 127; British withdrawing from, 67; and Clark, 66; copper ore in, 70; and Farnham, 58; galena in, 79; land cession treaty in, 98; lead mines in, 76; peace treaty (1825), 96; Pike in, 57; settlers moving to, 95; Taliaferro at, 119; trading in, 34; treaty signed at, 71–73, 93–95, 117
private property: concept of, 111–12; and natural world, 7, 113; and personal liberty, 7, 114; and race, 115; treaty signers relationship to, 92
private traders, 40, 48
Proclamation of 1763, 14, 15
property rights, 7, 111
Puget Sound, 85, 135

Quapaw, 69, 71, 87, 108, 143

race: academic discourse on, 114–15; American formation of, 50, 93, 112; and ethnic cleansing, 116; and private property, 115
Ramsey, Alexander: creation of land office in St. Paul, 149; and Dakota,

The text of *The Relentless Business of Treaties* has been set in Chaparral Pro, a typeface created by Adobe type designer Carol Twombly in 2000. Chaparral combines the legibility of slab serif designs popularized in the nineteenth century with the grace of sixteenth-century roman book lettering.

Interior book design by Wendy Holdman.

9 781681 340906